EVERMORE

EVERMORE

Edgar Allan Poe and the Mystery of the Universe

Harry Lee Poe

BAYLOR UNIVERSITY PRESS

Cover Design by J. Reiss Design
Cover image: Edgar Allan Poe (1809–49) 1907 (pencil on paper) (b&w
photo) by Ismael Gentz (1862–1914). Private Collection / The Bridgeman
Art Library.
Book Design by Diane Smith. The raven is a pen-and-ink drawing by
Richard Sardinha from *Last Flowers* published by The Poet's Press. Used
by permission.

Library of Congress Cataloging-in-Publication Data

Poe, Harry Lee, 1950–
    Evermore : Edgar Allan Poe and the mystery of the universe / Harry Lee
Poe.
      240 p. cm.
    Includes bibliographical references and index.
    ISBN 978-1-60258-322-1 (hardback : alk. paper)
    1. Poe, Edgar Allan, 1809–1849--Criticism and interpretation. 2. Poe,
Edgar Allan, 1809–1849--Philosophy. I. Title.
    PS2638.P68 2012
    818'.309--dc23

                                                    2011032293

BAYLOR
UNIVERSITY

Printed in the United States of America on acid-free paper with a mini-
mum of 30% PCW recycled content.

Dedicated to
Susan Tane and Peter Fawn,
my companions in collecting Poe,
and to Ben Warthen and Holt Edmunds,
my hosts in Richmond

CONTENTS

PREFACE

This book explores several of the major questions of life that Edgar Allan Poe considered. It does not explore all the questions he asked, nor does it attempt to exhaust the subject on those questions it examines. This book could have explored a single question, but it would have failed because Poe did not have a fragmented view of life that would allow us to examine a single aspect apart from its relationship with the whole. Poe was concerned with unity.

Until the last quarter of the twentieth century, virtually everyone, sympathetic Poe scholars included, regarded Poe's 143-page essay *Eureka* as bizarre evidence that he had gone round the bend. Over the last ten years, I have had the honor of conversing with many important Poe scholars, most of whom have acknowledged that they were at a loss when it came to *Eureka*. The easy road has been to dismiss it. This book is not for those who have taken the easy road. The issues Poe discusses in *Eureka* begin showing up in his poetry, tales, essays, and criticism at the beginning of his career. He quotes and paraphrases his own work throughout *Eureka*. In it, he proposes the Big Bang theory, speculates about what we call black holes, rejects the scientific understanding of the invisible ether through which gravity works, and declares that time and space are one thing, all while constructing a theology of creation and a philosophical answer to the problem of suffering. One of my areas of work for many years has been the intersection of science and religion. This crossroad fascinated Poe, and we see this fascination playing a major role in his development of the possibilities of science fiction, a type of literature so new when he began experimenting with it that it was often simply referred to as a "hoax" because the genre had no name until the twentieth century.

Because of its subject, this book does not pretend to be literary criticism. Instead, it examines Poe's life and work from a philosophical and theological perspective. The book necessarily interacts with Poe's work as literature and as scientific theory, but it strives to do so with humility. My doctoral degree is in theology rather than in American literature, but I did study literary criticism and the philosophy of language at the graduate level. I have tried not to overstep the bounds of my expertise, and when I have trespassed, I hope it will be acknowledged as an expression of enthusiasm rather than as a claim to authority I do not possess. While my efforts to show how Poe's thoughts on his big questions will have apparent flaws, I believe this book offers to literary scholars a tool to navigate some of the issues that permeate Poe's work, but which lie outside the province of literary scholarship.

As a descendant of Poe's cousin, William Poe of Augusta, Montgomery, and Baltimore, and as president of the Poe Museum of Richmond, I write with sympathy for Poe and with little patience for serious treatments of Poe that assume the Griswold myth. On the subject of this book, however, I began from an agnostic perspective. I had no idea what I might find. In the end, I found a complex interrelationship of ideas and beliefs.

This book took little time to write but many years to prepare. At one level it represents the substance of a series of lectures I delivered during the bicentennial of Poe's birth in 2009. At another level I grew up with Poe. When I was a child, my mother took us to the Charleston Museum, where I saw a shadow box on display with a small image of Poe standing on the shore of Sullivan's Island gazing out to sea. "He's your cousin," she explained. One night at home, my father was doing family research and pulled out a folder from his father's file drawers. "This is a letter that Edgar Allan Poe wrote to my father's grandfather," he remarked as he showed me the large photograph print and added, "but he had to sell it to pay my brother's medical bills."

When I was in the third grade, I first understood who Edgar Allan Poe was when I went to see Roger Corman's *House of Usher* starring Vincent Price. In the fifth grade my mother took us to Washington, D.C., for spring break. On the way back we went through Richmond and saw Poe's statue on the state house grounds. The summer after the ninth grade I had a job as a parking lot attendant, and as the long summer wore on, I staved off boredom by reading all of Poe's short stories. We read "The Tell-Tale Heart" in the ninth grade and "The Cask of Amontillado" in the eleventh grade. I was taught that Poe was a madman who wrote his stories while either drunk or on drugs.

A lifetime later in 1999 I spoke several times during the festivities of the 150th anniversary of Poe's death in Richmond. That week, at the First International Conference on Edgar Allan Poe, I became interested in *Eureka*. For some time I had been interested in science and religion, and I grew fascinated by how Poe dealt with the subjects. Over the next decade I wondered why no one seemed to notice that Poe had proposed the Big Bang theory long before any physicist could conceive of such a thing. At a conference on Poe, Emerson, and Hawthorne held at Oxford University in the summer of 2004, I made the acquaintances of Elvira Osipova, a Russian scholar who teaches at the University of St. Petersburg, and René Van Slooten, a Dutch scientist who had studied and written on the science of *Eureka*. Both have continued to stimulate my interest in the big questions that Poe addresses in *Eureka*.

The study of Poe and his writings has undergone a major transformation in recent years with the establishment of the Poe Studies Association and its journal. Objective and reliable assessment of Poe's work came remarkably slowly. At the beginning of the twentieth century, Professor James Harrison at the University of Virginia and Professor George Woodberry at Columbia University stood practically alone. In the next generation, Arthur Hobson Quinn at Penn State, Thomas Ollive Mabbott, and John Ward Ostrom established a new standard in biography and critical texts for Poe. The generation following them included Burtin Pollin, Ben Fisher, and Lasley Dameron who continued to advance Poe studies. Today the number of reputable Poe scholars is too broad to mention, but I am indebted to several leaders in the field who have kindly extended themselves to me. Scott Peeples has helped me appreciate the magnitude of Poe's legacy. Richard Kopley has shown me how Poe made use of real sources in constructing compelling tales, especially the mystery stories. I have also had beneficial conversations with Gerald Kennedy, Elvira Osipova, Dwight Thomas, Michael Deas, Barbara Cantalupo, Alexandra Urakova, and Steve Rachman.

I have had the opportunity to present most of the ideas contained in this book through forty lectures given during the Poe bicentennial. I must thank my cousin, Professor George Poe at the University of the South, for helping me conceive and carry out a series of exhibitions of my personal collection of Poe first editions and other ephemera in a variety of venues, beginning with the University of the South at Sewanee, where I had the opportunity to present my first lecture. Scott Peeples at the College of Charleston helped me with the exhibit at the Charleston Library Society and invited me to take part in a panel discussion with him, Rick Zender, and Jim Hutchisson of The Citadel. Randy Isaacs, executive director of the American Scientific Affiliation, kindly invited me to stage an exhibition for their annual conference at Baylor University, where I also presented a paper on Poe's Big Bang theory and had the opportunity to dialogue on Poe's cosmology with Jennifer Wiseman and David Leckrone, successive senior project scientists for the NASA Hubble Space Telescope.

Another opportunity to speak to Poe's scientific ideas came with an invitation from Eric Weislogel of the Metanexus Institute in Philadelphia. I also appreciate the opportunity this occasion provided for me to have a dialogue about *Eureka* with my responder, Ed Devinney, an astrophysicist at Villanova who developed the Wilson/Devinney computer code for binary star light-curve analysis. The

xii

annual Virginia Festival of the Book allowed me to speak at Poe's alma mater, the University of Virginia, and I wish to thank Nancy Damon, Kevin McFadden, and Kelly Miller for making the lecture possible. Ted Davis, professor of the history of science at Messiah College, invited me to address the Central Pennsylvania Forum for Religion and Science at Messiah College. Conversations with him about the ideas of science current in Poe's day were invaluable. The Third International Edgar Allan Poe Conference in Philadelphia provided me with the opportunity to explore Poe's understanding of imagination. The Edgar Allan Poe House National Historic Site also placed part of my collection on exhibit throughout the bicentennial and kindly invited me to speak at the 160th anniversary of Poe's death, where I addressed the presuppositions of the mystery story. I owe a deep debt of gratitude to Helen McKenna-Uff and Karie Diethorn of the U.S. Park Service for all the extraordinary courtesy and support that they rendered. Also in Philadelphia, I had some wonderful discussions with Edward Pettit.

The most extraordinary aspect of the bicentennial came with the invitation to place my collection on exhibit at the National Library of Russia in St. Petersburg, where Elvira Osipova also organized a major academic conference on Poe where I gave a plenary address. I can never repay Professor Osipova's thoughtfulness and hours of attention to me, not only in her tireless efforts to bring Edgar Allan Poe to Russia, but in her enthusiasm to introduce me to the glories of St. Petersburg. I could not have enjoyed the conference half so well without the help of the translators, Margarita F. Mudrak and Irina A. Nikitina. A number of agencies cooperated in order to hold the conference, and I would like to acknowledge and express my thanks for the support that came from the National Library of Russia, the Saint Petersburg Culture Committee, the United States Consulate General in St. Petersburg, Saint Petersburg State University, Saint Petersburg State Theatre Library, Saint Petersburg Association for International Cooperation, and Petersburg Arts Centre *AVIT.*

I must acknowledge the kindness and many attentions shown to me by the staff of the National Library of Russia, especially

Vladimir N. Zaytsev, Alexander Bukharev, Anton V. Likhomanov, Olga Nikolaevna Kulish, Irina Lynden, Aleksandr Bukreyev, Elena Bokhonskaya, and Nastia Kudriavtseva. I deeply appreciate the support provided for the exhibit and conference and to me personally by Sheila Gwaltney, United States Consul General for St. Petersburg, and her staff, especially Eric Johnson, Elena Smirnova, Maria Delova, Yekaterina Rubalskaya, and Vera Sevestyanova. While in St. Petersburg, I had the opportunity to speak at two universities. I am grateful to Elena Apenko of St. Petersburg State University for inviting me to speak to graduate students in the School of Philology and to Olga Filimonova of the St. Petersburg Pedagogical University for the invitation to speak to undergraduate students.

After St. Petersburg I spoke at universities in three other Russian cities. In Moscow I had the help of Maria Lvova and Lisa Gregory of the American Embassy who coordinated my schedule, accompanied me, and translated when necessary. I am grateful to the Gorki Literary Institute and to Elena Koshokova for the invitation to speak to a class of students and for the lovely luncheon with the president and faculty. I am grateful to Tatiana Venediktova for the invitation to speak at the Moscow State University School of Philology. I am grateful to Natalia Suchugova for the invitation to speak at the Russian State University for the Humanities. Alexandra Urakova, a professor of the Gorki Institute, provided me with great assistance and helped arrange my schedule. I am particularly indebted to her for her valuable insights into Poe and her willingness to share them with me as she "ushered" me through Moscow. In Yekaterinburg, Christopher G. Istrati of the American Consulate, with the assistance of Slavyana Sagakyan, arranged for two lectures at the Sverdlov Ural State University and a luncheon with local poets and artists. I deeply appreciate the courtesies of the faculty of the university, especially Valeriy Alexandrovich Gudov and Olga Grigoryevna Sidorova. I also had a delightful conversation with the poet Slava M. Rabinovich, who helped me understand some of the Russian appreciation of Poe. In Perm I had the support of Sofia Slesarchuk and her assistant Victoria Shakirova of the United States Consulate who hosted me at a lecture at the American Corner at the Perm Library. At the Perm

State Pedagogical University I had the honor of lecturing in the hall of the oldest part of the university where Scaliapin once sang. I am most grateful to Lyubov Alexandrovna Kryuchkova and the faculty for the invitation to speak and for their thoughtfulness in providing a lovely tea. I also want to express special thanks to U.S. Senator Lindsey Graham and to Chris Williams and Lauren Edwards, members of his staff, for their support and help in navigating the various offices necessary to bring about such a major cultural event as Edgar Allan Poe in St. Petersburg.

Several people whom I met during the bicentennial year reminded me how we gain new insights and understand old concepts in new ways simply through the process of talking and exchanging correspondence with others. I particularly want to thank Wally Coberg on matters of Poe biography, and Cynthia Popper and Selena Chambers on matters related to *Eureka*.

The Poe Museum continues to be a source of great joy because of the people involved. My research into Poe is certainly simplified by being president of the Poe Museum. I wish to thank Chris Semtner, our curator, for his cheerful helpfulness to me and to anyone else from around the world who seeks help from the museum. The members of the board who ensure the continuing work of the museum have always been a great support to me, but several members have been of extraordinary help. I mention Holt Edmunds and Ben Warthen in the text, and these two gentlemen have accompanied me through a number of Poe adventures. Two other members have ensnared me in collecting Poe. Susan Tane, who has assembled the most extraordinary Poe collection by a private individual, first suggested to me that I should put my collection on exhibit. Peter Fawn, who has assembled the largest Poe collection in the world (including a working pendulum) has helped me accept the fact that collecting Poe is a terminal condition. I also appreciate the participants in the Edgar Allan Poe Young Writers' Conferences through the years who prompted many of the questions I have considered here. Among the participants, I especially want to acknowledge Grace Williams, Caroline Raynor, and Eric Dickerson. The conferences could not have been the success and the joy they were without the help of the assistant directors who have worked with me through the years, including Frances Poe, Julianne Whitten Paxson, Chelsea Mytyk Schlegel, and Katherine Kipp.

English teachers who visit the Poe Museum from all over the country tell us that they struggle with their classes in American literature until they come to Poe, whom the students adore. I always speak to school groups if my schedule allows, and I want to thank those teachers, students, and principals who have provided me the opportunity to try out all of the ideas in this book on them first. I want to thank Molly Coffman of Madison Academic High School; Amy Blake Hearn, Adrienne Rainey, and Carla Freeman of Milan High School; Kathryn Weissenfluh and Anne Fine of University School of Jackson; Kathy McBroom of Liberty High School; and Candace Minor and Brian Norton of Scott's Hill High School. Because Poe's poetry and fiction are intended to be heard, I benefited from experiencing the effect of the rhythmical beauty of his poetry on audiences during performances of his works in which I collaborated with others. To my colleague Terry McRoberts of the Music Department at Union University, I offer my thanks and only hope we can do it again. Jay Orr of Lambuth University officiates at what has now become an annual Poe evening during the week of his birthday. Jay also coordinated a Poe reading event at the Madison County Library. I also appreciate the invitation from Heather Lawson to speak at the Hernando Public Library in Hernando, Mississippi.

As a professor at a university, I could not have embarked on my Poe adventures without the support of David S. Dockery, president of Union University; Carla Sanderson, the provost; Gene Fant, the vice president for academic administration; and Greg Thornbury, my dean. I especially appreciate the invitation from my dean to present a departmental colloquium in which I explored many of the ideas in this book. To all of them, I am most grateful for their encouragement. The staff of the Emma Waters Summar Library at Union University always has provided me with the resources I need, regardless of where they may have to go to find them. Marianna Dusenberry has provided exceptional support in helping me prepare this manuscript at a time when time mattered, and I appreciate it. My student assistant, Caleb Stallings, is always a great help.

In addition to my cousin George Poe, a number of other family members made an honorable showing at various Poe events during the year, and I appreciate their moral support. First, I must thank my mother Katherine Little Poe, who has always encouraged me. Among the cousins who attended lectures and exhibitions, I thank Beth Welborn and her husband Bill; Woo Thomason and her husband Bill; Carrie Poe; Harper Poe Vergel de Dios and her husband John; Toni Suiter, who serves with me on the board of the Poe Museum; and Charles Cannon, who encouraged me with letters.

My family has had to deal with Poe through thick and thin. My wife Mary Anne had not anticipated having a bust of Poe in the living room when we first married. My children did not realize what images their name evoked. I am grateful to them for their support over the years and for their journeys with me in 2009. My daughter Rebecca Whitten Poe Hays and her husband Joshua accompanied me to Richmond in January 2009, when I spoke at the launch of the Poe commemorative stamp produced by the United States Postal Service and at the official beginning of the bicentennial at the Poe Museum. My other daughter, Mary Ellen Poe, joined the whole family for the trip to Charleston for the lecture at the Charleston Library Society. Mary Anne and Mary Ellen traveled with me to St. Petersburg for the Consular Reception that opened the Poe exhibit. For those who know just how many of the family traits have survived the genetic intermingling of the past two centuries, I am grateful that you can keep a secret.

Harry Lee Poe
Jackson, Tennessee
January 2011

THE PROBLEM
OF EDGAR ALLAN POE

In the popular imagination, Edgar Allan Poe had a tragic life. Many people think of Poe as a figure who brooded over the tragedy of his life, and certainly he had his episodes of despair. The human condition, however, brings tragedy to each of us in our own time and in our own way. This common lot of humanity raises the problem of suffering. People in every culture and every age have pondered why we experience suffering and what, if anything, might be the meaning of life.

As we consider Poe's life, we see many moments of suffering or pain associated most often with the loss of a beloved person. The losses came with death, as with his mother, brother, foster mother, patroness, and wife. They also came through betrayal, as with his foster father and the fiancée of his youth (through her father's betrayal). In the midst of pain and loss, however, Poe knew vast periods of Love and Beauty. While many great thinkers through the ages have pondered the problem of suffering, very few have examined it alongside the *positive* problems of Love and Beauty. Even less do we find people who recognize the interrelatedness of these issues alongside the problem of Justice.

In order to ask why people suffer, we must first posit a universe of fairness and order in which things may be judged to be just or unjust. The problem of suffering questions the Justice of the universe, yet one cannot question the Justice of the universe unless the universe first presents to us the notion of Justice. It is a problem. Throughout his writing, whether in comic tales, stories of detection, horror, or science fiction, Poe continually pondered the *negative* problem of suffering alongside the *positive* problems of Love, Beauty, and Justice.[1] He also explored these ideas in his poetry and in his hundreds of essays and reviews.

One of the cardinal features of Poe's theory of writing, both for fiction and poetry, involved his conviction that the artist should strive to create a "unity of effect" in which all the elements of poetry or all the elements of plot combine seamlessly as a consistent whole to accomplish the purposed effect upon the audience. In *Eureka*, that mysterious prose poem/essay on the material and spiritual universe published in 1848, Poe concluded that suffering, Beauty, Love, and Justice come together in a meaningful and rational way in the unity of effect intended by the "author" of the universe. A fierce opponent of Descartes' culturally successful project to separate mind and body, matter and spirit, Poe argued in *Eureka* for the continuity of art and science and for the continuity of matter and spirit across the frontier of death. He recognized the imagination as the human faculty that forms the bridge across this seeming divide.

These suggestions, however, represent an alternative reading of Poe that cuts across the grain of several traditional readings of Poe. Benjamin Fisher has said that there are at least forty-nine ways to look at a work by Poe, and this reading of Poe's total work differs from the approach that a literary scholar would take.[2] It differs in method and style, for it does not approach Poe with questions of literary criticism but with questions of theology and philosophy.

We will most likely never have a common, much less a consensus, reading of Poe. Part of this situation has come about because of the way Poe invited his audience to participate in his tales and poems. He succeeded remarkably well at creating his "unity of effect" with his readers. The horror tales create an effect of horror.

2

His comic tales create an effect of comedy. "The Raven" creates an effect of somber melancholy. Because of the involvement of the reader in the stories, the reader also participates in their interpretation. This dynamic results in the discovery of layers of meaning that Poe most likely never intended but that his writing *evokes* in the reader. One reason Poe's writings work this way is because of what Poe leaves unstated. (This artistic skill represents a norm of polite Southern conversation in which the most outrageous scandals may be discussed in the presence of children without them ever knowing.) He leaves many things to the imagination. Different imaginations see different horrors. At critical moments, when one would normally expect a detailed description of Beauty or of horror, Poe evokes, instead of describes, through the means of the mood he has created. He leaves it to the reader to form images, connections, and implications from their own imaginations.

In *Eureka* Poe resolved for himself what kind of universe exists. In contradiction with all the philosophy and science of his age and for the next century, Poe saw an expanding universe in which time and space form a single reality. He saw a universe in which the laws of nature did not exist until the Big Bang. He saw all of this and much more because of science. He also saw a God for whom "the universe is the perfect plot." a plot in which pain, Love, Beauty, and Justice fit together and finally make sense.

Re-imagining Edgar Allan Poe

In order to explore this reading of Poe's works, it will be helpful to re-imagine Poe. In the summer of 1849 Edgar Allan Poe returned home to Richmond, where he had spent almost twenty years of his young life. During that year, he had renewed a relationship with the *Southern Literary Messenger*, the magazine in Richmond where Poe had held his first job as an editor. Flush with fame from writing "The Raven" and restored to financial prosperity through his lectures that earned him three months' wages in a single evening, Poe returned to his hometown with honor and praise. At the height of his poetic powers, he wrote "Eldorado," "Annabel Lee," and "The Bells" in the year of his return.

During the previous year, Poe had published *Eureka*, his self-avowed magnum opus and the single work upon which he based all of his hopes for intellectual recognition and reputation. He returned to Richmond with renewed confidence in his dream of establishing a national magazine of his own, for as the nation began to recover from the crippling series of recessions that had so stricken his own financial position, Poe began to acquire the necessary backing for his journal. Finally, Poe returned to Richmond to renew the affection that had once defined his relationship with Elmira Royster Shelton, a recently widowed lady of Richmond who had been Poe's childhood sweetheart. By the end of the summer, they were engaged to be married.

As the idyllic year faded into fall, Poe left Richmond for New York, where he went to bring his aunt Maria Clemm, the mother of his dead wife Virginia, back to Richmond for the wedding. Unfortunately, Poe died on the way to New York while passing through Baltimore.

Poe as David Copperfield

4

During this same happy year, a friend of Poe's in London began writing a serial novel published in a monthly magazine. The novel was titled *David Copperfield* and its author, Charles Dickens, had met Poe while visiting Philadelphia in 1842.[3] During his long and influential literary career, Dickens declared that Poe was the only author he had ever tried to help get published. Dickens already knew Poe by reputation in 1842 because Poe's literary reviews of his novels had helped establish Dickens as a popular author in America. When Dickens visited Philadelphia, he had two extended, private interviews with Poe, who lobbied everyone he could interest in his vision of international copyright laws that would protect the intellectual property of authors like Dickens who did not receive a penny for pirated copies of their works printed in America.

During his last tour of America in 1867, Dickens visited Poe's destitute aunt Maria Clemm in Baltimore, where she lived in the "poor house," and gave her a large purse of gold. We can only speculate about what bonds with Poe would have led Dickens to visit

Mrs. Clemm and bestow such a lavish gift. Any correspondence that Poe might have had with Dickens during 1848–1849 would have been destroyed in 1860, when Dickens burned all of his letters. As for letters written from Dickens to Poe—at the end, when he died, Poe's own papers were purloined by his literary enemy, Rufus Griswold, and everything else was lost. We have enough references to letters, however, to know that they corresponded.[4]

Coincidence and speculation are all we have to help us understand the strange tradition of *David Copperfield* as an autobiographical work by Dickens. Because he worked in a blacking factory at age twelve and lived alone in a boarding house while his family lived in debtors' prison, *David Copperfield* is almost universally regarded as a fictional account of Dickens' own life. Beyond this autobiographical touch, however, David Copperfield seems quite unlike Charles Dickens and quite like Edgar Allan Poe.

Like Poe, and unlike Dickens, David Copperfield's earliest childhood was spent without a father. Like Poe, and unlike Dickens, David's mother died when he was still a child. Like Poe, and unlike Dickens, David had a malicious and untrustworthy foster/step-father from whom he separated himself. Like Poe, and unlike Dickens, David found a loving home and support with a paternal aunt. Like Poe, and unlike Dickens, David's aunt lost her wealth through the faithlessness of another party (in the case of the Poe family, Maria's father had loaned his entire fortune to the fledgling government during the American Revolution, which afterward refused to repay the loan though never disputing the legitimacy of the debt). Like Poe, and unlike Dickens, David fell deeply in love with a young woman who could not keep house and who died very young. Like Poe, and unlike Dickens, David and his young wife spoke "baby talk" to one another—David was called Dody, and Edgar was called Eddy. Like Poe, and unlike Dickens, David's beautiful young wife died a slow, lingering death. Like Poe, and unlike Dickens, David went into a deep depression over the death of his beautiful young wife and turned to drink and isolation. Like Poe, and unlike Dickens, David returned to his childhood sweetheart in the wake of newfound literary fame.

This evidence is all circumstantial because not a single note, scrap of paper, or literary rumor exists to suggest that Dickens had Poe in mind in 1849 when he began writing *David Copperfield* in monthly installments. All we have to go on is that the story resembles Dickens hardly at all, but it resembles Poe in almost every particularity. If Poe were the model for *David Copperfield*, however, it would help clear up the confusion in Dickens scholarship over how David Copperfield and Pip of *Great Expectations* could both be autobiographical portraits of Dickens.[5]

Many people know of Edgar Allan Poe, but almost everything that people know of him is wrong. Poe has grown so shadowed in myth that only those who have an interest in knowing him will ever do so. He is not a difficult person to know, but most people prefer the myth. If someone wanted to know Poe, however, they could not find a better character sketch of him than what Charles Dickens has provided with David Copperfield.

Poe as Pop Icon

6   For the most part, Poe had a happy life and experienced great love and affection in it. In the telling of Poe's story, however, it seems to have been recorded by Uriah Heep, the villian in *David Copperfield*. Poe is known to most people today as a deranged, drunken, drug-addled, morbid, death-obsessed, antisocial bohemian living on the fringes of society. How do we account for such a strange misconception of Poe in the popular mind and even among otherwise competent literary scholars?

Edgar Allan Poe stands with a tiny group of Americans who have continued over many decades as internationally recognizable figures. The only true literary lion America has ever produced, Poe has also achieved icon stature as a popular mythic figure. The bicentennial of his birth in 2009 demonstrated a universal appreciation for Poe that can only be compared with the adulation normally reserved for rock stars. Poe shared a bicentennial with Abraham Lincoln and Charles Darwin, but those two giants in their fields received scant notice from the public at large compared with the yearlong frenzy of observances of Poe's two-hundredth birthday. Ironically, of the several billion people who took note of Poe in 2009, either through active participation or through passively absorbing Poe references in the media and entertainment industry, probably fewer than a thousand know the real Poe.

Griswold and the Making of a Myth

Edgar Allan Poe died while passing through Baltimore on his way to New York on October 7, 1849. The myth of Edgar Allan Poe began on October 9, when Horace Greeley published an obituary of Poe in the *New York Tribune* written by Rufus Griswold. Griswold did not sign his own name to the obituary but used the concocted name of "Ludwig." Griswold described Poe as a deranged, debauched, and loathsome creature and created the myth of Edgar Allan Poe.

Indeed, Griswold described Poe as a pathological, anti-social deviant with all the imaginative skill he could muster:

> He walked the streets, in madness or melancholy, with lips moving in indistinct curses, or with eyes upturned in passionate prayers (never for himself, for he felt, or professed to feel, that he was already damned), but for their happiness who at that moment were objects of his idolatry; or with his glance introverted to a heart gnawed with anguish, and with a face shrouded in gloom, he would brave the wildest storms; and all night, with drenched garments and arms wildly beating the wind and rain, he would speak as if to spirits that at such times only could be evoked by him from that Aidenn close by whose portals his disturbed soul sought to forget the ills to which his constitution subjected him.[6]

7

This description of Poe represents Rufus Griswold's only successful piece of fiction. The ghastliness of the prose gave just the right touch of verisimilitude to dupe the public. Griswold did not stop at his obituary of Poe. Within the week of Poe's death he called on Maria Clemm, Poe's mother-in-law, who had lived with Poe for eighteen years, and told her that Poe's fondest wish was that he should edit his works in the event of his death. Griswold then persuaded Mrs. Clemm to convey to him the power of attorney over Poe's literary works.[7] Mrs. Clemm never received a penny from the sale of the highly successful, four-volume, collected works of Poe edited by Griswold. He included a biography in the second volume that became the accepted account of Edgar Allan Poe. Because Mrs. Clemm turned over to Griswold all of Poe's papers, he was able to alter passages in correspondence to create his vision of the diabolical Poe.

In his highly successful, conversational engagement with Poe, with its idiosyncratic title of *Poe Poe Poe Poe Poe Poe Poe*, Daniel Hoffman remarked that Griswold "went to extraordinary pains, after Poe's death, to present the deceased writer in a manner designed to make his name a household word for the dissolute, immoral, recklessly debauched."[8] W. H. Auden observed of Griswold's desecration of Poe's character,

> That one man should dislike another and speak maliciously of him after his death would be natural enough, but to take so much trouble, to blacken a reputation so subtly, presupposes a sustained hatred which is always fascinating because the capacity for sustaining emotion of any kind is rare, and, in this instance, particularly so since no reasonable cause for it has been found.[9]

For most people, however, Poe remains the dark figure created by Griswold.

The extent of Griswold's unscrupulous character assassination did not come to full light until the definitive biography of Poe by Arthur Hobson Quinn was published in 1942. In this book Quinn published Poe's original letters alongside Griswold's altered letters. But by 1942 the damage had been done, and the myth of Poe had been unshakably established in all the anthologies. Scholars who had enough interest might have discovered Quinn's biography and the extent to which Griswold had falsified the facts of Poe's life, but the myth of Poe's depraved insanity had stuck in the popular mind and in the tradition of how American schoolteachers and college literature professors talked about Poe.

What is more, Griswold seemed such a respectable and reliable source. He styled himself "the Reverend Doctor" Griswold, which provided him with the credentials necessary to speak authoritatively on any subject with relative certainty that what he said would be accepted as gospel. To this day, prominent Poe scholars refer to

8

Griswold as a Baptist minister, but he was only a very successful fraud and con artist. Catholics have Mass, Anglicans have the Book of Common Prayer, but Baptists have the minutes of their monthly business meetings. The energy that liturgical churches devote to observing the Christian year with its moveable feasts and saints' days, the Baptists devote to record keeping. They count their members and their weekly attendance. They count their baptisms and their burials.

For our purposes, the Baptists keep track of whom they ordain and whom they license. Ordination and licensure among the Baptists are not the same. A lay person may present themselves before their congregation and request that the church "license" or permit them to preach. Licensure means that a church has agreed to allow someone to demonstrate their calling from God with the appropriate evidence of the gift of preaching from the Holy Spirit. Rufus Griswold flirted with preaching, but the flirtation passed, and he was never ordained to the gospel ministry by a Baptist church. Nonetheless, Griswold assumed to himself the ecclesiastical dignity of "reverend" with all the rights, privileges, and open doors that the title could afford him in the 1840s. By the mid-1840s, he promoted himself to the preferment of "Doctor" as he aspired to the ranks of St. Thomas Aquinas. Having represented himself as a member of the clergy, Griswold's attacks on Poe had significant influence on the clergy.

Whereas Griswold spread his venom judiciously throughout the lengthy memoir of Poe that he included in his edition of Poe's works, magazines that later published "sketches" of Poe's life tended to collect the juiciest bits of Griswold into one concentrated medley of vitriol. In London, *The Leisure Hour: A Family Journal of Instruction* published one of the most succinct statements of Griswold's interpretation of Poe in 1854. The article opened with a lambasting of Poe's parents and then drew the natural conclusion that one was expected to draw:

> He was descended from parents, one of whom at least, his mother, had a good deal of wild blood, as it is termed, in her veins, which was not likely to be sobered down by the profession she adopted,

namely, that of an actress. . . . Such, then, was the parentage of
the poet, and it is worthy of record, as elucidating many parts of
his mind and character.[10]

Thus, Griswold's picture of Poe became enshrined in the popular
imagination. Noticing that Poe had lived in England for five years,
the author upbraided him for not so much as alluding to any
of the settings or scenery of England in any of his stories.[11] Poe
actually set at least six of his most important stories in England:
"Ligeia," "William Wilson," "The Balloon-Hoax," "Three Sundays in
a Week," "The Man of the Crowd," and "The Fall of the House of
Usher." This slur demonstrates the sort of ignorance that began to
surround treatments of Poe.

The case of Augustus Hopkins Strong (1836–1921) will serve
to illustrate how successful Griswold was in his depiction of Poe.
A. H. Strong was one of the leading Calvinist theologians of the late
nineteenth and early twentieth century. A Baptist minister educated
at Yale, Strong served for forty years as president of Rochester
Theological Seminary. His *Systematic Theology*, first published in
1886, is still in print today. As documentary evidence of Griswold's
falsification of Poe's life gradually came to light, Strong came to the
defense of Griswold:

> Let us remember that Poe made Rufus Wilmot Griswold his liter-
> ary executor, and trusted him as his biographer. Griswold was the
> most capable compiler of his day. He was nearest to the scenes,
> and was most familiar with the facts of Poe's life. His story was so
> damaging to the poet's reputation that later writers attributed its
> dark colors to personal animosity. The half century that has fol-
> lowed, however, although it has witnessed the discovery of new
> material, has invalidated no essential of Griswold's conclusions.[12]

In many ways, Strong represents the American popular mind and
even the vast majority of American literary scholars who have not
researched Poe. Griswold's portrait is the one they want. Do not
bother them with the facts. Who wants David Copperfield?

Griswold and Critical Assessment of Poe

While Griswold's successful annihilation of Poe's character is sad, he did something far worse to Poe as a writer. Griswold began a literary tradition of how to read Poe that remains unparalleled in all literary studies. Griswold declared that Poe's dark stories were all about Poe himself:

> Every genuine author in a greater or less degree leaves in his works, whatever their design, traces of his personal character; elements of his immortal being, in which the individual survives the person. While we read the pages of the *Fall of the House of Usher*, or of *Mesmeric Revelation*, we see in the solemn and stately gloom which invests one, and in the subtle metaphysical analogies of both, indications of the idiosyncrasies,—of what was most peculiar—in the author's intellectual nature.[13]

Griswold set literary people off on a treasure hunt to find Poe's morbidity and pathology in his stories, and the literary world took the bait. Scholars of the stature of Richard Wilbur scurried off with spades in hand to exhume Poe from his stories.[14] Daniel Hoffman observed that "Griswold didn't hesitate to impute to Poe the opium-taking, laudanum addiction, drunkenness, and madness that Poe made the attributes of characters in his tales."[15]

Following Griswold's lead, critics have sought Poe in the characters of his stories, as no one has ever done with any other writer. We assume that a good writer will write about what they know. Faulkner wrote about North Mississippi and borrowed stories from his family. Fitzgerald wrote about Princeton. Hemingway wrote about World War I, the Spanish Civil War, and the ex-patriots of the Lost Generation. Tolkien wrote about Hobbits and the Shire, which were based on C. S. Lewis and other friends who liked nothing better than to eat, drink beer, and smoke pipe weed in Oxford.

Critical treatment of Poe, however, has been of a different kind that equates the pathologies of Poe's characters with Poe himself. A. H. Strong claimed, "His tale, 'The Imp of the Perverse,' well describes his own mental and moral unsoundness," and that "'The Haunted Palace' is a picture of Poe's own soul."[16] In all of Poe's tales

11

of horror, Strong insisted that he merely "depicted the lashings of his own conscience."[17] Basil Ashmore claimed that the *Narrative of Arthur Gordon Pym* "is, in fact, nothing less than his own allegorical autobiography."[18] Wolf Mankowitz insisted that "The Fall of the House of Usher" was autobiographical because it was "tinctured with opium."[19] Even though Virginia Poe contracted tuberculosis almost three years after the publication of "The Fall of the House of Usher," Mankowitz clearly saw Virginia in the consumption-withered Madeline Usher.

By the time of the centennial of Poe's birth in 1909, two generations of college educated teachers, professors, literary critics, pastors, journalists, and other influencers of public opinion had learned from the textbooks that repeated Griswold's picture of Poe. In one of the memorial volumes produced for Poe's centennial, Thomas R. Slicer wrote, "The facts of Poe's life are three: he was an inebriate, he did use drugs, his mind was of that character that gathers its best capacity under stimulant" and that Poe was a man "of nervous derangement—a neurotic."[20] For his memorial volume, Slicer invited his readers to "imagine a very beautiful porcupine, [and] you will have a fair idea of Poe's relation to most people."[21] In spite of this certainty of the character of Edgar Allan Poe, or perhaps because of it, Slicer confessed an odd situation in the historical record: "but it is singular that those who knew him best and saw him oftenest are not those who condemn him most freely."[22]

Those Who Knew Him Best

As soon as Griswold began publishing his smears of Poe, those who knew Poe best responded. When Griswold published the first two volumes of Poe's *Works* in 1850, George R. Graham immediately responded to Griswold's biography of Poe with a lengthy defense of Poe's character. Griswold had worked for Graham as editor of *Graham's Magazine* after Poe's departure. Graham blasted away at Griswold by saying, "I knew Mr. Poe well—far better than Mr. Griswold."[23] Having denied the ecclesiastical title in which Griswold cloaked himself, Graham declared Griswold's depiction of Poe as "*unfair and untrue.*"[24] Graham charged Griswold with writing his memoir "in a moment of spleen, written out and laid aside, and handed to the printer, when his death was announced, with a sort of chuckle."[25]

Graham charged Griswold with distorting Poe's life and defaming his character as reprisal for Poe's evaluation of Griswold's literary judgment in editing *Poets and Poetry of America.* Griswold had devoted enormous space to his friends in that volume while neglecting the greater lights like Longfellow. Graham further disputed Griswold's characterization of Poe's temper and arrogance:

> As to his "quick choler" when he was contradicted, it depended a good deal upon the party denying, as well as upon the subject discussed. He was quick, it is true, to perceive mere quacks in literature, and somewhat apt to be hasty when pestered with them; but upon most questions his natural amiability was not easily disturbed.[26]

Graham went on to contradict, dispute, and marshal evidence against one statement after another that Griswold had made against Poe's character.

Poe had made Graham a wealthy man, and he did not do it through weakness of character. Graham described Poe's manner:

> No man was more quickly touched by a kindness—none more prompt to atone for an injury. For three or four years I knew him intimately, and for eighteen months saw him almost daily; much of the time writing or conversing at the same desk; knowing all his hopes, his fears, and little annoyances of life, as well as his high-hearted struggle with adverse fate—yet he was always the same polished gentleman—the quiet, unobtrusive, thoughtful scholar,—the devoted husband—frugal in his personal expenses—punctual and unwearied in his industry—*and the soul of honor* in all his transactions.

13

Throughout the article, Graham makes continued references to Poe's friends. One of the most galling aspects of Griswold's obituary, for it had become known by 1850 who had written it, was Griswold's opening statement "*that few would be grieved by*" Poe's death (emphasis added).

One would have thought that such a strenuous essay that screamed "Liar!" in every paragraph might have stemmed the growing myth of Poe. Alas, Graham's article appeared only in one issue of his magazine. Griswold's memoir appeared in every edition of Poe's *Works*. Griswold's four-volume Redfield edition remained in print for decades, only to be replaced in 1884 by a six-volume edition published by A. C. Armstrong with a new introduction by Richard Henry Stoddard, who hated Poe!

Sarah Helen Whitman, to whom Poe was engaged briefly in 1848, published a defense of him in 1860. Whitman responded to the growing myth of Poe's degeneracy; for example, an article she quotes from an 1858 issue of *Fraser's Magazine* claims that Poe had caused his wife to die of starvation. She cited another case in which Poe was alleged to have caused Virginia's death so that he could write funeral dirges about her.[27] Elmira Royster Shelton, Poe's fiancée at the time of his death, asked Dr. John Moran to write an account of Poe's death to counter the version that Dr. J. E. Snodgrass had begun to expound on the sawdust trail once he joined the temperance movement.[28] While Snodgrass had arranged for Poe to be taken to the hospital, Moran was the doctor who attended him at the hospital. Like Snodgrass' version of Poe's death, Moran's version suffers from many inaccuracies as Moran sought to wrest Poe from the clutches of the temperance movement, which found Poe to be a most helpful poster child. The movement wanted a lurid picture of a depraved Poe. Susan Talley Archer wrote an account of Poe's last summer in Richmond for *Scribner's* in 1878. She was a young woman and the member of a family acquainted with Poe's family and friends in Richmond. He gave his last public recitation at a party given by the Talleys at their home, which still stands in Richmond in the Fan District. She challenged Griswold on several points related to Poe's relations with his foster father based on what she had heard from "venerable ladies of Richmond."[29]

Several efforts at rival biographies by Poe defenders appeared in the 1870s. In 1874 John Ingram, an Englishman who devoted his life to the restoration of Poe's reputation, published a four-volume edition of Poe's *Works* in Edinburgh which he prefaced with a new

14

"Memoir" of Poe. In 1877 Eugene L. Didier published a new mem-
oir in *The Life and Poems of Edgar A. Poe*. The same year, William
Fearing Gill published his long, belabored, and much promoted *The
Life of Edgar Allan Poe*. Ingram then published a two-volume *Life,
Letters, & Opinions of Edgar Allan Poe* in 1880. Unfortunately, this
early group of biographers hated each other as much as they hated
Griswold. They feuded and carried on a dreadful row that did noth-
ing to enhance Poe's precarious reputation.

The beginning of reasonable Poe scholarship came in the next
generation. Professor George Edward Woodberry of Columbia University published a *Life of Poe* in 1885. In 1895 Woodberry and
Edmund Clarence Stedman, a respected businessman and poet, produced a ten-volume edition of Poe's *Works*. In 1902 Professor James
A. Harrison of the University of Virginia published a seventeen-
volume edition of Poe's *Works* that remains the most complete and
definitive edition in spite of several errors.[30]

Leading up to the fiftieth anniversary of Poe's death in 1899
and the centennial of his birth in 1909, a number of new editions
appeared along with numerous articles about him in the popular
magazines. Woodberry brought out a new two-volume biography in
1909. Mary E. Phillips and Hervey Allen both published two-volume
biographies in 1926, but these tended to take several steps backwards in their "creative nonfiction" approach at romanticizing Poe's
life. More helpful were the volumes of Poe's letters that began to
be published beginning in *Century Magazine* in 1894 and continuing with Harrison's two-volume edition of Poe's letters in 1903 and
Poe's correspondence with John Allan published as *Edgar Allan Poe
Letters Till Now Unpublished in the Valentine Museum, Richmond,
Virginia* in 1925.

Arthur Hobson Quinn published the definitive biography of Poe
in 1942. His inclusion of primary sources and careful assessment of
secondary sources has given Poe scholars a reliable starting place in
understanding Poe, the man. The second essential reference work
for Poe biography is John W. Ostrom's *The Collected Letters of
Edgar Allan Poe*, methodically revised, corrected, and expanded in
2008 by Burton R. Pollin and Jeffrey A. Savoye (Staten Island, N.Y.:

15

Gordian Press). Finally, an indispensable tool is the meticulous *The Poe Log*, edited by Dwight Thomas and David K. Jackson (Boston: G. K. Hall, 1987), which provides a daily account of the life of Poe with reference to the original sources. It is a treasure map that would neatly fit with "The Gold-Bug." Understanding the real Edgar Poe is important because of the curious twists and turns of literary criticism of Poe's work since his death. Some people work with the wrong treasure map.

The Critical Tradition

It is not surprising that reader response theory has such a strong, early connection with a study of Poe's "The Purloined Letter," because the history of criticism of Poe is the history of individuals who have imposed their agendas on the body of Poe's work.[31] What is surprising is that generations of American literary critics have pilloried Poe, yet his works continue to survive and thrive. His legacy and influence do not diminish, regardless of the ferocity with which his critics have insisted that his skill was rather superficial and vulgar. In the wake of Poe's bicentennial in 2009, it may be helpful to examine how the Poe critical tradition arose and why it could be so wrong in its contradictory assertions about Poe's works.

16

While much stress has been given to the role of Rufus Griswold in creating the myth of Edgar Allan Poe, comparatively little attention has been given to the "official" assessment of Poe's abilities as a poet and a story writer in his own lifetime. Griswold at least praised Poe for his literary genius. In New England, however, the literary establishment did not honor Poe's memory as a significant poet. Emerson referred to him as "the jingle man." The official arbiters of taste in New England, and especially the American academic world, with its capital in Cambridge, dismissed Poe. Harvard and the literary circle that thrived in its vicinity taught those who taught those who wrote the essays and edited the anthologies that explained Poe's place in American letters.

Poe's Contemporaries

Poe's contemporary literary enemies continued to exert enormous influence until the end of the nineteenth century. Richard Henry Stoddard never forgave Poe for saying that his "Ode on a Grecian Flute" was a flagrant plagiarism of Keats' "Ode on a Grecian Urn." In the second half of the nineteenth century, a poet of the stature of Stoddard had great standing with a new generation that accepted the judgments of literary lions like him. Stoddard wrote a number of essays about Poe in the popular magazines of the last half of the nineteenth century. In 1889 he wrote an article that would be embarrassing for him if it had not been so venomous. After quoting Malvolio's claim that "some have greatness thrust upon them," Stoddard claims that Poe belongs to this category of writer. He goes on to say in his introduction that it was his "good—or bad—fortune" to meet Poe when he was twenty-one. In contrast with Poe, Stoddard assured his readers that Rufus Griswold was a man of great kindness. After referring to Poe as a "highly-gifted but ill-balanced man of genius," Stoddard recounts how unjust Poe was to reject his poem "Ode on a Grecian Flute" in a rambling, pathetic, self-indulgent attack on Poe in which he accused him of everything but stealing the crown jewels. He reckoned that Poe was "not of the race of Chaucer, for he was not gracious, and was without honor."[32] Hervey Allen called this run at Poe "One of the most self-complacent articles ever written."[33]

17

Under this pervasive pillorying of Poe in the academy, young Henry James (1843–1916) came of age. James represented a new generation that did not know Poe, but which accepted the prejudices of its teachers. In an essay on Charles Baudelaire (1821–1867), James advised Americans to be wary of the French poet because Baudelaire was an avowed apostle of Poe. He added that "it seems to us that to take him with more than a certain degree of seriousness is to lack seriousness one's self."[34] Nonetheless, James considered Poe a "greater charlatan" than Baudelaire.[35] He viewed Poe's criticism as "the most complete and exquisite specimen of *provincialism* ever prepared for the edification of men" and that his judgment was "pretentious, spiteful, vulgar" though he was capable of the occasional "happy insight embedded in a patch of the most fatuous pedantry."[36]

With all of Poe's negative publicity, it is not surprising that he failed to gain enough votes in a literary survey conducted by *The Critic* in 1893 to be included in "The Best Ten American Books." Worse yet, he did not receive enough votes to be included among the twenty runners up. Edmund Gosse wrote a scathing letter to the editor from London to protest the oversight that he regarded as "sinister." He declared,

> While every year sheds more luster on the genius of Poe among the most weighty critical authorities of England, of France, of Germany, of Italy, in his own country prejudice is still so rampant that he fails to secure a paltry twenty votes when Wallace (who on earth is, or was, Wallace?) secures 252, Mrs. Jackson 57, and Mitchell (who is, or was, Mitchell?) 42. You must look to your own house, but it makes one wonder what is the standard of American style.[37]

As James reported in his review of Baudelaire, Poe had taken France by storm. Baudelaire translated *The Narrative of Arthur Gordon Pym*, Poe's short stories, and *Eureka* in five volumes between 1856 and 1865. Of his science fiction, Baudelaire said that Poe "ingeniously fabricated hoaxes flattering to the pride of *modern man*."[38] He read Poe philosophically and took great interest in Poe's insight into human nature: the human perversity which "modern philosophy does not wish to take into consideration."[39] Baudelaire said that even though Poe suggested that God may use human perversity to achieve his purposes, he preferred to think only about human perversity. Though Baudelaire championed Poe, we see in his appraisal of Poe the occasion to make of Poe what he would. As much as Poe's literary detractors in the twentieth century, Baudelaire's criticism of Poe is actually an exposition of himself.

When he bore in on Poe's ideas about literary composition and criticism, however, Baudelaire stood on firm ground. In recapitulating Poe, Baudelaire contrasted Poe's idea of Beauty with the prevailing American interest in utility. He grasped Poe's idea of imagination in a way no American critic ever did:

18

Imagination is not fantasy; nor is it sensibility. . . . Imagination is an almost divine faculty which perceives immediately and without philosophical methods the inner and secret relations of things, the correspondences and the analogies.[40]

Baudelaire grasped Poe's concept of the short story with the advantages of brevity for unity of impression. In his discussion of Poe's poetry, he grasped how Justice relates to Poe's vision of Beauty. The artist cannot have a sense of Beauty unless they also have a sense of deformity or disproportion. Thus, a true poet is particularly sensitive to injustice. Poe's reputed "temper" had nothing to do with the vulgar notion, but with "a more than usual clear-sightedness in respect to Wrong:—this clear-sightedness being nothing more than a corollary from the vivid perception of Right—of Justice—of proportion—in a word, of the beautiful."[41] In point after point, Baudelaire accepted Poe's instruction about short poems, that poetry is not meant for instruction, and that great art requires methodical effort: "There are no insignificant details in matters of art."[42]

The French interest in Poe would continue into the twentieth century.[43] Paul Valéry (1871–1945) was devoted to Poe and wrote an introduction to a 1927 edition of Baudelaire's translation of *Eureka*. Marie Bonaparte (1882–1962) published a controversial and largely discredited psychoanalytical study of Poe through his works. She relied heavily upon Griswold's assurance that the stories of Poe are all about Poe. At the height of the Cold War, Jacques Lacan (1901–1981) and Jacques Derrida (1930–2004) engaged in a dispute over the interpretation of "The Purloined Letter." Lacan proposed Structuralism, a controversial psychoanalytical theory, and Derrida disposed of it with Deconstruction, which denied any pure, original form. Thus, Poe lay at the heart of two of the major literary theories that were taken up in the United States.

About the same time that Baudelaire championed Poe in France, Fyodor Dostoevsky (1821–1881) translated three of Poe's tales into Russian and published them in his magazine, *Time*, in 1861. Dostoevsky demonstrated that Poe differed markedly from Hoffman, who depended upon the occult and otherworldly settings for his fantasy, while Poe established his fantasies with reality. Poe's imagination was invested with "the power of detail."[44] He said that Poe had the ability to present something that has never occurred before and never could, yet led the reader to believe in its possibility and even its reality. Dostoevsky mentioned in particular Poe's stories that we now call detective or mystery stories, and the stories that we now call science fiction. Though Dostoevsky did not forsake the novel for Poe's vision of the short story, Poe's "The Tell-Tale Heart" inspired his *Crime and Punishment*. Russian artists from Rachmaninoff and his magnum opus with orchestra and chorus based on "The Bells" to Nabokov's *Lolita* have taken inspiration from Poe.[45] It would be difficult to identify all of the substantial literary and cinematic figures who acknowledge having been influenced by Poe.[46]

Academic Literary Criticism

Major changes in the American academic curriculum that began in the last quarter of the nineteenth century had an impact on the critical study of Poe. In 1876 Francis James Child (1825–1896) of Harvard University, a philologist, received the first appointment as a professor of English literature in the United States. Until then, modern or contemporary literature had no recognized place in the curriculum of colleges and universities in the United States. By 1894 English language literature had become an established part of the high school curriculum. Vernacular literature had slipped into many colleges through studies in rhetoric and oratory, but as an academic discipline, English came late to the modern university along with the social sciences and the professional disciplines.

The classical curriculum had a centuries old tradition governing what it involved and how it was pursued. Mathematics and the sciences of chemistry and physics had clearly established disciplines and methods of study. The new English faculties across the English speaking world had the challenge of establishing what they actually studied and how they studied it. English was an academic discipline without a methodological discipline. The tradition of Poe studies throughout the twentieth century reflects the journey of academic literary criticism to find itself and establish, if not a common method, accepted standards of critical study of literature. Early studies of Poe provide more insight into the concerns of the critic than into the prose and poetry of Poe.

By the turn of the twentieth century, Poe's international reputation had grown so enormously as the only recognized American man of letters in Europe, that American critical opinion was forced to acknowledge that Poe had some ability. In a 1907 issue of *The Book News Monthly*, William Aspenwall Bradley presented his appraisal of Poe. Bradley began his "critical estimate" of Poe with an acknowledgment that America was forced by Poe's international acclaim to recognize his genius at last. Bradley warned, however, against too idolatrous a regard for Poe and suggested that Henry James may not have been far from the mark when he wrote, "An enthusiasm for Poe is the mark of a decidedly primitive stage of reflection." Bradley reminded his readers that Poe's "preoccupation was profoundly with the mechanical side of his art to the exclusion of all moral or intellectual significance," that he "took a puerile pleasure in mystification," and that he "loved, with the vanity of a Caglioastro, to adopt the cheap allures of a charlatan." He further explained that Poe's "aesthetic theories are in large means the characteristic product of the shallow spiritual soil from which they sprang."[47]

In contrast to Bradley, J. Brander Matthews (1852–1929), while musing on the work of the "natural historians" of literature in their efforts to discover the origins of the lyric or of elegy, declared that at least the origin of one species of literature is certain: "[t]he history of the detective story begins with the publication of the 'Murders in the Rue Morgue,' a masterpiece of its kind, which even its author was unable to surpass; and Poe, unlike most other originators, rang the bell the very first time he took aim."[48]

The introduction of English departments into the American universities came just a few years before the centennial of Poe's birth in 1909. The observation of this anniversary at the University of Virginia provided an occasion for a debate over Poe as a regional or national writer. Harvard professor Barrett Wendell delivered an address in which he argued that Poe represented his time and the entire country. In praising his fiction and poetry, however, Wendell

21

rejected Poe's essays and criticism as insignificant. In response to Wendell, Eugene Didier of Baltimore, who had written an early biography of Poe, published "Poe's Cult and Other Papers" (1909) in which he presented Poe as a southern hero along the lines of Robert E. Lee.[49]

C. Alphonso Smith, head of the English Department at the U.S. Naval Academy in Annapolis, contributed an article in 1922 for a special issue of *The Mentor* devoted to Poe. While many critics acknowledged Poe's skill at the short story, few had anything good to say about his poetry. Smith saw much in Poe's poetry to commend: "So far as I know, no new stanza had been coined in English literature since Spenser's time, till Poe appeared. The stanza structure of 'The Raven,' of 'To Helen,' and of 'Ulalume' are altogether new creations."[50] Because of the "flexibility and malleableness" with which Poe dealt with stanza structure, Smith claims that Poe "found the stanza a *solid*, but left it a *liquid*."[51] Smith took Poe at his word about how he wrote "The Raven" and considered the self-attentiveness that it expresses as one of Poe's great contributions to the craft of writing. As such, Poe remains the preeminent "spokesman of those who believe that genius, whether in literature, painting, sculpture, or music, must toil painstakingly and self-consciously to bridge the chasm between the first rapture and the well-ordered expression of that rapture in concrete form."[52] Smith defended Poe against the charge that he was not a true American writer because he had not written about American history, American scenery, American geography, American traditions, or American characters. Smith insisted that Poe's Americanism lay in his constructive genius which is the hallmark of American culture.[53]

Several important scholars played a key role in the establishment of Poe studies through textual criticism. Killis Campbell issued a scholarly edition of Poe's poems in 1917 followed by an edition of his tales in 1927.[54] Thomas Ollive Mabbott undertook a fifty-year project to establish the definitive text of Poe's works. Because Poe continued to refine and alter his work in an unending effort to improve his poetry and prose, Mabbott had a massive undertaking that was not finished when he died in 1968. The work was

22

carried forward by Maureen Cobb Mabbott, Eleanor Kewer, Patricia Edwards Clyne, and Burtin Pollin, who completed the project.

Theoretical criticism flowered after World War II, and Poe studies had more than its share of theoretical enthusiasts. For the most part, these varied approaches to literary criticism as the discipline developed in the United States derived their method and purpose from the social sciences and philosophy, particularly psychology, sociology, anthropology, and the philosophy of language. Very few efforts at academic literary criticism until the late twentieth century dealt with the kinds of things Poe would have thought important in his literary reviews. Poe assumed a standard of quality by which a piece of literature or, indeed, any work of art might be judged, and he critiqued his contemporaries in view of this standard. In the twentieth century, however, the academy abandoned the concept of any sort of standard of artistic excellence and sought something to discuss about literature in other disciplines. To complicate matters for Poe, it was not unusual for prominent American literature professors like Harold Bloom, who had no particular expertise in Edgar Allan Poe, to edit volumes of Poe's works or collections of essays about Poe to which they appended introductions that made little contribution.[55] With the consistent work of those scholars who have devoted themselves to studying Poe and the formation of the Poe Studies Association in 1972, however, recognized Poe scholars are increasingly available who have assumed the editing responsibilities for these books.[56] As much as the New England tradition had continued to vilify Poe and curse his writing, desperate to explain how the great figures of nineteenth-century French literature could have considered Poe a significant writer, the French renewed their appreciation for Poe who stood at the center of the new directions in literary theory.[57]

Variety

Poe did not care for the selection of short stories chosen by Evert Duyckinck for inclusion in Wiley & Putnam's 1845 edition of Poe's *Tales*. He did not think the selection gave a broad enough sample of his work to demonstrate his versatility as a prose fiction writer.

In a letter to Philip Cooke on August 9, 1846, Poe expressed his understanding of the relationship between individual stories to the whole body of his work:

> In writing these Tales one by one, at long intervals, I have kept the book-unity always in mind—that is, each has been composed with reference to its effect as part of *a whole*. In this view, one of my chief aims has been the widest diversity of subject, thought, & especially *tone* & manner of handling.[58]

Poe does not make a farfetched claim to Cooke. When he first began writing short stories in Baltimore in the early 1830s, he did so with the intention of publishing a collection of short stories produced by members of the fictitious "Folio Club." The members of the club, like Chaucer's pilgrims, would each contribute a tale, and the variety of club members would account for the variety of forms found in the collection. Poe tried for years to interest publishers in his *Tales of the Folio Club*. Though he never published the collection, he intentionally wrote diverse types of stories, fearing the possibility that he might ever be "typecast" as the author of only one type of tale. To a great extent, Poe has been typecast as the master of horror by the selection of his stories included in the anthologies for the study of American literature in high school and college.

Poe's tales may be grouped in a variety of ways and scholars will disagree over which category a tale most closely represents. Some fit nicely into more than one category; such as "Three Sundays in a Week" which is a love story, a comic story, and science fiction all at once.[59] In an article about Poe's genius in 1854, George R. Graham said that Poe's stories could be divided into three groups: his science fiction, his mysteries, and his tales of pure imagination. Notably, Graham called the mystery stories tales of ratiocination, as Poe had done. Yet, he had no name to call the science fiction. Nonetheless, he gives us an important early definition of the literary form that would not have a name for another seventy years. Graham said that these tales had in common

> an appearance of reality and a *vraisemblance* so perfect as almost to compel credence to what we know to be impossible, is

maintained by earnestness of style, vigor of description, minute attention to the most seemingly immaterial and trivial details, the mingling of known truths of nature with the wildest and strangest fancies, and "the application of scientific principles, so far as the whimsical nature of the subject would permit," to subjects whimsical, absurd and impossible.[60]

The following tabulation, however, suggests the variety and scope of Poe's writing. We tend to forget that Poe was the Mark Twain of the first half of the nineteenth century, for his tales of humor and satire far outnumber his tales of terror.[61]

Humor and Satire: 24

"King Pest"
"The System of Doctor Tarr and Professor Fether"
"Mystification"
"Loss of Breath"
"The Man That Was Used Up"
"Diddling Considered as One of the Exact Sciences"
"The Angel of the Odd"
"The Thousand-and-Second Tale of Scheherazade"
"The Business Man (Peter Pendulum)"
"A Tale of Jerusalem"
"The Sphinx"
"Why the Little Frenchman Wears His Hand in a Sling"
"Bon-Bon"
"The Duc De L'Omlette"
"The Literary Life of Thingum Bob, Esq."
"How to Write a Blackwood Article"
"A Predicament"
"X-ing a Paragrab"
"The Devil in the Belfry"
"Lionizing"
"Some Words with a Mummy"
"The Spectacles"
"Four Beasts in One"
"Never Bet Your Head to the Devil"

Science Fiction: 11

"The Balloon-Hoax"
"Mesmeric Revelation"
"The Unparalleled Adventure of One Hans Pfaall"
The Narrative of Arthur Gordon Pym
"Mellonta Tauta"
"Three Sundays in a Week"
"The Colloquay of Monos and Una"
"The Conversation of Eiros and Charmion"
"The Island of the Fay"
"The Power of Words"
"Von Kempelen and His Discovery"

Mystery and Crime: 10

"The Murders in the Rue Morgue"
"The Mystery of Marie Rogêt"
"The Purloined Letter"
"The Gold-Bug"
"Thou Art the Man"
"The Man of the Crowd"
"The Imp of the Perverse"
"The Tell-Tale Heart"
"The Black Cat"
"The Cask of Amontillado"

Supernatural Horror: 10

"Ligeia"
"A Tale of the Ragged Mountains"
"Morella"
"Metzengerstein"
"The Oval Portrait"
"William Wilson"
"The Facts in the Case of M. Valdemar"
"MS. Found in a Bottle"
"Shadow"
"The Mask of the Red Death"

Natural Horror: 8

"A Descent into the Maelström"
"Berenice"
"The Fall of the House of Usher"
"The Pit and the Pendulum"
"The Oblong Box"
"The Premature Burial"
"Silence—A Fable"
"Hop-Frog"

Beauty: 5

"The Island of the Fay"
"The Domain of Arnheim"
"Landor's Cottage"
"Eleonora"
"Morning on the Wissahiccon"

This listing makes no claim to be definitive. Rather, it suggests the variety of stories that Poe told. Yet some modern critics will tend to identify one kind of story as the kind of story Poe wrote, just as he feared during his lifetime.[62] Alternatively, critics may latch onto one theme or topic that Poe addressed as the single key to unlatching Poe.[63] Allen Tate, one of the most respected literary critics of the twentieth century and one who admired Poe, famously remarked, "Everything in Poe is dead: the houses, the rooms, the furniture, to say nothing of nature and of human beings."[64] In making this statement, of course, Tate has reduced Poe's body of work to only his tales of horror.

Poe's Poetry and the Modern Critique

Little has been said so far about Poe's poetry. It did not serve the utilitarian purpose set by the New England moralists that poetry should teach a moral lesson and instill patriotism. In the twentieth century, however, Poe's poetry sinned against a new fashion. In a candid bit of self-awareness, T. S. Eliot came to understand one of the reasons for the French enthusiasm for Poe that he had

27

never shared. The French tended to read Poe in terms of his total body of work, while Americans tended to see Poe only in fragments (though Henri Justin has pointed out that even Baudelaire neglected to translate Poe's comedies[65]). In other words, American taste was affected by the social impetus toward fragmentation and against Poe's aesthetic and philosophical concern for unity. Eliot observed:

> If we examine his work in detail, we seem to find in it nothing but slipshod writing, puerile thinking unsupported by wide reading or profound scholarship, haphazard experiments in various types of writing, chiefly under pressure of financial need, without perfection in any detail. This would not be just. But if, instead of regarding his work analytically, we take a distant view of it as a whole, we see a mass of unique shape and impressive size to which the eye constantly returns.[66]

Eliot criticized Poe for "dabbling" in so many different forms instead of settling down into one genre. He also finds fault with Poe's detective stories for a strange reason: modern detective writing had made great advances over Poe's original mysteries. I suppose in the same way, the 747 is a much more comfortable way to travel than the Wright brothers' original biplane, but that would be cynical of me. As for why the French liked Poe's poetry, Eliot concluded that it must be because they do not speak English.[67] Eliot has no regard for *Eureka* because Poe was not a specialist in philosophy, theology, or science. In a world of fragmentation and specialization, any attempt at unity of thought has no place because only the specialist has warrant to speak, yet cannot speak in an area without specialization.[68]

Eliot's greatest criticism of Poe, and of the French poets Baudelaire, Mallarmé, and Valéry, whom Poe influenced, is the dedication to self-conscious writing. He levels his greatest disdain for "The Raven" and Poe's description of how he wrote it in "The Philosophy of Composition." Eliot declared, "It is difficult for us to read that essay without reflecting, that if Poe plotted out his poem with such calculation, he might have taken a little more pains over it: the result hardly does credit to the method."[69] In fact, Eliot concluded that "The Philosophy of Composition" was a hoax because no one would go to that much trouble to write a poem. Eliot's unstated

28

reason for not regarding Poe as a poet is that the fashion had changed. Eliot played the critical and definitive cross-the-Rubicon, can't-go-back-now, burn-the-bridges role in changing poetry in the twentieth century in a way that poetry had never changed before in world history. Poe defined poetry as the creation of rhythmical Beauty, but Eliot had something entirely different in mind. Poe was concerned with creating an effect in the audience, but the tradition of poetry that followed Eliot did not have the same concern for the audience.

When the twentieth century began, the American people enjoyed poetry as a popular form of entertainment, as people in most cultures have since the beginning of recorded history and no doubt earlier than written language. After World War I in the West, we see one of the most startling cultural events in world history: a culture lost its poetry. Poets continued to write, but not in a way that the culture could hear. Poets experimented with forms for themselves but grew disconnected from the ear of the culture. Poe had little regard for the opinions, artistic judgment, or aesthetic taste of the mob, but he understood that the poet does not write for himself.

Conclusion

In spite of critical opinion, "The Raven" is the best known poem ever written by an American.[70] People in the United States and abroad do not merely know the name of the poem and its author, they freely quote lines from it—one of the only poems many Americans can quote. Poe continues to save high school American literature classes from utter boredom.[71] Regardless of the changes in academic, critical opinion about what constitutes good literature, Poe's audience has never failed. He continues to be read for pleasure. His critical judgments about his contemporary writers have all proven true. Apart from Hawthorne and Longfellow, he has few contemporaries who have survived, and even Hawthorne and Longfellow survive largely as required reading. Poe still "sells," but he would be the last person to have regard for an author simply because of popularity. His continued success has little to do with current fashions. His

29

appeal over many generations suggests that he transcends the latest literary fads of the mob. In spite of the confusion over the mythology of Poe and the disarray of critical opinion, Poe continues to speak to successive generations.

I have heard Poe dismissed because he does not treat the great universal issues, but I believe that view completely misses the reason that Poe speaks so powerfully to such a global audience. Poe deals with the questions that people ask in every place, in every time, and in every culture.[72] As Holt Edmunds, longtime member of the board of trustees of the Poe Museum in Richmond, constantly reminds me, "I don't care about Poe's life; it's his stories that I want to hear."

THE PROBLEM OF SUFFERING

By temperament and habit, Edgar Allan Poe had a cheerful and optimistic disposition. Like everyone else, however, Poe's life had highs and lows during which he responded appropriately. During periods of tragedy or loss, Poe experienced bouts with grief. In moments of injustice, Poe expressed righteous anger. On the whole, Poe's life could be called happy. He had his share of disappointments and tragedies, but he also succeeded at his only real ambition—to become a significant poet.

Like most of the people of the world, Edgar Allan Poe wondered about the problem of suffering. Why do the innocent suffer? Why does pain and death stalk the lives of everyone? This question haunted the Buddha and Job. It lay in the background of the work of Poe's contemporary Charles Darwin. For most people, the question does not represent merely a philosophical curiosity but an existential dilemma. The same could be said for Poe. He experienced the problem of suffering.

The child of actors before motion pictures made the celebrity of actors near worshipful in American culture, Poe was orphaned in 1811 when only two years old. Only the strenuous insistence of several ladies in Richmond upon their influential husbands made it possible for Poe's mother to be buried at the edge of the church-yard of St. John's church, where Patrick Henry had made his famous "give me liberty" speech on the eve of the Revolution. Poe and his younger sister Rosalie were taken in by two families of Richmond: the Allans and the Mackenzies. Their older brother, William Henry Leonard Poe, was sent to Baltimore to live with their grandfather, General David Poe. Having loaned his fortune to the patriot cause during the Revolution, General Poe lived in impoverished circumstances in Baltimore awaiting the government's willingness to repay the loan.

Love and Affection

Young Edgar Poe made his home with Frances Allan and her husband John Allan, a Scottish-born merchant in Richmond who engaged in trade with Britain. Mrs. Allan's sister Ann Moore (Aunt Nancy) Valentine completed the household. The War of 1812 wrecked John Allan's business, so after the war, he took his family with him to London for five years in an effort to rebuild his trade. Though not wealthy, the Allans had a comfortable, middle-class life. In Richmond they lived for a time in the rooms above the warehouse of the firm of Ellis and Allan in Shockoe Bottom beside the James River. In England they lived for a time in Stoke Newington, a pleasant village near London where Cowper had lived. Young Edgar attended Dr. Bransby's Manor School in Stoke Newington from 1817 until 1820. John Allan's attempts to revive his business did not succeed, and the family returned to Richmond in June 1820.

Having lived almost half his life in England, the eleven-year-old boy had seen things and heard tales that would stimulate his imagination for the rest of his life. He sailed the Atlantic twice, providing vivid material for "MS. Found in a Bottle," "The Oblong Box," and *The Narrative of Arthur Gordon Pym*. On trips to Scotland to visit Mr. Allan's relatives, Poe would have seen romantic landscapes, ruined manor houses, and a rich array of customs and behavior that would ornament his poetry and tales. At the Tower of London he would hear the dark stories of Henry VIII and the killing of his wives, Richard III and the murder of his little nephews, and the Tower ravens. According to legend, if the ravens ever leave the Tower, the British monarchy will fail; therefore, the wings of the ravens are clipped so that they may flit but never quit the Tower.

Upon returning to Richmond, the Allans spent the summer with John Allan's business partner Charles Ellis, who lived on the hill above Shockoe Bottom, and settled into a new house near the Ellis family on Clay Street at the end of the summer. By all accounts of those who knew him as a child, these were happy days for Edgar Poe, though it was hardly a time of luxury and extravagance for the Allans. John Allan's debts continued to accumulate and his properties were mortgaged to the hilt. The family lived with Scottish frugality and young Edgar learned to live simply.

Poe developed his strong sense of honor as a schoolboy in Richmond. The story was retold by his schoolmates that on one occasion a much bigger boy had said that Poe was a liar or a rascal. Poe confronted the offender and a fight ensued. The larger boy soon was on top of Poe, beating his head mercilessly until he grew weary, at which point Poe turned the tables on the larger boy and won the fight. Such episodes were rare, and Poe's school days were remarkable for his exemplary conduct which spared him the rod that school masters of that day so enjoyed exercising on their pupils.

Despite his slight size, Poe was the leading athlete at William Burke's school.[1] Of his athletic ability, Andrew Johnston said, "In athletic exercises he was foremost: especially, he was the best, the most daring, and most enduring swimmer that ever I saw in the water."[2] John Preston recalled Poe's athletic ability during their days at Joseph Clarke's Richmond Academy: "In the simple school athletics of those days, when a gymnasium had not been heard of, he was *facile princeps*. He was a swift runner, a wonderful leaper, and what was more rare, a boxer, with some slight training. . . . For swimming he was noted, being in many of his athletic proclivities surprisingly like Byron in his youth."[3] Poe's most famous feat came when he swam the six miles from Ludlow Wharf to Warwick against the tide of the James River on a hot June afternoon.[4]

Despite his superior athletic and intellectual abilities in school, Poe had few close friends in Richmond because of what many

33

considered an unsuitable social background as the child of stage actors. Preston remarked, "Of Edgar Poe it was known that his parents were players, and that he was dependent upon the bounty that is bestowed upon an adopted son."[5] Rather than shrink from acknowledging his parents, however, Poe joined the Thespian Society where he demonstrated talent on the stage, much to the displeasure of Mr. Allan.[6] Years later as the country's most famous literary critic, Poe wrote in the *Broadway Journal,* "The writer of this article is himself the son of an actress—has invariably made it his boast—and no earl was ever prouder of his earldom than he of his descent from a woman who, although well born, hesitated not to consecrate to the drama her brief career of genius and beauty."[7]

Poe was not devoid of friends during his youth. Among his best friends, Robert Stanard often invited Poe home. Stanard's mother would play one of the most significant roles in young Poe's life, for she encouraged him to write poetry. He had written love poetry for the benefit of the girls in the boarding school run by Jane Mackenzie, the sister of Rosalie Poe's foster father. Jane Stith Stanard, however, encouraged Poe to take his talent more seriously. She was a beautiful woman known for her graciousness. She gave Poe attention as he grew from childhood to early adolescence, and he responded with devotion. Jane Stanard embodied for Poe true Beauty which went beyond physical appearance to innate character. She also provided something troubling and painful to watch, for she began a rapid decline into insanity about the time Poe met her. She was soon confined, and on April 28, 1824, she died. The transformation had been swift and relentless. Poe witnessed the frailty of the human mind, and for the first time, he experienced the loss to death of someone he loved deeply. At the age of fifteen, Poe had his first taste in his memory of tragedy.

Justice and Righteous Anger

Edgar Poe had a profound sense of Justice and integrity that marked his work as a literary critic and permeated his personal relationships. The first great instance of Poe's outrage at injustice occurred in his late teens while still living at home in Richmond with his foster parents. He had known great love and affection from Frances Allan and her sister, Nancy Valentine. According to Elmira Royster Shelton who was Poe's childhood sweetheart, "He was devoted to the first Mrs. Allan and she to him."[8] Mr. Allan had always seemed generous and indulgent of the boy. In a letter to his cousin William Poe in 1835, Edgar remarked that he had been raised with the expectation of inheriting a great fortune from the childless Mr. Allan.[9]

As it turned out, Mr. Allan had been rather prolific with several illegitimate litters scattered about Richmond. As long as John Allan lived in Shockoe Bottom in an apartment above his warehouse, he could have a variety of lady friends without fear that his secret would be known. Being a mere merchant in an aristocratic community, he was far too inconspicuous to notice. All of that changed on March 16, 1825, when John Allan's uncle, William Galt, died and left him the bulk of his vast estate. From the lowest point in Richmond in the warehouse district on Shockoe Creek, Allan moved to the highest point in the city. He purchased the grand, brick mansion named Moldavia, with its handsome double piazza that allowed him to look down on the entire city and survey the countryside up and down the James River. The Allans had arrived. Wealth thrust them into the first place of society, for William Galt's three plantations that stretched across Goochland and Fluvanna Counties made John Allan one of the wealthiest men in Virginia when Virginia was the wealthiest state in the republic.[10]

In the period leading up to William Galt's death, the warm affection that had existed between John Allan and Edgar had deteriorated to frigidity. Poe's most important biographers agree that Allan's affairs became known to the family about this time.[11] With a reputation to protect, it appears that John Allan began discrediting Edgar as the child of actors to ensure that no one would believe anything that he might say about Allan's extramarital romps. Given Poe's affection for Frances Allan, the last thing he would have wanted was for her to be exposed to public humiliation, but John Allan's sudden change in attitude toward Edgar is apparent in his letters and other papers.[12] Allan sent Edgar off to the recently opened University of Virginia in Charlottesville during its second term of operation in February 1826. The fabled wealth in which Edgar had been raised lasted for less than one year. Allan sent him to the university, but he declined to pay the full bill for his tuition and fees.

Poe had an outstanding record at the university as a student of ancient and modern languages, focusing his attention on Latin and French. Unfortunately, Allan not only declined to pay Poe's full university expenses, but he also failed to provide him with living expenses. Some of the other young Virginia gentlemen at the university endeavored to teach young Edgar to drink. In the process, he discovered that he did not take to it very well. (The Poe family, on the whole, has shown a predisposition to alcoholism for some 250 years that we can document.)[13] Poe finally resorted to gambling to cover his expenses but lost terribly, incurring a "debt of honor" which he could not pay.[14] Poe had to leave the university, but the University of Virginia has preserved the financial records of that period and regularly places the noteworthy page on exhibit to vindicate their most illustrious alumnus, something John Allan would never have anticipated. Ironically, the truth about Allan's affairs came out by his own admission when he died, for he included several of his illegitimate children in his will but left Edgar nothing.

Leaving Edgar out of his will and cutting him off without support was not the worst thing that Allan did. During the same period of the growing estrangement between Edgar and Mr. Allan, Edgar had fallen in love with a beautiful girl in the neighborhood named Elmira Royster. When Edgar left for the university, they had an understanding. The prospect of a marriage to the only logical heir of the wealthy John Allan would have made good sense to Elmira's father. Once Edgar had gone to the university, however, Elmira never heard from him again. She wrote and wrote, but he never replied. By the end of the year, Mr. Royster had arranged for Elmira to marry Barrett Shelton, a well-to-do planter. According to Elmira Royster Shelton, recalling the events in 1875, she did not learn until she was married that Edgar had written to her continually.[15] Elmira's father had intercepted the correspondence, which would only make sense if John Allan had assured Mr. Royster that Edgar would not inherit or receive any support from him. Edgar returned to Richmond after his humiliating departure from the university because of Allan's nonpayment of fees to learn that Elmira was engaged.

We have numerous accounts from the life of Edgar Poe in which he had conflict with people, beginning with John Allan. These situations all have a common feature: someone has been injured through injustice. The conflict with Allan began because of Allan's faithlessness to Mrs. Allan, but it enlarged to include multiple acts of malice that injured Edgar tremendously. Allan injured Edgar in a variety of ways that left no way for Edgar to defend himself or repair the damage. Worst of all, Elmira was lost to him as one dead. The episode left Poe with one of his most constant and sustained poetic images: death as a metaphor for what has been lost forever. In this sense, murder becomes a metaphor for injustice of any kind.[16]

On His Own

Poe left the Allan home and Richmond on March 19, 1827, following a quarrel with Allan over his future. Allan would not allow Poe to remain in his house if he pursued a literary career. Poe at least knew his own mind and knew that Allan would suffocate him if he submitted to the kind of living entombment that Allan required. By now, Poe would have understood that Mr. Allan's newfound wealth would not be a part of his own future. Wealth seemed to have corrupted the once happy home, and Edgar walked away from it forever.

He went to Boston, the town where he was born and where his mother had known great success on the stage. Biographers assume that Mrs. Allan provided Poe with travel money out of the meager household funds that John Allan made available to her. Poe had no memory of his mother, but he had a miniature portrait of her and a small watercolor of Boston harbor that she had painted while living there. On the back she had written a brief inscription to Edgar as she lay dying: "For my little son Edgar, who should ever love Boston, the place of his birth, and where his mother found her best, and most sympathetic friends."[17] Poe had no connections of his own in Boston who could help him, and on May 26, 1827, he did what so many other young men nursing a broken heart and without prospects have done—he joined the army.

Poe enlisted in H Battery of the first artillery which was stationed at Fort Independence in Boston Harbor. Between his enlistment and January 1, 1829, less than two years later, Poe rose in the ranks to regimental sergeant major, the highest rank possible in the army for those who had not attended West Point. Such advancement normally took a man his entire military career to attain. His self-discipline, his attention to his appearance, his methodical attention to detail, and his sense of honor and duty contributed to his success in the army. Though his education had always focused on language, Poe demonstrated mathematical skills so necessary in the artillery. While the prospect of serving as a clerk in Allan's warehouse held no charm for Poe, he served with distinction as a clerk in the artillery. In contrast to the susceptibility of so many enlisted men to drink away their slight wages, Poe was known to the officers for his sobriety and steady ways. Army life came long before the stories of Poe's bouts with alcohol.

38 During his first summer in the army, Poe published his first book of poems and named it for the longest poem in the collection, *Tamerlane*. The slight book is little more than a forty-page pamphlet with paper wrappers, and its poetry written during Poe's adolescence touches on the two subjects of all adolescent poetry: unrequited love and death.[18] The signature poem runs on for 406 lines as it tells the tale of a great Mongol conqueror who forsook love for earthly gain. Poe does not deal kindly with the man whose pride (a frequently repeated word) led him to abandon love for wealth. John Allan had made a fool's bargain, if we may suppose that Allan provides part of the impulse for so long a poem. The character, Tamerlane, could not represent Poe himself, who views Love as the only thing in life worth aspiring to. When the scene shifts to Tamerlane's youth and "Young Love's first lesson," we may assume that the poem focuses on Edgar and Elmira. In its early lines we find a hint of the very last poem Poe wrote:

O, she was worthy of all love!
Love—as in infancy was mine—

'Twas such as angel minds above
Might envy; her young heart the shrine

These early lines seem to have their echo in "Annabel Lee," in
which Poe writes of his childhood sweetheart:

With a love that the winged seraphs of Heaven
Coveted her and me.
. . . .
The angels, not half so happy in Heaven,
Went envying her and me;

Death plays two parts in "Tamerlane." For Tamerlane, it comes as
a judgment on his injudicious choice. The death of the beloved,
however, represents a loss of such finality that no hope remains of
its recovery. Thus, the desolation of a young broken heart.

In November of his first year in the army, Poe embarked with
his battery on a ten-day voyage to Fort Moultrie on Sullivan's Island
which protected Charleston harbor. He spent a year on the remote
and wild island with leisure time to enjoy the long walks he had
always favored. This barrier island was a shell collector's paradise
before the jetty was constructed off the coast. Poe would have
become casually acquainted with the shells he wrote about in *The
Conchologist's First Book* several years later. More importantly for
his career, on Sullivan's Island Poe imbibed the romance of the
pirate lore still told by local Charlestonians about the days when
Black Beard, Stede Bonnet, and their ilk raided Charleston. Tales of
pirate treasure formed part of the local lore Poe would have heard
and provided the atmosphere out of which he drew his tale "The
Gold-Bug," which he set on Sullivan's Island. Poe set most of his
tales in no distinct place, which allowed the reader to appropriate
the tale to their own imaginary place, but he set several tales in and
about Charleston, including "The Gold-Bug," "The Balloon Hoax,"
and "The Oblong Box."

In December 1828 Poe's brigade was reassigned to Fortress
Monroe at Point Comfort, Virginia, near the mouth of the Chesa-
peake Bay. Poe's officers had encouraged him to seek an appointment to West Point, but to seek such an appointment he must first

39

secure a replacement who would serve out his term as an enlisted man. Poe wrote three letters to John Allan to request his aid in paying the bounty but heard no reply until Allan wrote to say that Frances Allan was dying. By the time Poe was granted a furlough, she had died on February 28, 1829. The mainstay of Poe's happy childhood and the source of stability and security in his life was now gone. Poe now had a deeper acquaintance with loss and grief.

Poe and Allan were on their best behavior for the funeral and period of mourning. Allan had a black mourning suit quickly made for Poe. This suit would appear in numerous descriptions of Poe over the next twenty years until his own death in 1849. A suit would have been more necessary for Allan's reputation than for Edgar's comfort. It would have been humiliating to Allan for the neighbors to learn that his foster child was a common enlisted soldier serving in the ranks. The army was a perfectly respectable profession for a gentleman who was an officer, but not an enlisted man. Allan agreed to help Edgar secure his place at West Point, but this rather inexpensive act probably had more to do with his social standing than any desire to renew affection with Edgar now that Mrs. Allan was dead. At West Point, Poe would be far, far away.

On April 17, 1829, Poe was replaced in his brigade by Sergeant Samuel Graves, a solider whose term of enlistment had expired, who agreed to reenlist in place of Poe. The normal bounty that Poe expected to pay was $12, but Graves demanded $75, which outraged John Allan. Instead of returning to Richmond to live at Moldavia while awaiting news of his acceptance to West Point, Poe went to Baltimore to seek out his family.

Poe's family in Baltimore had fallen on hard times. In the War of 1812 the aged General Poe had gone to the barricades in Baltimore to fight the British again during the battle in which Francis Scott Key wrote "The Star Spangled Banner." He had died soon after the close of the war and his widow subsisted on a government annuity of $240 because the Maryland legislature refused to pay the forty thousand dollars owed to the general. The general's widow, Elizabeth Poe, lived with her daughter, Maria Clemm, whose husband William had died in 1825, leaving her impoverished with two small children. The household also included Poe's older brother Henry, who had gone on an extended sea voyage to seek his fortune only to return as an alcoholic.

Poe lived in a boarding house during this first sojourn in Baltimore and took steps to advance his career as a poet. Though the Poe family now lived in poverty, they were still known to many prominent Baltimoreans, including William Witt, who had publishing connections in Philadelphia. The firm of Carey, Lea, and Carey declined the opportunity to publish Poe's poetry, but Hatch and Dunning of Baltimore agreed to publish his second book without requiring Poe to subsidize it. In addition to the poems collected in his first little book, *Al Aaraaf, Tamerlane, and Minor Poems* included the poetry that Poe wrote while in the army. When he had submitted the collection to Carey, Lea, and Carey, he described the title poem:

> It's [*sic*] title is "Al Aaraaf"—from the Al Aaraaf of the Arabians, a medium between Heaven & Hell where men suffer no punishment, but yet do not attain that tranquil & even happiness which they suppose to be the characteristic of heavenly enjoyment. . . .
>
> I have placed this "Al Aaraaf" in the celebrated star discovered by Tycho Brahe which appeared and disaapeared [*sic*] so suddenly. It is represented as a messenger star of the Deity, &, at the time of its discovery by Tycho, as on an embassy to our world. One of the peculiarities of Al Aaraaf is that, even after death,—those who make choice of the star as their residence do not enjoy immortality—but, after a second life of high excitement, sink into forgetfulness & death—This idea is from Job—"I would not live <them> always—let me alone." I have imagined that some would not be pleased . . . with an immortality even of bliss.[19]

41

The poem is important for understanding the development of Poe's interests more than for its merit as a poem. We find Poe's interest in astronomy influencing his art twenty years before the publication of *Eureka*. The relationship between the physical and the spiritual, between science and God, was not a late development, but a prolonged issue reflected in the little untitled poem that served as the preface to *Al Aaraaf.*

Science! meet daughter of old Time thou art
Who alterest all things with thy peering eyes!
Why prey'st thou thus upon the poet's heart,
Vulture! whose wings are dull realities!
How should he love thee—or how deem thee wise
Who woulds't not leave him, in his wandering,
To seek for treasure in the jewell'd skies
Albeit, he soar with an undaunted wing?
Hast thou not dragg'd Diana from her car,
And driv'n the Hamadryad from the wood.
To seek shelter in a happier star?
The gentle Naiad from her fountain-flood?
The elfin from the green grass? and from me
The summer dream beneath the shrubbery?[20]

At the age of twenty, Poe had two books of poetry in print and he had settled on the primary themes that would run through his poetry, culminating in *Eureka* in 1848.

With his book in hand, a sign of his success as a poet, Poe returned to Richmond for a brief visit before starting his entrance exams at West Point in June 1830. Poe did well at West Point. With his army experience, he was an exemplary cadet and easily fit into the routine of military discipline. He stood third in his class in French and seventeenth in mathematics out of a class of eighty-seven cadets.[21] Unfortunately, the military academy did not provide free books or mathematical instruments. Poe found himself in the same situation he had been at the University of Virginia. He could not continue his studies unless Mr. Allan would provide the funds. Poe wrote to Allan requesting the he either provide the necessary money for his school supplies or provide a letter agreeing to Edgar's resignation from the academy, since Allan was still the legal guardian of the underage Poe. Poe said that if Allan would not respond, he would have no choice but to neglect his duties in order to be dismissed from the academy.[22]

When Allan did not respond, Poe neglected his duty by being absent from parade and roll call and by not attending classes. Poe also disobeyed orders to attend church on January 23 and not to leave the academy on January 25. Poe's court-martial took place on January 28, 1831. He was found guilty of the charges and dismissed from the cadet corps. No doubt Poe's cadet comrades understood what was happening, and the superintendent, who was aware of Poe's solicitations of his wealthy foster father, was sympathetic enough to allow Poe to continue living at West Point until he left for New York on February 9, 1831. He carried with him his military great coat in which he would be photographed at the end of his life and which he draped over the blanket of his tubercular wife in an effort to keep her warm as she lay dying. He also carried with him the encouragement of 131 of the 232 cadets who subscribed seventy-five cents each to publish Poe's third book of poetry, which was simply entitled *Poems*. Poe dedicated the book to the U.S. Corps of Cadets.

Poe's *Poems* contained six new works, including "Israfel" and "To Helen." In his preface he laid out several of his principles of poetry that he would develop in "The Rationale of Verse" and "The Philosophy of Composition." He daringly disagreed with Wordsworth, the greatest poet of the age, by insisting that instruction should not be the aim of poetry. Poe explained:

43

> A poem, in my opinion, is opposed to a work of science by having for its *immediate* object, pleasure, not truth; to romance, by having for its object an *indefinite* instead of a *definite* pleasure, being a poem only so far as this object is attained: romance presenting perceptible images with definite, poetry with indefinite sensations, to which end music is an *essential*, since the comprehension of sweet sound is our most indefinite conception: Music, when combined with a pleasurable idea, is poetry; music without the idea is simply music; the idea without the music is prose from its very definiteness.[23]

Poe did not remain in New York for long. He was there long enough to publish his book and to grow deathly ill. Strong and vigorous until this point, Poe almost died from his fever and suffered from broken health the rest of his life.

As soon as Poe was strong enough to travel, he returned to his family in Baltimore. While Poe had been at West Point, John Allan had remarried, and the new Mrs. Allan had no interest in visits from

Edgar Poe. He joined the family household in Baltimore in late winter or early spring in 1831. By August, Poe's brother Henry died of tuberculosis at the age of twenty-four.

Poe's literary life changed in an unexpected way during the summer of 1831. The *Philadelphia Saturday Courier* announced a one-hundred-dollar prize for a tale of fiction. Poe tried his hand at prose fiction, but he did not win. His effort, however, caught the attention of the editor and in January 1832 he published "Metzengerstein." The journal went on to publish four more of Poe's tales that year, and they demonstrated at this early stage of his prose fiction career that Poe had a large palette of forms at his disposal, from humorous satire to psychological thriller.

In 1832 the *Baltimore Saturday Visiter* [*sic*] offered a fifty dollar prize for the best tale and a twenty-five dollar prize for the best poem. Poe won the fiction prize for his tale "MS. Found in a Bottle," but did not win for his poetry. When he learned that John Hewitt, the editor of the *Baltimore Saturday Visiter*, had entered the poetry contest under a false name and won the prize, Poe's sense of Justice grew inflamed and he went to see Hewitt. Though the prize was awarded by an independent panel of judges, Poe believed that Hewitt's action was inappropriate. Hewitt had committed a double injustice: he had competed in his own competition, and he had created an impression that the honorable judges were not honorable. When confronted by Poe, Hewitt began swinging, and the two had to be separated.[24] The story is important because it illustrates that Poe's sense of honor and integrity were matters he did not take lightly. He was a man of conviction, and this aspect of his character weighs heavily in any evaluation of his conduct and motives.

Besides winning a money prize for "MS. Found in a Bottle," Poe came to the attention of John Pendleton Kennedy, one of the judges for the competition. Kennedy was a well-known literary figure who later served as Secretary of the Navy following several terms in Congress. Kennedy helped Poe place a number of his tales and reviews with a new magazine in Richmond edited by Kennedy's friend Thomas Willis White.

For his first submission to White's *Southern Literary Messenger*, Poe sent "Berenice," a horror tale that involved premature burial and the mutilation of the undead body. White was horrified, which is the effect that a horror story should create. He wrote to Poe and said that he feared the tale of Berenice was in bad taste and not appropriate for his readers. A certain tradition of Poe criticism reads "Berenice" as an example of his neurosis and severe pathology. Actually, "Berenice" demonstrates Poe's grasp of the popular market and what it would take for a popular magazine to succeed in the second quarter of nineteenth-century America. With "Berenice," Poe set out to do exactly what he said a writer must do—aim for the effect they want to create.

After agreeing with White that "Berenice" was "by far too horrible" and not a piece of writing that he would want as the basis for judging his capability as a writer, Poe explained to White his grasp of the magazine business:

> The history of all Magazines shows plainly that those which have attained celebrity were indebted for it to articles *similar in nature—to Berenice*. . . . You ask me in what does this nature consist? In the ludicrous heightened into the grotesque: the fearful coloured into the horrible: the witty exaggerated into the burlesque: the singular wrought out into the strange and mystical. You may say all this is bad taste. I have my doubts about it. . . . But whether the articles of which I speak are, or are not in bad taste is little to the purpose. To be appreciated you must be *read*, and these things are invariably sought after with avidity.[25]

In short, "Berenice" was the result of the same calculated process that Poe claimed had produced "The Raven," as he later explained in "The Philosophy of Composition."

Poe's analysis of the successful magazines proved correct. He provided White with a series of tales designed to appeal to the reading market, and the *Southern Literary Messenger* prospered. In the summer of 1835 White invited Poe to join the editorial staff of the magazine in Richmond. The job came at a critical time for the small household in Baltimore. Poe's grandmother died that summer, and with her death the small annuity came to an end. Maria Clemm and her daughter, Virginia, had no means of support. Their cousin, Neilson Poe, who had married Maria's half sister, Josephine, offered to take Virginia into his home.

The death of Elizabeth Poe and Neilson Poe's offer precipitated a crisis that need never have arisen. Had Elizabeth Poe lived a few more years, the fears of destitution would not have arisen, and the prospect of any change in the family would never have occurred. Whether Poe was fully aware of his own feelings prior to Neilson Poe's offer, it is impossible to say. When the offer came, however, Poe wrote an intense letter to his aunt in which he expressed his deep love for his thirteen-year-old cousin. Instead of writing to Virginia, Poe followed the convention of honor and first approached her mother. He loved Virginia, but he did not want to stand in the way of the security that Neilson Poe could offer.

In the end, Maria Clemm allowed Virginia to make her own choice. Some Poe critics take the position that Maria Clemm pushed Virginia into the marriage to guarantee that Edgar would take care of them, but this view ignores the much more secure offer of Neilson Poe. Edgar went back to Baltimore for Virginia's decision. She chose him.

The little family returned with Edgar to Richmond at the beginning of October 1835. Maria and Virginia boarded with Mrs. Yarrington until May 16, 1836, when Edgar and Virginia were married. She was almost fourteen and he was twenty-seven. The age difference seems alarming today, but Poe's cousin, Washington Poe of Macon, Georgia, married Selina Shirley Prince when she was fourteen as well.

In the midst of the crisis over Virginia and the prospect that he would likely lose her forever to a new circle and new relationships, Edgar began drinking. When he drank, he could not work, and White threatened to fire him. With the assurance of Virginia's love, however, Poe returned to normal and became an editorial machine. Poe never had editorial control of the *Southern Literary Messenger*, but he produced an enormous number of tales, essays, and reviews for the magazine. His reviews quickly stood out from what magazines had printed until then. He soon had a reputation for viciousness that can only be understood in terms of Poe's assessment of American literature and the state of magazine publishing.

An old joke compares English *literature* with American *writing*. Poe believed that American literature would never come into its own as long as American writers aped European authors, British authors in particular. Poe wanted a uniquely American literature, but it would never come about as long as the literary industry maintained such a low standard of quality. Poe strove to improve his own writing, and we can trace improvements he made to his stories and poetry as they went through various printings. In his reviews he fearlessly analyzed the weakness of poor writing to challenge Americans to do a better job or not to write. The other consideration for his fierce reviews, of course, was that they attracted readers.

Following the Dream: The Publishing Centers

In 1837 Poe and his family moved to New York where he hoped to found his own magazine. Unfortunately, the American economy collapsed as a result of Andrew Jackson's bank scheme into the greatest depression the young nation had seen. Mrs. Clemm took in boarders in the way that Mrs. Micawber took in David Copperfield in order to cover their basic needs for food and lodging. Poe only managed to sell a few of his "Folio Club" tales and one review to the *New York Review*. During this episode, however, he managed to complete his only novel, *The Narrative of Arthur Gordon Pym*.

During the summer of 1838, Poe gave up on New York and moved to Philadelphia with continuing hopes of starting a magazine and with greater prospects for selling work to the magazines situated there. Instead of Philadelphia magazines, however, Poe sold his stories to the *American Museum*, a young and short-lived journal published by his friends N. C. Brooks and J. E. Snodgrass in Baltimore. The *American Museum* published "Ligeia," "The Haunted Palace," and his satires on horror stories, "The Psyche Zenobia" and "The Scythe of Time" (later retitled "How to Write a Blackwood Article"). Poe picked up a freelance job, editing a book on shells for Professor Thomas Wyatt entitled *The Conchologist's First Book*. A few years later it earned him a charge of plagiarism from the *Saturday Evening Post,* but the Harvard biologist Stephen Jay Gould defended it as a breakthrough work because of Poe's decision to present life forms from simplest to most complex instead of the traditional practice of presenting more complex forms first.[26]

From December 1839 until early May 1840, Poe edited *Alexander's Weekly Messenger* in Philadelphia. For this weekly newspaper he came up with a new gimmick to attract readers in addition to his reviews. He started a column about secret codes in which he challenged his readers to devise complicated codes that he would then decipher. The scheme worked and Poe ran fifteen successive columns before leaving *Alexander's* to take up editing responsibilities with *Burton's Gentlemen's Magazine.*

William Burton was a successful comic actor who had unwarranted literary aspirations and the funds to pursue them. He hired Poe to edit his magazine, but he never gave Poe the authority to make editorial decisions without his approval, a formula for conflict that eventually led to Poe's resignation. In a typical issue of the monthly magazine, Poe contributed short stories, poetry, essays, columns, and book reviews. These writing assignments came in addition to the actual work of securing and editing copy from other contributors. In the pages of *Burton's,* we find the first appearance of "The Fall of the House of Usher." While working for Burton, Poe also published his two-volume collection of short stories entitled *Tales of the Grotesque and Arabesque.*[27] Frustrated with the working arrangement with Burton, Poe left in order to start his own magazine in June 1840. With the lingering financial depression, however, Poe could not raise the necessary money, so he accepted a position as editor of *Graham's Magazine* in April 1841.

George R. Graham had purchased *Burton's* after it faced collapse under William Burton's sole administration. He had also purchased *The Casket.* The combined circulation of the two magazines numbered around five thousand. At the end of one year, Poe had raised the circulation to around forty thousand. He made George R. Graham a wealthy man, and he confirmed his own conviction that if he were ever to have financial security, he must own his own magazine. To commemorate his new job, Poe devised something different for

48

the magazine that he hoped would set it apart. He modestly referred to the tale as "something in a new key." Poe had created the first mystery story, "The Murders in the Rue Morgue." With this tale, Poe created a form of storytelling that would become, along with science fiction, one of the most popular forms of narrative in modern culture.

Poe was diligent in his work and achieved a level of financial prosperity. He earned eight hundred dollars a year at *Graham's* and had a lovely three story home that is now a National Historic Site. He was also able to buy a piano and a harp for Virginia, who was noted for her musical talent. Poe also loved music and entertained his guests by singing duets with Virginia or playing his flute with her on the harp or piano. Still, Poe did not have full editorial control of the magazine. He differed with Graham, a cabinet maker by profession, over matters of literary judgment as well as the visual appearance of the magazine. Poe could not help but be offended when Graham paid more than twice Poe's annual salary for a single story by James Fenimore Cooper. Inevitably, Poe left *Graham's Magazine* flush with success and firm in his intention to start his own magazine.

As Poe began to make plans for the new magazine that he planned to call *The Stylus*, tragedy struck the Poe household. In January 1842 while singing at her piano, Virginia ruptured a blood vessel in her throat and blood gushed from her mouth. Virginia had tuberculosis and Edgar would watch her slowly die for the next five years until January 1847. A famous letter from Poe written in 1848 describes how he felt as he watched her die:

> Six years ago, a wife, whom I loved as no man ever loved before, ruptured a blood-vessel in singing. Her life was despaired of. I took leave of her forever & underwent all the agonies of her death. She recovered partially and I again hoped. At the end of a year the vessel broke again—I went through precisely the same scene. Again, in about a year afterward. Then again—again—again & even once again in varying intervals. Each time I felt all the agonies of her death—and at each accession of the disorder I loved her more dearly & clung to her life with more desperate

pertinacity. But I am constitutionally sensitive—nervous in a very unusual degree. I became insane, with long intervals of horrible sanity. During these fits of absolute unconsciousness I drank, God only knows how often or how much. As a matter of course, my enemies referred the insanity to the drink rather than the drink to the insanity.[28]

Biographers and critics frequently misquote the letter to suggest that Poe was insane when it clearly deals with the horror of anticipatory grief that so many people experience when someone they love battles a terminal disease.

Piece Work

While Poe threw himself into the task of raising support for his new magazine, he had to continue to earn money to support a sick wife and her mother. He wrote at a feverish pace and placed his work wherever he could. Poe contributed a criticism of the poetry of Rufus Dawes in the October 1842 issue of *Graham's*. He published "The Landscape Garden," an ephemeral tale that extolled the Beauty of nature and the art of gardening, in the October issue of *The Ladies' Companion*. Also in October he placed "Raising the Wind; Or, Diddling Considered as One of the Exact Sciences," a humorous tale, in the *Philadelphia Saturday Courier*. The next month, *The Ladies' Companion* published the first installment of "The Mystery of Marie Rogêt," the first sequel to "Murders in the Rue Morgue." This second Dupin mystery story ran in installments for three issues.

In 1843 James Russell Lowell published "The Tell-Tale Heart," a murder story with a confession, in his short-lived *Pioneer*, as well as "Notes Upon English Verse" and the poem "Lenore." *Graham's* published the poem "The Conqueror Worm" as well as four essays and reviews. N. P. Willis paid Poe to translate two pieces from French for *The New Mirror*. Poe also embarked on a venture in 1843 to publish his stories in cheap, paperback editions for a popular audience. The first issue contained two stories, "The Murders in the Rue Morgue" and "The Man That Was Used Up," which demonstrated the range of Poe's writing ability from mystery to humor. Published as *Prose Romances*, the project failed to lead to a second issue. Poe won a hundred-dollar prize for "The Gold-Bug," a variation on the detective mystery that involved pirate treasure and a secret code, which the *Dollar Newspaper* published in two installments in June 1843. In August the *United States Saturday Post* published "The Black Cat," another murder story that involved a confession.

In 1844 Poe sold three stories to *Godey's Lady's Book.* In "A Tale of the Ragged Mountains" Poe set the tale in his beloved Blue Ridge Mountains that surround Charlottesville and the University of Virginia. He published "The Oblong Box," based on an actual attempt to conceal a murder, in the September issue. In the November issue of *Godey's,* he published "Thou Art the Man," an effort at combining humor with the mystery story. He published "The Spectacles," one of his funniest stories, in the *Dollar Newspaper. Graham's* bought Poe's poem "Dreamland" and five other reviews and criticisms during the year.

During this period, Poe also wrote for the annual Christmas "gift" books. He placed "Morning on the Wissahicon," another tale that mused on the Beauty of nature, in *The Opal* in 1844. "The Pit and the Pendulum," an exploration of institutionalized injustice, appeared in *The Gift* for 1843. *The Gift* for 1845 (published in the late fall of 1844) included "The Purloined Letter," the third Dupin mystery and the prototype for the espionage story. A pirated, condensed version of the story appeared in *Chamber's Edinburgh Journal.*

The failure of James Russell Lowell's *Pioneer* after three issues in 1843 suggests the economic times in which Poe labored to raise funds for his own magazine. No sooner had Poe resigned from *Graham's* but the country plunged into another economic depression. Businesses closed. Fortunes were lost. Most American writers had invisible means of support, like Longfellow who held an academic post at Harvard, Emerson who inherited money, and Hawthorne who managed to land a government patronage position at the Boston Custom House. Poe tried, through the influence of several of his friends, to secure a government post in the Tyler administration, but this effort led nowhere.

In desperation, Poe moved his family to New York in April 1844. If he had to peddle his writing to newspapers and magazines, New York had the advantage over Philadelphia because of its larger population and greater number of presses. He soon placed one of his science fiction tales, "The Balloon-Hoax," in the *New York Sun*. By the end of the year, Poe secured a job with N. P. Willis and George Pope Morris at the *Evening Mirror* and *Weekly Mirror* for fifteen dollars a week. Poe had little time to write poetry since leaving *Graham's* because he had to devote his energy to writing tales that would appeal to the public. With the steady, if meager, income he had from Willis and Morris, however, he could spare the energy to write another poem: "The Raven."

"The Raven" appeared in late January 1845 for the February issue of the *American Review*. Some regard it as the greatest poem ever written by an American while others consider it vulgar or too perfect. Critical debate that will not disappear continues to rage over the poem. Undoubtedly, it is the most familiar of all American poems. It created a sensation when it was published and made Poe famous in a matter of weeks as it was reprinted in journals and newspapers all over the country, beginning with the *Evening Mirror*. In many ways, it spoke for the experience of most people in the nineteenth century who knew death so intimately when family members died at home and so many children died before reaching maturity. Poe's poem of anticipatory grief captured the heart of the nation. It is not so much a poem about Poe, but about Everyman. And so it continues to be.

Poe left the *Evening Mirror* soon after the publication of "The Raven" to assume a third interest in the *Broadway Journal*, a young, struggling weekly with a circulation of less than one thousand. Poe also supplemented his income with public lectures. His February lecture on "Poets and Poetry of America" drew a crowd of three hundred, who paid twenty-five cents apiece to hear Poe dismember the New England poets. The seventy-five dollars he took home from one evening's lecture was more than he made at the *Evening Mirror* in a month. In July the publishing firm of Wiley and Putnam published a collection of Poe's short stories entitled simply *Tales*, for which he received eight cents for each of the fifty-cent books that sold. At the end of the year the firm brought out a collection of Poe's poetry that featured his triumph, *The Raven and Other Poems*. The Poes lived in several locations during their first year in New York, but by late spring they had settled into what would be their final home. Poe rented a cottage across the river in Fordham in hopes that the country air would be better for Virginia's health.

Poe's partners in the *Broadway Journal* gradually withdrew, and Poe tried to hold on by purchasing John Bisco's interest for fifty dollars cash. Horace Greeley loaned Poe the fifty dollars, but the money only managed to buy for Poe the journal's indebtedness. The *Broadway Journal* published its last issue on January 3, 1846.

Even while publishing his weekly journal, Poe had submitted work to other magazines. Besides "The Raven," the *American Review* published three other poems, a major essay on the state of American drama, and the short story "The Facts of M. Valdemar's Case." *Graham's* published two of Poe's short stories, issued a favorable review of his *Tales*, and contracted James Russell Lowell to write an article about Poe that was published with a steel engraving portrait of Poe before he grew his iconic moustache. In 1846 Poe published "The Philosophy of Composition" and three of his "Marginalia" columns with *Graham's*.

Poe's work for *Godey's*, however, brought him the most attention. During 1845 and 1846, Poe wrote a number of criticisms of American literary figures that culminated in a series on "The Literati of New York." In this last year of Virginia's life it was critical to Poe to have an income and his treatment of the New York literary establishment boosted circulation for *Godey's* and kept Poe busy with his often scathing assessment of what passed for talent in New York. Hiram Fuller, the new editor of the *Evening Mirror* after the departure of N. P. Willis, attacked Poe and accused him of forgery, insanity, and of carrying on an immoral relationship with the poetess Frances Sargeant Osgood. Poe sued and won a verdict of $225 on February 17, 1847, but it came too late to help Virginia, who had died only days before on January 30.

Eureka

Marie Louise Shew nursed Virginia during her last illness, and as soon as Virginia died, she took care of Edgar, whose heart had not been strong since his severe fever in the winter of 1831. She noted the irregularity of his heartbeat and his high fever punctuated by delirium that sent Poe to bed following Virginia's death. The money from Poe's defamation lawsuit gave him enough to live on while he recovered his strength, but the tremendous production of stories, essays, criticism, and poetry virtually ceased with Virginia's death. Other than a poem of appreciation to Marie Louise Shew and the poem "Ulalume," which expressed his grief over Virginia's death, he published little. Grief held him in a vise, and he turned to the questions that had danced around his head and decorated his writing for the previous twenty years.

After the highly productive year of 1846, Poe did not publish during 1847. Instead he devoted himself to the question of how everything fit together. The problem of suffering and evil was assumed. Bad things happen. On the other hand, the world is filled with Beauty and Love. Some things simply do not seem fair, but to speak of fairness implies a pervasive sense of Justice that lies beneath and over the fabric of the universe. And then there was the universe. Why is there a universe? The same vision of unity that had guided his aesthetic judgments now guided his contemplations on "the universe, God, and everything."

When his health recovered, Poe resumed his favorite pastime of taking long walks of miles and miles through forests, over hills, and beside rivers and streams. He visited the Catholic brothers and their young institution with its respectable library in nearby Fordham. Just over a year after Virginia's death, Poe gave a public lecture at the Society Library in New York on February 3, 1848, in which he read from the essay he had spent the year writing. In July 1848 George Putnam published *Eureka* in a run of five hundred copies.

Few literary critics then or now know what to make of *Eureka*, for in this 143-page essay Poe disputed the fundamental scientific understanding of the universe. Poe confused many of his readers by calling the essay a "prose poem" and insisting that he wanted it to be judged as a poem. Buried in his discussion of scientific knowledge and the pursuit of Truth, however, Poe had revised his position on the nature of poetry. Poe had always distinguished Beauty from Truth, but in *Eureka*, he argues for their identification and for the "poetical essence of the Universe." In other words, he argued that whenever geniuses discuss the discovered truths of the universe, they speak poetry.

What truths had Poe discovered? Contrary to the best science of the Enlightenment, which took its cue from Aristotle, Poe argued that the universe had not existed forever as an infinite extension of stars and space. Instead, he speculated that the universe began from a tiny "primordial particle" and that it had expanded outward in all directions.[29] He also insisted that Time is not the absolute thing that Aristotle and Newton decreed but that it is an aspect of space and is relative to space, there being no privileged place in the universe.[30] He further argued that the universe is curved and that light and electricity belong to the same continuum. In short, Poe proposed the basic ideas of the Big Bang theory and much of the theory of relativity. The learned community assumed Poe had lost his mind completely.

Poe did not stop with the universe. A universe that just exists needs no explanation. A universe that begins, on the other hand, needs a cause. Poe concluded that a God exists who created the universe for his pleasure. Love and Beauty provide a glimpse of God, for they are the source of the universe and the goal of the universe. Pain, suffering, evil, and death are the contingencies of physical existence that are left behind. Poe conceived the universe in its span from beginning to end as one great story, and we encounter suffering because the story is not yet over. He argued, "The Universe is the perfect plot. The Universe is the plot of God."[31]

At the end of *Eureka*, Poe conceived of a conscious deity, unlike the unconscious God of Plato or Buddhism, who dispersed himself through physical creation so that all matter was a part of God but did not exhaust him, who in the end would draw all matter back into himself so that individual beings would lose all identity and

55

differentiation as God becomes "all in all." This view of God was as far as natural theology based on a fresh look at the universe could take Poe. After Poe published *Eureka* in the summer of 1848, however, he could not leave it alone. Poe was known for revising and improving his poetry and stories, but he went far beyond small adjustments with *Eureka*. While he was convinced about the reality of an expanding universe, he continued to wrestle with what an expanding universe told us about God. In Susan Tane's copy of *Eureka*, Poe made over four hundred substantive changes to the text. With *Eureka* we have a work in progress.

Success and Happiness

Poe moved through the classic stages of grief in the "textbook" twelve-month period after Virginia died, but he would reexperience his grief from time to time until he died. In 1848 and 1849, Poe gave several lucrative lectures, produced a variety of "Marginalia" columns and other essays, wrote some of his most important poems, and published a variety of short stories ranging from humor to science fiction. He gave lectures in Lowell, Massachusetts, in July 1848; in Providence, Rhode Island, on December 20, 1848; in Richmond, Virginia, on August 17, 1849; in Norfolk, Virginia, on September 14, 1849; and again in Richmond on September 24, 1849. The Providence lecture alone brought Poe approximately five hundred dollars.

Still, Poe was a man dealing with the death of a wife whom he desperately loved and probably felt some guilt for not having provided for her more substantially. In his biography of Robert E. Lee, Douglas Southall Freeman made an observation of "Light Horse Harry" Lee that might have been made of Poe or countless other men following the death of a beloved wife: "Like many another widower he found consolation for a lost love in a new."[32] Poe had several romances. For a few months in the fall of 1848, he was engaged to Sarah Helen Whitman of Providence. From June 1848 until the fall of 1849, he found security in a complex friendship with a safely and virtuously married woman. She provided sympathy without the complications of physical love. In July 1849, however, Poe returned to Richmond, his boyhood home, and there he renewed the acquaintance of Elmira Royster Shelton, the sweetheart of his youth, whose husband had died in 1844.

The summer of 1849 brought happiness back to Edgar Poe. He was warmly received by his friends in Richmond, vindicated of the slurs of John Allan when Allan's will was read and he made provision for his illegitimate children. By August, Poe and Elmira were once again in love. Then Poe did something extraordinary. He had always placed great confidence in his intellect and strength of will, but after years of failed promises he realized that he could not deal with his alcoholism on his own. As the summer wore on, Poe went forward at a Sons of Temperance revival meeting. The Sons of Temperance was an evangelical organization active throughout the nineteenth century like the Young Men's Christian Association or the Salvation Army. Poe's biographers, including Arthur Hobson Quinn, have neglected to mention the religious nature of this organization. Going forward to take the pledge at a Sons of Temperance meeting in the nineteenth century would be similar to going forward at a Billy Graham meeting in the twentieth century. Within the context in which he made such a dramatic and public step, for newspapers all over the country reported his action, Poe had made a statement about his religious convictions. We do not have, however, any statement from Poe himself about the meaning of his identification with the Sons of Temperance. We can only weigh the probability that Poe had further evolved in his conception of God since he wrote *Eureka* against the probability that he was only making a cynical gesture to gain Elmira's good opinion. How we understand the significance of Poe's public gesture at the Sons of Temperance meeting becomes in the end a judgment of Poe's character.

By the end of September, Poe and Elmira were engaged. Poe's detractors have suggested that Poe was only interested in the young widow's money. By the terms of Barrett Shelton's will, however, Elmira would forfeit all but a small share of the inheritance if she remarried. Poe left Richmond by steam packet to return to New York in order to close his affairs there and bring Mrs. Clemm back to Richmond for the wedding. He had a fever when he left

Richmond, and both his doctor and Mrs. Shelton urged him not to make the trip. Full of love, hope, and confidence for the future, however, Poe embarked on his last journey. While passing through Baltimore on his way to New York, Poe disappeared.

No one knows to this day what happened to Poe. He was found in a semiconscious state on October 3, 1849, at the Fourth Ward polls, following one of Baltimore's notoriously violent elections. He was able to ask that a message be sent to his friend Dr. J. E. Snodgrass who lived nearby. Poe, always known for the care he took with his clothes and general appearance, was wearing old, unkempt clothes that did not belong to him. Poe was taken to Washington Hospital. Dr. John J. Moran, the attending physician, testified that there was no sign that Poe had been drinking.[33] He drifted in and out of consciousness with passing episodes of delirium until Sunday morning, October 7, when he quietly said, "God help my poor soul," and died.

THE PROBLEM OF BEAUTY

The problem of Beauty does not strike the average person as a problem. For an artist who deals with Beauty day in and day out, however, this problem may raise its ugly head. Poe came to deeper and deeper convictions about Beauty over the course of his career. As a boy he assumed Beauty, as his poem "To Helen" suggests. Inspired by the mother of his best friend, emblematic of the schoolboy crush, Poe pays tribute to Jane Stith Stanard, his ideal of female beauty, a rival to Helen of Troy. Tragically, Jane Stanard descended into insanity and died shortly afterward, and Poe witnessed the contrasting ugliness of life. Beauty and ugliness have a complicated relationship that goes beyond a mental construct to the very nature of things. Thus, death plays a profound part in understanding Beauty.[1]

As he established himself as a literary critic, Poe needed a basis for evaluating prose and poetry. He had to resolve in his own mind some objective criteria, some just basis for evaluating literature. More importantly, he had to set a standard for his own writing. In his essays and criticisms about writing, Poe reveals his developing understanding about the nature of Beauty and what it tells us about the world. Despite the emphasis that he lays on Beauty throughout his work, he is not known for his descriptions of beautiful subjects. He suggests and he evokes, but he relies upon the reader to participate by using their own imaginations to picture the scene. In this way, readers rely upon the cosmic source of Beauty rather than the poet's restrictive impressions. Thus, the common experience of Beauty provides a basis for unity between that which evokes Beauty and those who experience it.

The Philosophy of Furniture

Poe presented some of his thoughts on taste in "The Philosophy of Furniture," published in May 1840. Without an aristocracy of blood, as in European countries, Americans defaulted to an aristocracy of money, displaying wealth the way Europeans display their heraldic arms. Because of the role of money in society in America, the general population tends to confuse "magnificence and beauty."[3] Poe lamented that in such an environment, the cost of something determines its artistic merit. Given this cultural situation, Poe offered a number of opinions regarding good taste in the decoration of a room with an important qualification that relates to his understanding of literature in general and the universe. Decoration and the combination of furnishing elements depend "upon the character of the general effect."[4] Good taste in furniture and the arrangement of a room involves the general effect, or as he would come to describe this situation in writing, "the unity of effect."

Poe did not hesitate to make extravagant statements about the variety of carpets he did not appreciate. Because he does not write about his fellow poets and tale writers, but about the people reading the magazine in rooms adorned with the kind of furnishings Poe ridicules, his comments speak directly to his public audience. He wrote,

> As for those antique floor-cloths still occasionally seen in the dwellings of the rabble—cloths of huge, sprawling, and radiating devices, stripe-interspersed, and glorious with all hues, among which no ground is intelligible,—these are but the wicked invention of a race of time-servers and money-lovers—children of Baal and worshippers of Mammon—Benthams, who to spare thought,

and economize fancy, first cruelly invented the Kaleidoscope, and then established joint-stock companies to twirl it by steam.[5]

Besides flashy carpets, overpowering curtains, and glaring lamps, Poe also took issue with the overuse of mirrors. He decried all the glitter that Scarlet O'Hara adored and speculated that a bumpkin would realize something was wrong in a room so crammed with such "discordant and displeasing effects," but that the same person in a room tastefully furnished "would be startled into an exclamation of pleasure and surprise."[6]

Poe does not provide a developed standard for taste other than indicating that Beauty involves a general effect that brings pleasure and surprise. He also regards Beauty as the antithesis of discord and displeasure. After his general criticism of the prevailing vulgarity of American taste driven by the accumulation of expensive furniture, Poe gives a description of a tastefully furnished room. The description has a startling similarity to Monticello, Thomas Jefferson's home near Charlottesville, except for the shape of the room. The placement of paintings, the color and design of draperies, the size and construction of windows, and the size of the door describe the home where Poe would have dined with Jefferson during his first term at the University of Virginia. One of the most obvious features of Poe's tastefully furnished room is its simplicity. The idea of simplicity would form a critical aspect of Poe's thoughts on plot and his thinking about Beauty.

Twice-Told Tales

Poe wrote a lengthy review of Hawthorne's *Twice-Told Tales* for the May 1842 issue of *Graham's Magazine* in which he established the norms of the modern short story and presented his fundamental ideas about composition, which he would continue to refine until the time of his death.[7] Poe had a high regard for Hawthorne as a writer, but did not fail to mention his shortcomings, which was typical of his reviews. Hawthorne's greatest fault, from Poe's perspective, lay in his insistence upon the use of allegory, a literary form that Poe disliked, to teach moral lessons. The problem with allegory is that it does not reveal but conceals, except for the initiated who already possess the secret code to the allegory. In his facetious critique of allegory, Poe declared, "The deepest emotion aroused within us by the happiest allegory, *as* allegory, is a very, very imperfectly satisfied sense of the writer's ingenuity in overcoming a difficulty we should have preferred his not having attempted to overcome."[8] Under the rarest of circumstances, Poe allowed that a writer might utilize allegory without doing too much damage to a story:

> Where the suggested meaning runs through the obvious one in a *very* profound undercurrent, so as never to interfere with the upper one without our own volition, so as never to show itself unless *called* to the surface, there only, for the proper uses of fictitious narrative, is it available at all. Under the best circumstances, it must always interfere with that unity of effect which, to the artist, is worth all the allegory in the world.[9]

This review, however, gave Poe the opportunity to discuss many of his major ideas. Poe had no admiration for the book *as* a book, a great mass of words and pages. He insisted upon measuring a work of art, not by its size or by the effort it took to produce it, but "by the object it fulfills, by the impression it makes, than by the time it took to fulfill the object, or by the extent of 'sustained effort' which becomes necessary to produce the impression."[10] Poe believed that every story succeeded as a story to the extent that it created an effect upon the reader. All stories should aim toward this effect. While repudiating any supposed value in long works of prose by virtue of their bulk, Poe insisted, "The fact is, that perseverance is one thing and genius quite another; nor can all the transcendentalists in Heathendom confound them."[11]

At this point in his critical development, Poe believed that the capacity to create intense excitement formed the essence of poetry. He argued, "Excitement is its province, its essentiality. Its value is in the ratio of its (elevating) excitement."[12] Poe would later modify this view to focus on a particular kind of excitement that he termed Beauty. Because a sense of excitement cannot be sustained for very long, Poe held that a poem should not be longer than a person could read within an hour. Epics like "Paradise Lost" come in waves of excitement followed by troughs of platitudes, leaving the reader with a mixture of pleasure and weariness that equals out. Poe argued that such poems are really "a succession of brief poems."[13] Too brief a poem, however, does not have the momentum and continuity necessary to create an effect. Without enough duration and repetition, a poem cannot leave an "enduring impression."[14]

Poe's remarks on the pitfalls of long poems came in a climate in which the great poets were valued by the number of lines they wrote. Wordsworth's *Prelude* set the tone. Longfellow strove to write the great American epic with "The Song of Hiawatha" and "Evangeline." Poe understood that he swam against a tide of fashion, metaphorically the way he swam six miles against the tide on the James River as a boy. While he recognized that the overwhelming body of critical opinion stood against him, Poe believed that he would eventually be vindicated. He said confidently, "By and by these propositions will be understood as self-evident, and in the meantime will not be essentially damaged as truths by being generally condemned as falsities."[15]

Poe preferred the short prose tale to the novel because of its advantages in allowing the author to create an effect.[16] Poe's preferred length for a short story ran from a half hour to two hours of reading time.[17] The story that can be read in one sitting places "the soul of the reader . . . at the writer's control."[18] Poe argued that when a writer constructs a tale,

> He has not fashioned his thoughts to accommodate his incidents, but having deliberately conceived a certain *single effect* to be wrought, he then invents such incidents, he then combines such events, and discusses them in such tone as may best serve him in establishing this preconceived effect. If his very first sentence tend not to the out-bringing of this effect, then in his very first step has he committed a blunder. In the whole composition there should be no word written of which the tendency, direct or indirect, is not to the one pre-established design. And by such means, with such care and skill, a picture is at length painted which leaves in the mind of him who contemplates it with a kindred art, a sense of the fullest satisfaction. The idea of the tale, its thesis,

has been presented unblemished, because undisturbed—an end absolutely demanded, yet, in the novel, altogether unattainable.[19]

Poe recognized the analogy between his understanding of the parts of a plot and the parts of the universe in his essay on "The American Drama" (which will be discussed in chapter 6). Poe grew in his conviction that the artist had an obligation to create an effect, and this conviction informed his view about plot.[20] In this way, when a story contains a moral lesson or exposition of Truth, as the lesson on vanity in "The Spectacles" or the lesson on the truth about time in "Three Sundays in a Week," it conveys the lesson as self-evident truth through the effect created, rather than through a logical discourse.

The Philosophy of Composition

Part of the popular mythology of Edgar Allan Poe involves the belief that Poe had a morbid preoccupation with death. Poe had a preoccupation, but it did not concern death. His preoccupation focused on Beauty. In "The Philosophy of Composition" Poe claimed "that Beauty is the sole legitimate province of a poem," yet he wrote poetry about the worms that devour a corpse and about the descent from sanity into madness.[21] What do we make of this situation? The apparent contradiction probably occurs for most people because of the recent tendency to think that Beauty refers to something that is merely pretty.[22]

Most modern critics dismiss Poe's theory "that Beauty is the sole legitimate province of a poem."[23] The predominant body of Victorian American and English poetry extolled patriotism and taught life lessons. Of course, the lasting value of much of this body of poetry is insubstantial. The body of twentieth-century poetry also repudiated Poe's view. In the twentieth-century poetry became the medium for teaching ideology and philosophical views. Of course, twentieth-century poetry became inconsequential to its culture, regardless of how highly it was regarded by poets—a remarkable accomplishment without parallel in all of human history. No culture had ever lost its poetry before. Poe's view of the relationship between poetry and Beauty rooted in the very nature of poetry as an art form may help explain why poetry ceased to play a significant role in American society after World War I.[24] Another way critics have dealt with "The Philosophy of Composition" is to regard it as a clever hoax. Poe loved his jokes, but the theme of unity of effect that frames the entire discussion is one that he emphasized across his career. Of this aspect of his essay, we may be certain.

In the aftermath of the phenomenal popularity of "The Raven," Poe undertook to describe the process by which he wrote the poem, and in so doing, presented his own philosophy of composition. Some authors begin at the beginning and stroll about the narrative until something happens and the piece comes to an end, often surprised along the way or befuddled at how to get the plot to a conclusion. Poe, on the other hand, believed that a plot began with the end in mind. The purpose of the story or poem was to get to the intended end.

Effect

For Poe, the artist's craft focused on determining what effect the work of art should have. While Poe believed that most writers lack the self-awareness of how their compositions come to be written, he claimed to be aware of the writing process for all of his compositions, largely because he wrote with the self-conscious intention to create an effect. In his analysis of how he wrote "The Raven," he stresses the importance of writing a poem "that should suit at once the popular and the critical taste."[25] Poetry is not a solitary art form, for it depends upon its audience.

To be accessible to the modern audience, the length of a poem matters. The importance of unity lay at the foundation of Poe's literary theory. It formed the basis for his preference for short poetry and short fiction. Poe insisted that the length of all literary works should be limited to what can be read in a single sitting.[26] He preferred the short poem to the epic, and he preferred the short story to the novel. While it may be possible to continue a rhyme scheme or a rhythmical pattern for thousands of lines, Poe realized that the unity of such a poem could not be sustained. Returning to a theme he had explored in his essay on Hawthorne's *Twice-Told Tales*, Poe

65

argued, "What we term a long poem is, in fact, merely a succession of brief ones. . . . For this reason, at least one half of the *Paradise Lost* is essentially prose."[27] Poe seems to blame the affairs of the world for interfering with a person's ability to attend to the unity of a work of literature. The demands of modern urban life had robbed most of society of the freedom to attend to long literary works. This fundamental assumption of storytelling in a complex urban society became the rule for technological storytelling through motion pictures and television in the twentieth century. Movies rarely exceed Poe's rule. Movies normally last less than two hours and television stories normally last less than one hour. The connection with Poe's view of storytelling is probably not coincidental, for credit for the creation of the true movie as a complete storytelling form normally goes to D. W. Griffith, a disciple of Poe, who based several of his early "feature length" movies on Poe and his stories.

Poe believed that for a poem to have a universal audience it must not accommodate itself to utilitarian purposes, but it must be grounded in the Beautiful. Poe allowed that Truth and Passion may be attained in poetry, but that they are "far more readily attained in prose."[28] He argued that Truth requires a precision not suited to the metaphors and imagery of poetry; thus, *Eureka* and all of his other essays required a prose form. Poe does not mean that Beauty is necessarily the subject of poetry, but that Beauty is the form of poetry.[29] The nature of poetry differs from prose at this point. Poetry, by its very nature, produces pleasure that prose does not. A stanza of poetry and a paragraph of prose may treat the same ideas and observations, but poetry creates an entirely different effect than prose. Poe argued that Beauty is not so much a quality as it is an effect that Poe calls "that intense and pure elevation of *soul—not* of intellect, or of heart."[30] Beauty is not neutral, brute fact. It causes something to happen within a person. It is the kind of universal, spiritual experience that Rudolf Otto named the *numinous*.[31] The striking element, of course, is the connection between a work of art and the person who perceives it. It is not like a morsel of food and the animal looking for something to eat. The animal seizes the food, but with the work of art, Beauty seizes the audience.[32]

66

One may best understand Poe's point more than one hundred and fifty years later by examining the great art form of the twentieth century—the movie. The mechanics of film may be used to train soldiers or for propaganda. Films may educate or indoctrinate. To succeed as a movie, however, the many aspects that make up a movie must be brought together into a harmonious whole by the artist who directs the picture. The director must use the script, the actors, the set, the light, the sound, and the costumes in a way that creates a unitary effect upon the audience. A misstep with any of the major elements of a film will throw the movie off. Some of the greatest movies of the twentieth century were produced for Hitler and Stalin as propaganda films, but they succeeded as great art because they remained focused on the elements of film. Thus, a movie that has a brutal message might create a beautiful effect regardless of how the viewer may abhor the message.

Tone

Understanding that Beauty provides the province of a poem, Poe then settled on the tone he wanted to use. Since he wanted to speak to a universal audience in a poem that appeals to both critical and popular audiences, Poe settled on a tone that would achieve the maximum effect, "and all experience has shown that this tone is one of *sadness*."[33] Sadness has an effective power because it can produce tears; therefore, Poe argued that Melancholy is "the most legitimate of all the poetical tones."[34] He does not mean that "To Helen" and "Eldorado" are illegitimate because they do not have melancholy for their tone. He simply means that Melancholy almost always hits the mark. Thus, we remember John Donne's line: "Send not to ask for whom the bell tolls; it tolls for thee." Humor is too transitory to achieve the same effect.

Artistic Tools

Poe next explained how the tools available to the poet provide the structure for creating a beautiful effect. Just as the movie director has sound, lights, costumes, and set available to create an effect, the poet has a variety of tools. Poe decided to use a *refrain* because of its historic value in poetry of the type he had in mind. Poe decided, however, to be creative with the normal monotone of the refrain by maintaining the sound of the monotone but varying the thought conveyed from stanza to stanza.

In order to vary the refrain continually through the poem, Poe resolved to have a brief refrain that would require little alteration. In deciding for a single-word refrain, Poe then had to determine the *character* of the word. For maximum effect at the close of a stanza intending to heighten sadness, Poe chose "the long *o* as the most sonorous vowel, in connection with *r* as the most producible consonant."[35] He claimed that the first word he thought that fulfilled this combination was "Nevermore." The problem with such a refrain, however, lay in its monotonous repetition that seemed to offend reason. The solution would be for the refrain to come from an unreasoning source like a parrot, but Poe quickly switched to a raven as more in keeping with the tone.

Only after these issues of structure had been settled does Poe claim to have turned to the question of topic:

68

> "Of all melancholy topics, what, according to the *universal* understanding of mankind, is the *most* melancholy?" Death—was the obvious reply. "And when," I said, "is this most melancholy of topics most poetical?" From what I have already explained at some length, the answer, here also, is obvious—"When it most closely allies itself to *Beauty*: the death, then, of a beautiful woman is, unquestionably, the most poetical topic in the world— and equally is it beyond doubt that the lips best suited for such topic are those of a bereaved lover."[36]

This statement has been repeatedly misrepresented. Poe did not say that the death of a beautiful woman is the most beautiful idea imaginable. He stressed that the death of a beautiful woman is the *saddest* topic imaginable. Poe's detractors frequently confuse Poe's statements about the nature of poetry rooted in Beauty with the topic of a poem.[37]

Poe has received a great deal of derogatory comments over the years for his choice of the death of a beautiful woman as the topic that will have the greatest effect upon the reader. Many critics regard Poe's discussion of how he composed "The Raven" as a grand hoax, largely because of his statement about the selection of the death of a beautiful woman as the topic for the poem. Poe merely states one of the basic axioms of literature. In the classic romance the couple lives happily ever after, but in the classic tragedy the beautiful girl must die.

Shakespeare understood this assumption of storytelling when he wrote *Romeo and Juliet*. Juliet's death is necessary; Romeo's death is optional, as in Hemingway's *A Farewell to Arms*. The death of a warrior in battle, as we find in *The Song of Roland*, does not have the same effect upon the reader as the death of the Lady Elaine who pined away for love of Sir Lancelot in *Le Morte d'Arthur* and "The Lady of Shalott." The death of Siegfried does not have the same effect as the death of Brünnhilde. Hamlet's death does not have the same impact as that of Ophelia. In *Little Women*, Aunt March's death does not have the same impact as Beth's death. Reflecting on why William Faulkner considered *Anna Karenina* the greatest novel ever written, Pat Conroy acknowledged, "The suicide of Anna still ranks as one of the saddest moments in world fiction."[38] Anna Karenina, Madame Bovary, Cathy Earnshaw (*Wuthering Heights*), Marguerite Gauthier (*Camille*), and Tess Durbeyfield (*Tess of the D'Urbevilles*) all had to die in their novels in the nineteenth century.

Movies in the twentieth century were no different. In *Mrs. Miniver*, only the death of Carol can achieve the effect of rousing American support for Britain during World War II. Churchill said that the movie did more good for the war effort than a flotilla of destroyers. Even into the twenty-first century, Padmé must die in *Revenge of the Sith*. Poe understood the basic truism of storytelling that no theme has a greater emotional impact on the audience than the death of a beautiful woman.

Perhaps Poe has received such rough treatment over his presentation of death because he does it so well. Everyone else did it, but not as well as Poe. Consider his ruthless critic, Richard Henry Stoddard, and his poem "Oblivion," which opens with the lines:

There is a land of darkness and gloom,
A stern and solemn region in the Past,

To which, fulfilling their appointed doom,
The multitudes of earth are hurrying fast.[39]

It is not so bad, but it is not "The Haunted Palace" or "The Conqueror Worm." Poe did not write about death the way the transcendentalists did. For Poe, death was not a lovely thing like "crossing the bar" or growing out of one's restrictive chambered shell to go off on some great new adventure. Death is dreadful.[40] It separates people.

Poe discussed how he varied the raven's refrain of "Nevermore." The raven does not converse so much as it responds to the grieving lover's inquiries. The first query should be commonplace, the second less so, and the third even less so that subsequent responses succeed in rousing the lover to an agitated and superstitious state, in which the lover propounds wild ideas that he cannot believe but which drive him further to ask questions for which he knows the answer will be "Nevermore." With the possibilities of this kind of exchange in mind, Poe conceived the last query to which the last "Nevermore" "should involve the utmost conceivable amount of sorrow and despair."[41]

Poe claimed that he actually wrote stanza fifteen of the eighteen stanza poem before any of the others. Following his method of development, he fixed the highest moment of the poem in order to work out the scheme that would lead up to it. With the climax he determined the rhythm, the meter, and the details of the stanza to ensure that no earlier stanza would surpass the climax. Poe's combination of rhythm and meter for "The Raven" represents true originality for which Poe modestly admitted "nothing even remotely approaching this combination has ever been attempted."[42] The originality lies in how he combined existing forms to combat monotony and build intensity. Poe varies the length of the lines in an alternating pattern in which the feet (trochees) "consist of a long syllable followed by a short [such as 'prophet']: the first line of the stanza consists of eight of these feet—the second of seven and a half (in effect two-thirds)—the third of eight—the fourth of seven and a half—the fifth the same—the sixth three and a half."[43] The complexity of Poe's entire scheme heightens the pleasure for the audience in terms of its musicality, but combined with its topic of melancholy, the total impact made it an instant success with the public and a permanent resident in American literature anthologies.[44]

Poe completed "The Philosophy of Composition" by summarizing the setting and narrative events of the poem to demonstrate that everything about the poem is realistic and rational, from a man sitting up late reading to an escaped pet bird seeking a refuge in a storm. (Poe was notorious for taking in stray cats.) In spite of the effect that Poe achieves, he uses realism of narrative to achieve it, yet it is known as an otherworldly poem. Poe said that suggestiveness and undercurrent rather than overt and excessive attention to the meaning of the poem brings about the end he desired. In contrast to his approach, Poe ridiculed the transcendentalists who insisted upon making the theme the upper—rather than the under—current and thereby succeeded only in turning poetry into prose.

In the closing paragraph Poe clarifies his understanding of the relationship between poetry and the "moral lesson" that so many poets of the nineteenth and twentieth centuries insisted upon. Not until the next to the last line does Poe claim to have introduced any metaphorical expression: "from out my heart." Poe explains that at the very end of the poem, these words,

> With the answer, "Nevermore," dispose the mind to seek a moral in all that has been previously narrated. The reader begins now to regard the Raven as emblematical—but it is not until the very last line of the very last stanza, that the intensity of making him emblematical of *Mournful and Neverending Remembrance* is permitted distinctly to be seen.[45]

In this way Beauty, rather than logical argument, conveys the message Poe wants to send.

"The Rationale of Verse"

In "The Rationale of Verse," published in November 1848, following the publication of *Eureka*, Poe sought to explain more than mere artificial rules of poetry. He sought to explain why and how poetry works. He had no use for rules that did not have some rational basis in fact. In this essay he explains why the combination of rhythm, meter, and rhyme has such an effect on people when skillfully employed.[46] He also explains why the effect fails when the elements of poetry are not used well. His rationale for why poetry works also provides an explanation for his understanding of Beauty when applied to poetry. For Poe, Beauty does not mean the description of pretty things. Beauty in poetry refers to the quality of the sound of the poem to the ear.

Poe declared that issues of rhythm, rhyme, meter, and versification involve one-tenth ethics and nine-tenths mathematics.[47] He argued that verse originated in "the human enjoyment of equality," which includes the concepts of similarity, proportion, identity, repetition, and adaptation (or fitness).[48] Poe suggests that this pleasure in equality occurs when a person sees a crystal with repetitive sides and angles. The compounding of the experience of equality increases the pleasure derived from it mathematically. The more, the merrier. Music finds its basis in the pleasure related to the equality of sounds. Those with a more highly cultivated musical taste have the capacity to hear and grasp more complex forms of equality in music, but Poe doubted that such "scientific" music had a claim to "intrinsic excellence."[49] He believed that simpler melodies and harmonies must prevail. Poe's warning fell on deaf ears. In the twentieth century, academic orchestral and concert music pursued increasingly complex mathematical, musical formulas that smaller and smaller audiences were trained to appreciate.

Poe saw a strong relationship between poetry and music. Aldous Huxley faulted "The Raven" and Poe's poetry in general for being too musical and, thus, vulgar.[50] Poe's grasp of this relationship is not surprising if we consider the origins of poetry and music in human society. Neither art form arose as a solitary human experience even though they may be practiced in solitude. They probably began as communal chants and laments associated with battles, funerals, and supplications before the dreaded spirit world. Before there was music, there was the rhythmical chant, eventually to the accompaniment of the beating of sticks and other objects. Once in an age may people witness the birth of poetry, and we can see something of its rise in the phenomenon of "rap" at the

72

close of the twentieth century in a culture that had lost its poetry. Cut off from its rhythmical origins, poetry dies. Poetry dissociated itself from Poe's requirement of rhythm in the twentieth century, and the culture in its turn dissociated itself from this disembodied form of poetry.

Poe regarded verse as an "inferior or less capable Music."[51] He speculated that the origins of verse lay with the *spondee*, a two-syllable word in which both syllables have equally long accents. Because of the monotonous sound of such words piled upon one another, two-syllable words like *upon* with uneven accents (short and long) called an *iambus* would relieve the monotony. Experimentation along this line eventually produced the *trochee*, a two-syllable word like *raven* consisting of a long and short accent, the *dactyl*, a three-syllable word like *beautiful* consisting of one long accent followed by two short accents, and the *anapest*, a three-syllable word like *Ulalume* consisting of two short accents followed by one long accent.[52] Each of these basic forms is called a *foot*. An unending sequence of any one of these feet would eventually sound monotonous, so the *line* developed to break and define the sequence length.

73

Lines with equal numbers of feet probably developed first followed by lines of varying proportion. Equality of sound between the final syllables of lines resulted in *rhyme*.[53] A one-syllable rhyme like *moon* and *June* simply lacks the pleasure of a trochaic rhyme like *duty* and *beauty*. The pleasure rises with the more complex dactylic rhyme of *dutiful* and *beautiful*. Poe believed that the next advance came by collecting proportional masses of lines into *stanzas*.[54] Eventually, *natural feet* formed by a single word were augmented by *artificial feet* created by the combination of syllables across more than one word. Finally, embellishments came in the form of *refrains*, which repeat one or more words at the close of a stanza, and with the introduction of *alliteration*, which repeats the beginning sounds of words across feet within a line.

While many poets adjust words and their pronunciations to make them fit an appropriate foot (silv'ry, murm'ring), Poe believed that words "should be written and pronounced *in full*, and as nearly as possible as nature intended them."[55] Poetry should have the conversational tone of plain language, rather than an artificial tone. Poe also objected to substituting a foot of unequal "time" within a line of different feet, such as replacing a dactyl for a trochee. Timing matters to the ear.[56] This equality of time explains why much modern poetry and classical music may please the intellect of the highly trained, but they fail to please the ear of the ordinary person.[57] On the other hand, Poe had no difficulty with occasionally substituting a trochee for an iamb, because they had equality of time even though their accents were reversed. This occasional variation to break the monotone should not occur, however, until after the ear has had sufficient time to comprehend the rhythm of the poem.[58] If a poem proves false in its rhythm, it proves unmusical. It has failed in its appeal to the ear.[59]

In this discussion Poe continually points out that he is not an advocate of maintaining the rules of verse. Instead, he wants people to understand what kind of verse "works" and why some verse is better than other verse. The failure to recognize how rhythm acts upon people can only lead to sloppy poetry that does not act upon people. A disruptive pattern of feet works like a road with pot holes. Hitting the bumps creates a jarring sensation that distracts the ear from the content of the poem. An unequal number of feet within a line, once the expectation of a poetic pattern has been established, creates the effect of stalling and not quite reaching the mark.[60]

Poe did not insist that poetry necessarily developed exactly as he speculated, but he did believe that his proposal illustrated the evolutionary nature of poetry. In his whole discussion, designed to acquaint the average reader with how poetry "works," Poe is concerned with how poetry strikes the ear. The sound of poetry either gives pleasure to the ear, or it does not. In his essay "The Rationale of Verse," he seeks to offer the reader a rationale for why some verse gives more pleasure than other verse. A poem may have a noble subject and teach an important moral lesson, but if it does not sound pleasing to the ear, it will fail to impress the reader.

Poe thought that a skilled reader might adjust the enunciation of a poem so as to render an unmusical line into a musical line through sheer force of declamation. After leveling a charge against Coleridge's "Christabel" on this score, he gave a more familiar example with a nursery rhyme that people have been taught to make musical by inserting strategic pauses to make the feet and lines come out equally:

Pease porridge hot—pease porridge cold—
Pease porridge in the pot—nine days old.

If the poet can train people to read the poem in the right way by deliberately pausing in the midst of the reading, then all is well. It will sound right. With printed verse, however, poets do not have this opportunity. When poets mix their feet indiscriminately—here five short syllables and there three short syllables—Poe sarcastically charges them with demonstrating "what all the mathematicians have stupidly failed in demonstrating—that three and five are one and the same thing."[61] Through his analysis of Byron's "Bride of Abydos," Poe demonstrates that the length of a line is a purely arbitrary matter, and the division may be given at any place as long as the line has at least two feet. Again, he relates his claim to mathematics: "As in mathematics two units are required to form number, so rhythm . . . demands for its formation at least two feet."[62]

Throughout his essay, Poe illustrates his points about the components of verse and the scanning of lines of poetry in debate with conventional scholarly treatment of the same lines. Poe disputes the basis for many scholarly "rules" of verse which have no basis other than authority.[63] Poe had begun this debate about rules and where they come from in "The Mystery of Marie Rogêt" in which Dupin disputed a so-called rule of how long a body must remain submerged before it floats to the surface.[64] For centuries, many rules of science were merely traditions handed down from Aristotle. In poetry the authorities explained the rules of verse, but Poe wanted to explain *why* verse works the way it does. His analysis presents a strong argument for why many of the conventional rules of verse amount to nothing more than traditional ignorance and should be abandoned. Here, Poe takes exception with the traditional scholarly approach to scanning lines on the same basis that he rejected the conventional physics of his day in *Eureka*: it was based on tradition rather than on actual analysis. Just as Poe found a mathematical beauty in the structure of the universe that relates to time, he found the same mathematical beauty in poetry, which involves the time required to speak parallel lines of verse.

Ironically, one school of critics faults Poe's poetry for being too cerebral and cold, yet it is his insistence on a strong rhythmical quality that literally gives his poetry "heart." Poetry becomes disembodied without its regular heartbeat. Poetry has a visceral aspect that connects it to people by means of its rhythmical quality. Absent its heartbeat, poetry retreats to a mental framework. This gnosticism captivated Western art forms throughout the twentieth century as artists retreated into their own mental studios, expressing themselves without any necessary intention to communicate to, through, or with the broader culture. Meaning became unnecessary for some artists with the resultant effect that the art became unnecessary to the culture. Poe understood why poetry cannot be separated from rhythm and still continue to exist, and a few important critics have agreed with him. At the beginning of the twentieth century, poetry was a popular art form. People read poetry for entertainment and pleasure. People memorized reams of poetry. Every kind of magazine published poetry. At the beginning of the twenty-first century, few Americans can recite any lines of a poem . . . except "The Raven." Without the rhythmical creation of Beauty, regardless of the subject matter, poetry withers.

The Domain of Arnheim

In 1842 Poe had published a tale concerned with Beauty named "The Landscape Garden" in *Snowden's Ladies' Companion*, but in 1847 he expanded it and renamed it "The Domain of Arnheim" when he published it in the *Columbian Lady's and Gentleman's Magazine*. Like "The Gold-Bug," it is a tale of the sudden acquisition of unimaginable wealth. Whereas "The Gold-Bug" dwells on how a man acquired a treasure, "The Domain of Arnheim" focuses on how a man spent a great treasure.

A poet by temperament, Ellison, who inherits 450 million dollars, feels the greatest satisfaction in "the creation of novel forms of beauty."[65] Because he holds materialistic convictions, however, Ellison believes that the sole legitimate expression of the poetic imagination lies in creating physical works of art. Though he loves poetry and music, his materialistic convictions do not allow him to pursue them. Instead of painting or sculpture, he turns to landscape gardening as the greatest poetic outlet. For him, landscape gardening provides an endless opportunity for the imagination to combine multiform and multicolor flowers and trees in the creation of Beauty. Ellison believed that landscape gardening, which adapted nature to the eyes that would see it, not only allowed him to fulfill "his own destiny as a poet, but of the august purposes for which Deity had implanted the poetic sentiment in man."[66] Poe's association of poetry and landscape gardening provides a critical key to understanding how he can call his scientific and theological essay, *Eureka*, a prose poem. It is a poem, as are all scientific theories, in the same way that a garden is a poem. All three cases involve the expression of Beauty.

The narrator believes that his friend Ellison has solved an important problem in art: "That no such combination of scenery exists in nature as the painter of genius may produce."[67] The painting or sculpture of the human form only approaches and imitates its subject, but in landscape gardening, the artist recomposes the scene. In the composition of the objects of nature, the way all of the pieces fit together, do we behold Beauty. The harmony, fitness, and proportion of nature as a unified whole betokens Beauty, yet the broken limb, the muddy gully, and the withered flower disrupt our apprehension. Dissatisfied with nature as we find it, the landscape painter and the landscape gardener bring Beauty out of the corruption of jungle or desert by altering what they find. While the natural style of gardening seeks to remove the offensive and restore nature to its original state, the artificial style of gardening seeks to introduce "extent and novelty of beauty, as to convey the sentiment of spiritual interference."[68]

77

In "The Fall of the House of Usher" (1839) the narrator contemplates how the combination of the simple objects of nature has an effect upon people, and he anticipated the landscape gardener by remarking, "It was possible, I reflected, that a mere different arrangement of the particulars of the scene, of the details of the picture, would be sufficient to modify, or perhaps to annihilate its capacity for sorrowful impression."[69] Like the arrangement of furniture in a room or words in a line of poetry, the landscape gardener arranges plants to achieve an effect upon the person who shall behold the garden. The garden is not for the gardener.

Ellison explained to his friend the narrator that "in the most rugged of wildernesses—in the most savage of the scenes of pure nature—there is apparent the *art* of a creator; yet this art is apparent to reflection only; in no respect has it the obvious force of a feeling."[70] John Wisdom would develop this idea in his parable of the gardener in which one person only sees a neglected garden while another sees the work of the gardener.[71] Some see the hand of God, and some do not. Poe stressed the importance of reflection in 1847 when he spent the entire year reflecting upon the universe before writing *Eureka*.

In very few of his stories does Poe write *about* Beauty. "The Domain of Arnheim" and "Landor's Cottage" are notable exceptions, yet Poe's deep attraction to the awesome wonder of nature appears in story after story. The ability of nature to create an effect on the viewer forms the introduction to "The Fall of the House of Usher." For the most part, Poe avoids calling nature beautiful in the same way he recoils from teaching a moral lesson at the end of his tales or in his poems. As he allows horror and terror to create their own effect to which the reader assents, he allows the description of nature to create its effect. Just as Poe would elucidate Justice in urban society, he elucidates Beauty in the midst of the majesty of nature.

Without calling attention to Beauty, Poe's stories set in the natural world are filled with a picture of Beauty in all its dreadfulness, solitude, solemnity, and power in order to point beyond Beauty toward something eternal. It happens with the mist, the moss, and the untrodden depths of the forest in "A Tale of the Ragged Mountains." It happens with the fury and power of the sea in "MS. Found in a Bottle," "A Descent into the Maelström," "The Oblong Box," and *The Narrative of Arthur Gordon Pym*. It happens in "William Wilson" with the "misty-looking village" with its "gigantic and gnarled trees" where the title character studied as a boy in a place that "was a dream-like and spirit-soothing place."[72] It happens with the view from the airship, the deep silence over the sea, and the mountainous waves raging under the force of the gale in "The Balloon-Hoax." It happens with the vegetation and wildlife that forms the jungle, the marshes, and the swamps of the South Carolina low country in "The Gold-Bug." What Poe realizes is that Beauty can create a variety of effects, but he also realizes that it points to something beyond itself.

The Poetic Principle

During the last year of his life, when Poe refined his poetic theory in "The Poetic Principle," he still defined a poem as "*The Rhythmical Creation of Beauty*." In "The Poetic Principle" Poe took major sections from "The Philosophy of Composition" and rewrote them. Since writing "The Philosophy of Composition," Poe had modified his view about the relationship between Beauty, Truth, and Goodness. In "The Poetic Principle" he modified his earlier statement and added an important qualification:

> It by no means follows, however, that the incitements of Passion, or the precepts of Duty, or even the lessons of Truth, may not be introduced into a poem, and with advantage; for they may subserve, incidentally, in various ways, the general purposes of the work:—but the true artist will always contrive to tone them down in proper subjection to that *Beauty* which is the atmosphere and the real essence of the poem.[73]

Between "The Philosophy of Composition" and "The Poetic Principle" Poe had written *Eureka*, which had allowed him to grasp the relationship between Beauty, Goodness, and Truth as he grasped the relationship between science, poetry, and God. Poe's understanding of the importance of unity helped him grasp this relationship.

Poe's concept of Beauty was realized in *Eureka*, in which he describes Beauty in relation to math, physics, and the cosmos. Poe realized that Beauty involves more than merely an emotional response to some stimulus but constitutes a cognitive criterion for judgment and response.

In contrasting the means of communicating Truth and Beauty, Poe argued that Truth has severe limitations:

> She has no sympathy with the myrtles. All *that* which is so indispensible in Song, is precisely all *that* with which *she* has nothing whatever to do. . . . In enforcing truth, we need severity rather than efflorescence of language. We must be simple, precise, terse. We must be cool, calm, unimpassioned. In a word, we must be in that mood which, as nearly as possible, is the exact converse of the poetical.[74]

Poe explains further by his division of the mind into the Pure Intellect concerned with Truth, the Moral Sense concerned with Duty, and Taste which stands between the other two and concerns Beauty. Taste wages her own war upon Vice, but on the grounds "of her deformity—her disproportion—her animosity to the fitting, to the appropriate, to the harmonious—in a word, to Beauty."[75] With this statement, Poe provides the basic elements of his understanding of Beauty: the fitting, the appropriate, the harmonious which contrast with deformity and disproportion.

Poe goes far beyond his other essays that touch on Beauty in "The Poetic Principle," for he now makes plain his growing understanding of what Beauty tells us about the universe. He considers Beauty an "immortal instinct" of the human spirit. Beauty is a thirst that "belongs to the immortality of Man."[76] The apprehension of Beauty represents a transcendent experience that points beyond physical existence: "Inspired by an ecstatic prescience of the glories beyond the grave, we struggle, by multiform combinations among the things and thoughts of Time, to attain a portion of that Loveliness whose very elements, perhaps, appertain to eternity alone."[77] The tears that come from poetry or music are not merely the result of an excess of pleasure. Rather, they are the jab of sorrow, the momentary pain over our separation from "those divine and rapturous joys" of which poetry and music can only provide "brief and indeterminate glimpses."[78]

The poetic sentiment which enables these glimpses of eternity finds expression in all the arts from painting, to sculpture, to landscape gardening (of which more will be mentioned later). For Poe, however, music provided the most certain prospect on Beauty, and any poetry which neglects music is simply silly.

The balance of "The Poetic Principle," which Poe originally delivered as a lecture and poetry reading, deals with samples of poetry upon which Poe comments. He quotes eleven stanzas of Longfellow's "Waif," in the midst of which fall the lines:

> Not from the grand old masters,
> Not from the bards sublime,
> Whose distant footsteps echo
> Through the corridors of time.

Six stanzas later Poe observes that these lines have been greatly admired, and he adds the brief observation that

> Nothing can be better than—

> —The bards sublime,
> Whose distant footsteps echo
> Down the corridors of Time.[79]

I am indebted to Benjamin Warthen for pointing out to me what Poe has done.[80] In one of Poe's little jokes, he changed Longfellow's line from "Through the corridors of time" as earlier cited, to "Down the corridors of Time." Thus, Poe thinks his line is the best line in Longfellow's poem. Poor Longfellow. Poe's change is the way people remember one of Longfellow's most memorable lines. The joke, however, indicates how seriously Poe regarded the choice of words in creating the intended effect. The wrong word ruins the beauty of a line.

Poe continually revised his poetry as he sought greater and greater perfection in his pursuit of the poetic ideal. He revised "To Helen" twice after its initial publication in *Poems* (1831) as he

81

searched for the right words. The most significant alteration came in the lines that are among Poe's most memorable. The original version read:

> To the beauty of fair Greece,
> And the grandeur of old Rome.

The lines scan well enough, but Poe was not satisfied until his second revision:

> To the glory that was Greece,
> And the grandeur that was Rome.

In "To Helen" we have something most rare among Poe's poems: a beautiful poem with Beauty actually as its subject. Just as the medieval allegorical internal war (the *bellum intestinum*) was not best represented by warfare, so for Poe, the beautiful poem would not normally have Beauty as its subject. In this case the poem most likely honors Jane Stith Craig Stanard, the mother of Poe's boyhood friend, who first encouraged him to write poetry and the embodiment of feminine beauty to Poe.[81]

82

Conclusion

Poe began "The Philosophy of Composition" with a discussion of how an artist's plot should begin with the ending that the artist has in mind. The perfection of proportion and the way all of the elements combine to create the unity of effect constituted Poe's vision of Beauty. The concept of plot and Beauty would play a critical role in Poe's understanding of how all of reality adheres and makes rational sense as he explored these ideas in *Eureka*.[82] Perhaps nowhere did Poe capture this sentiment about Beauty better than in his review of Longfellow's *Ballads* for *Graham's Magazine* in April 1842:

> There is still a longing unsatisfied, which he has been impotent to fulfill. There is still a thirst unquenchable, which to allay he has shown us no crystal springs. This burning thirst belongs to the *immortal* essence of man's nature. It is equally a consequence and an indication of his perennial life. It is the desire of the moth

for the star. It is not mere appreciation for the beauty before us. It is a wild effort to reach the beauty above. It is a forethought of the loveliness to come. Inspired with a prescient ecstasy of the beauty beyond the grave, it struggles by multiform novelty of combination among the things and thoughts of Time, to anticipate some portion of that loveliness whose very elements, perhaps, appertain solely to Eternity. And the result of such effort, on the part of souls fittingly constituted, is alone what mankind have agreed to denominate Poetry.[83]

Poe realized that Beauty and the human experience of it constitute an "indication" and a "forethought" that tells us an actual "*immortal*" beauty lies "beyond the grave." Beauty constituted to Poe evidence that human experience is not bound by time but belongs to eternity. In *Eureka,* Poe would finally resolve his understanding of the continuity of physical and spiritual beauty, of science and poetry, of Love and Truth.

THE PROBLEM OF LOVE

The problem of pain and suffering presents a major challenge to monotheism, and Poe felt the problem strongly. On the other hand, Love presents an equally challenging problem for materialism. In a purely material world, it is not difficult to account for pain and suffering, but how do we account for Love?

Love formed the central core of Edgar Poe's life experience. Surprisingly little has been written about Love in relationship to Poe's works. Much has been written about his view of Beauty, especially in relation to his idea expressed in "The Philosophy of Composition" that Beauty is the province of poetry and his remarks about the death of a beautiful woman. Poe did not tell all, however, when he spoke about the melancholy sadness of the death of a beautiful woman. For it to have its effect, the death must be of a *beloved* woman who is beautiful.[1] The death of a beautiful villainess does not produce the desired effect. Poe employs a clever trick when writing of lovely women. He barely describes their features at all. He requires the reader to enter the narrative with their imagination and picture the woman themselves, using their own experience of loveliness. In order for it work, Beauty and Love must be universally known, even if only in their absence. For Poe, the reality of Love, a nonmaterial experience associated with physical persons, serves as a pointer to a spiritual reality from which Love and Beauty come.

Love is a multidimensional aspect of human experience, though the English language uses the same word to speak of all these dimensions. In other cultures, however, different words express the various aspects of Love. It is impossible to understand Edgar Poe's references to Love without understanding the various ways in which he experienced and valued Love. For Western culture, the Greeks provide a helpful framework for understanding the various dimensions of Love.[2] *Storge* refers to the affection between parents and children, and between people and their pets. *Philia* refers to the bond of friendship. *Eros* involves sexual attraction and passion. *Agape* encompasses the realm of charity without thought for return. Unless we recognize that each of these dimensions of Love played an important and complex part in Poe's life and his writing, we may miss some of the essential connections Poe made between the physical and the spiritual.

Poe's love poetry represents the variety of loves he felt. In "The Raven," "Annabel Lee," "Eulalie," and "Tamerlane" we find the passion of *eros* as the driving force. In "To My Mother" and "Elizabeth" we find the calm affection of *storge*. For the friendship of *philia*, we turn to "A Valentine to __ __ __," "To M. L. S.," and "An Enigma."

Storge: *Affection*

Poe lost both his parents by the time he was two years of age. This loss did not mean, however, that he went without parental affection. If ever a soul experienced love throughout his life, that person was Edgar Allan Poe. Cherished by a mother who died too young, Poe was raised by Frances Allan, who loved him deeply and showed him every affection. Poe also experienced the betrayal of parental affection from John Allan, who turned on Poe viciously after Allan entered into a series of adulterous affairs. Finally, he found the constant affection of his Aunt Maria Clemm, who also became his mother-in-law and surrogate mother. Poe understood the need for affection, and his tales depict both the positive side of affection and affection's betrayal.

People

Poe experienced the depth of affection with Maria Clemm that he had never known from his own mother and that had been lost to him with the death of Frances Allan when he moved to Baltimore and came into the home of Maria, his father's sister. One of the most sentimental poems of affection ever written came from the pen of Poe when he composed a poem for her, which he entitled "To My Mother." Few people know it, for it violates all the basic mythology about Poe for him to have written such a poem. It has been printed on Mother's Day cards, gift boxes, and advertisements, and it reveals Poe's essential attitude about normal human affection:

> Because I feel that, in the Heavens above,
>   The angels, whispering to one another,
> Can find, among their burning terms of love,
>   None so devotional as that of "Mother,"
> Therefore by that dear name I long have called you—
>   You who are more than mother to me,
> And fill my heart of hearts, where Death installed you
>   In setting my Virginia's spirit free.   87
>
> My mother—my own mother, who died early,
>   Was but the mother of myself; but you
> Are mother to the one I loved so dearly,
>   And thus are dearer than the mother I knew
> By that infinity with which my wife
>   Was dearer to my soul than its soul-life.[3]

Written in the last year of his life, it does not have the evocative power of "Annabel Lee" or "The Bells" or "Eldorado," which were written during the same period. It provides us, however, with a rare glimpse into Poe's personal life in which he dispenses with images and metaphors. He expresses himself in a way that his audience of only one can understand. This lowering of his art for affection's sake embodies the significance of Love, in all its many aspects, in Poe's life. In a more subtle fashion, the Dupin tales may also throb with affection. Richard Kopley has argued that each of the tales involves the attempt to vindicate a woman "of uncertain reputation," which was the common slur against Poe's mother.[4]

Biographers and critics write with wide ranging effect about the episode with Sarah Anna Lewis, a mediocre poetess of sentimental verse who used the pen name "Stella." Her prosperous lawyer husband provided the necessary funds to advance her career, which included gifts to Mrs. Clemm, who had the responsibility of managing the struggling household at Fordham. Poe wrote a favorable review of Mrs. Lewis' book *The Child of the Sea and Other Poems* for the April 1849 issue of *Graham's Magazine*, but he published it anonymously. Mrs. Clemm had placed Poe in the impossible position of compromising his critical reputation by promising Mrs. Lewis that he would write a favorable review. He had spent fifteen years establishing a model for integrity in literary criticism that he cast aside with one review. He had no choice. He could dishonor himself or dishonor Mrs. Clemm, whom he always called by the affectionate term "Muddy." In many ways, he belonged to the courtly love tradition expressed in Sir Lancelot's resignation to ride in a cart in order to fulfill his lady's commission even though riding in a cart dishonored him as a knight. When affection becomes costly, it moves to a rarer form of love called *agape*. Whereas Lancelot undertakes his lady's commission in order to win her love, a mere transaction, Poe sacrifices his literary freedom and reputation because of love.

In *The Gold-Bug* a strong mutual affection bound Legrand and Jupiter, a freed slave. The narrator observed that Jupiter was more supervisor and guardian of Legrand than servant, speculating that the Legrand family had instilled in him the responsibility to look after the young manic-depressive. As the story unfolds, however, it is affection that prompted attention on both sides—a complicated affection in the antebellum South.

Animals

Poe had a deep affection for animals and reflected on the bond that formed between them and people. This experience with animals appears in several stories. In "The Gold-Bug," Jupiter had a large Newfoundland that rushed into the room and leapt up on the shoulders of the narrator upon his arrival. The massive dog continued to lick him and show his affection, the narrator believed, because he had shown the dog a great deal of attention on previous visits.[5] In "Landor's Cottage" the traveler treads the byways of New York with his dog, Ponto. Upon encountering a mastiff, who bounded toward him "with eyes and whole air of a tiger," the narrator held out his hand to the massive animal and received the expected effect: "He not only shut his mouth and wagged his tail, but absolutely offered me his paw—afterwards extending his civilities to Ponto."[6] Significantly, the narrator claims he never knew a dog that would not respond similarly.

In "Instinct vs. Reason—A Black Cat," Poe provides a glimpse of his regard for all animals, but cats in particular. In the essay Poe discusses the power of intuition generally and of his cat in particular. Poe's famous black cat had learned or taught itself or intuited how to open the spring latch to the kitchen door. This essay, written in 1840, prefigures Poe's discussion of imagination in the introduction to "The Murders in the Rue Morgue" the following year. Respect and amazement, of course, are not the same as affection for an animal. It is the sort of ability of an animal that contributes to regarding it as something more than a mere beast that one would fear in the wild. In a sense, affection for an animal depends at some level on the recognition of a common origin which notion Poe would explore in *Eureka*. For now, Poe merely observed of his pet that she "must have made use of all the perceptive and reflective faculties which we are in the habit of supposing the prescriptive qualities of reason alone."[7]

The Corruption of Affection

Poe's short story "The Black Cat" has an entirely different tone, but it leaves the reader condemning cruelty to animals. The narrator grew up loving animals and had many pets. He had always taken great pleasure from animals. As he explains:

> To those who have cherished an affection for a faithful and saga-
> cious dog, I need hardly be at the trouble of explaining the
> nature or the intensity of the gratification thus derivable. There
> is something in the unselfish and self-sacrificing love of a brute,
> which goes directly to the heart of him who has had frequent

89

occasion to test the paltry friendship and gossamer fidelity of mere *Man*.[8]

When the narrator married, his wife gave him, among other pets, a black cat, which became his favorite.

As the narrator gives himself to alcohol, his temperament changes, and he grows violently abusive to his wife and the animals. In describing his violent and destructive behavior, he attributes his disintegration to the spirit of perverseness in terms Poe had elaborated in "The Imp of the Perverse." Not only does he offend against Justice, but he offends against Love. His degeneration rouses a sense of disgust and revulsion in the reader, who must agree with the effect Poe strives to create. The horror of sin against Love by cruelty only serves to confirm the reality of Love. Cruelty to animals would have been an unutterable horror to Poe, whose affection for all animals seemed endless in its expression. This love of animals also suggests the possibility that Poe's tendency to approach strays might have put him in the way of a rabid cat or dog that might have caused his death.

90

In Poe's first short story, "Metzengerstein," he contrasts his natural affection for animals with the unnatural affection shown by the young baron. In order to compare the heir of the Metzengerstein barony with Caligula, Poe introduces a gigantic horse for which the young baron has a "perverse attachment," which all reasonable men in the story regard as having "a hideous and unnatural fervor."[9] While affection for an animal is an appropriate sentiment, confusing the affection for animals with the friendship for people amounts to a violation of Love.

Familial affection is betrayed in "Ligeia," in a way similar to how Poe might have judged the father of his childhood sweetheart, Elmira. The narrator of "Ligeia" deplored the family's "thirst for gold" that would permit the marriage of the Lady Rowena Trevanion of Tremaine to him, an opium fiend who did not love her, simply because he had money.[10] Poe's most vivid examples of this kind of corruption of affection among people comes with tales, such as "The Fall of the House of Usher," in which the suggestion of incest has corrupted the natural affection of a brother and sister. We also find this corruption of affection between the young man and his landlord in "The Tell-Tale Heart." Horror stories work upon a person's understanding of what is natural, normal, and appropriate, and through them, Poe expresses his most vigorous moral indignation and outrage.

Philia: *Friendship*

Poe wrote easily about friendship, and many of his most well-known tales depend upon friendship for the telling. We find this feature of his stories especially true in his mysteries in which a close friend relates the events. The narrator of the Dupin mysteries first met the Chevalier C. Auguste Dupin at a rare book shop, where they had a mutual interest in the same rare volume.[11] Healthy friendships usually form through common interests. Unhealthy or deformed imitations of friendship frequently develop through the desire to advance one's position in life or to vicariously experience life through another person or in some form of dependency in which a person's self-image and identity takes its shape from another person. Dupin and his new friend liked the same things enthusiastically, which provided them with a basis for friendship. They derived similar pleasure in these interests, and the narrator notes that they had a "common temper."[12]

Both Dupin and his friend preferred solitude apart from the social life of Paris. They chose to live in an old house in an isolated section of the city, and Dupin's new friend did not inform his former associates of his new address. The narrator contrasts the term *former associates* with the term he chose for Dupin—*friend*.[13] He makes no pretense that they would have been thought normal in a city like Paris with its international renown as a city of gaiety. He admits that they were "madmen of a harmless nature" for their reclusive habits and for being "enamored of the Night for her own sake."[14] They enjoyed reading, writing, and talking together, shut up from the world in the old mansion by day. At nighttime they loved to roam the city and enjoy her excitement as voyeurs, observing from a distance. The importance of friendship comes in having someone with whom to enjoy the same pleasures so that the company ceases to merely enhance the pleasure and becomes the greater pleasure.

While friends have common interests, they are still different. Dupin and his friend have different financial status. While the friend has money, Dupin has "background." Friendship transcends social barriers. The friend is clearly intelligent because he shares Dupin's intellectual interests, but he is not the equal of Dupin. No one is. If friendship were based upon absolute equality, then no one would have friends because no two people are exactly alike. Friendship in its healthy form is one of the strangest forms of Love. Arthur Conan Doyle overlooked this critical issue in bringing Sherlock Holmes and Watson together. In his effort to elaborate the eccentric nature of Holmes and the contrasting nature of plain old Watson, he neglected to provide a common interest upon which friendship could be built. In that sense Holmes and Watson were never friends.

In the second of Poe's mystery stories, a discussion of how the two friends passed their time comprises the introduction to "The Mystery of Marie Rogêt." The murder interrupted their pleasant reveries. Unlike Sherlock Holmes, who had to have a difficult case to stimulate his brain to keep him from turning to drugs, friendship provided the only stimulant that Dupin needed. Such friendship involves shared confidences, and one of the features of the Dupin stories is that he often tells his friend how he has worked out the solution to a problem that he never tells the police. The friend knows the financial arrangements by which Dupin is induced to take up the case of Marie Rogêt, but the friend would never tell.

Poe's last Dupin story, "The Purloined Letter," begins with the narrator neck deep in the joy of friendship, "enjoying the twofold luxury of meditation and a meerschaum, in company with my friend C. Auguste Dupin, in his little back library."[15] He could just as easily sit by himself alone in the dark, but the pleasure of friendship comes with the company we keep. The friends did not require a continuous conversation, though they enjoyed conversation. As the story opens they sit silently in the dark smoking and thinking for over an hour. Into this state of reverie, the prefect of police intrudes. The friends have a shared regard for the prefect, who strikes them as equally contemptible and entertaining. Friends do not agree about everything, but friends often have similar opinions punctuated by occasional differences. They have common jokes and share private jokes, seeing humor and injecting humor into situations that no one else notices, as Dupin and his friend do when in the company of the prefect. They are not vicious or rude; they are discreetly amused by the forensic pomposity. While the friendship provides Poe with a means to tell the story, the friend is not merely a literary device. The literary advantage would not exist unless a peculiar thing like friendship exists whereby people share their lives.

"The Gold-Bug," perhaps Poe's most popular tale during his lifetime, also depends upon friendship, not only for narration, but for the successful completion of the treasure hunt. The narrator became acquainted with William Legrand, an impoverished aristocrat like Dupin, and the acquaintance "ripened into friendship."[16] As Poe made clear in "The Murders in the Rue Morgue," there is a difference between acquaintance and friendship. In a few brief sentences Poe makes clear the shared interests that formed the basis of the friendship. Legrand was well educated and intelligent. He enjoyed the sports of the South Carolina low country—hunting and fishing. He also took long walks on the beach of Sullivan's Island and through the myrtle jungle that covered the island as he collected shells and bugs. The narrator seems to have shared Legrand's interests, for the discovery of the mystery of the gold-bug begins when Legrand wanted to show his friend the wonderful new bug he had found.

In addition to the mutual interests, however, Legrand has his flaws. He has mood swings that range from enthusiasm to melancholy. Poe makes clear that manic-depression, or bipolar disorder, does not present impediments to friendship. Rather, difficult conditions become the occasion for demonstrating a difference between acquaintance and friendship. Care and concern take on a heightened dimension. Friendship brings pleasure, but it also involves a mutual regard that passes far beyond the original basis for friendship. The story could not move forward without this care that made the friend solicitous for Legrand's mental health. As the

93

story unfolds, the drama heightens because of the friend's concern for Legrand's mental health as he grows increasingly agitated over buried treasure.

Only a true friend could accomplish the comedy of "The Spectacles." Adolphus Simpson Esq. has a true friend, indeed, in the person of Talbot, who is his friend in spite of Simpson's foolishness. Born Napoleon Bonaparte Froissart, Simpson had his name changed in order to inherit a fortune from a distant relative. Simpson's fatal flaws are vanity and pride. He will not wear the glasses without which he cannot see because he thinks they will "disfigure" his youthful appearance.[17] We do not know the basis for the friendship between Simpson and Talbot, for it had far advanced long before the tale begins. What we see in the story is how far a friend may go in order to rescue a friend from his own silliness. When Simpson falls in love with an eighty-two-year-old lady whom he sees across the theater at the opera without his glasses, Talbot decides it is time to teach his friend to wear his glasses or become a laughing stock. That the old lady turned out to be Simpson's great-great-grandmother only added to the high comedy, giving Poe the reputation as one of the greatest American humorists before Mark Twain. Without an intimate friend, the romantic comedy would have ended as a tragedy. All of the events could have been orchestrated by a villain with lives left in ruins, and without the happy marriage at the end. The depth of friendship makes the difference. The knowledge of another person and their motives that gives rise to trust and the suspension of judgment marks the difference between friends and enemies. Poe knew both classes of people very well.

"Never Bet the Devil Your Head" is such an outrageous farce and parody of the moral tales of the transcendentalists that one struggles to treat the idea of friendship seriously in its text. The narrator, who appears to be Poe himself, lectures his friend endlessly. Tobias Dammit takes all the lectures good-naturedly and ignores them. Poe cannot correct his friend's bad habits, yet Poe does not abandon Dammit, and Dammit does not reject Poe. Friends may part company, but it takes much more than lectures and disapproval to end friendship. As the Apostle Paul remarked, Love "beareth all things, believeth all things, hopeth all things, endureth all things. Love never faileth" (1 Cor 13:7-8a).

"The Fall of the House of Usher" shows us a picture of the power of childhood friendship, even when years and miles separate childhood friends. The narrator had not seen Roderick Usher in years when he received an agitated letter asking him to visit. Usher wrote of "acute bodily illness—of a mental disorder which oppressed him—and of an earnest desire to see me, as his best, and indeed his only personal friend, with a view of attempting, by the cheerfulness of my society, some alleviation of his malady."[18] The request left the friend "no room for hesitation," and he traveled the great distance to Usher's home. That Usher thought of his childhood friend in the midst of his fall from sanity, and that the friend responded, tells us a great deal about the lifelong significance of first friendships. The great change that had taken place in the body and mind of Usher does not alter the friendship, and the narrator makes desperate efforts to stop the disintegration. When Usher grows hysterical in the storm, the friend attempts to soothe him by reading an old romance. But this tale is terror and not comedy. The friend can be present and loyal, but he cannot forestall the end.

95

Diseased Friendship

With "The Cask of Amontillado" we see the corruption and disease of what often passes for friendship. The tale of Fortunato and Montresor suggests why some social scientists argue that what we call friendship is merely a transaction of self-interest. They use the language of friendship and endearment with one another, giving the linguistic analysts cause to argue that language has no objective meaning. While Montresor activates his murderous policy of revenge, he speaks of his "dear Fortunato" and calls him "my friend."[19] They do not have the kind of relationship that allows for whatever Montresor considers Fortunato's injuries, to which he had added insult. No doubt Fortunato had overstepped the boundaries of courtesy, to which Montresor responded with duplicity: "It must be understood, that neither by word nor deed had I given Fortunato cause to doubt my good will. I continued, as was my wont, to smile in his face, and he did not perceive that my smile *now* was at the thought of his immolation."[20] Belonging to the same order of society by wealth and position, Fortunato and Montresor represent one of the tawdriest mockeries of friendship that often leads to vindictiveness and treachery of spirit, if not actual murder.

With "William Wilson" we find Poe's exquisite antifriend. Wilson has no interest in friendship. He demands subordinates. He requires acquiescence to his "arbitrary dictation" and "submission to his will."[21] The greatest offense perpetrated by William Wilson's namesake was his equality that left Wilson fearing he was superior. The namesake lacked the ambition which drove William Wilson, yet he continued to excel. The namesake also had a manner of "*affectionateness*" that Wilson regarded as "most unwelcome."[22] Though they were on speaking terms, the imperious William Wilson resisted the option of friendship. Poe paints William Wilson as the most miserable of men, a man who has rejected the possibility of friendship. The ghastliness of it makes "William Wilson" one of Poe's most horrible tales because it is so firmly rooted in normal experience. The reader knows this man.

"William Wilson" is one of Poe's stories that has true and unveiled autobiographical elements. Poe describes the Manor School he attended in Stoke-Newington during the five years his family lived in England. He even gives the headmaster in the story the name of his own schoolmaster, Dr. Bransby. He gives William Wilson his own birthday of January 19. When he names Wilson's flaws, however, he describes how he himself had been victimized by card cheats at college like Wilson. Poe's eminent trusting spirit had made him easy victim to people who profess friendship and then manipulate and abuse those whom they draw into their web. Poe lost money at cards at the University of Virginia and apparently never gambled again, but he was always susceptible to people like William Wilson who insisted that he have a drink with them. Wilson's card game with Lord Glendinning draws forth the contempt and condemnation of the reader against him for offending against friendship. Wilson cannot enjoy someone who shares his interests. He must prevail against them, for they are his competitors, and his competitors are his enemies.

Eros: *Passion*

Edgar Allan Poe's capacity or desire for physical love and passion has long been a topic of literary conversation. It presents a fallback position for academic papers and sophomore themes. Sexuality always arouses interest in American culture. Poe's interest in sex has been complicated by incompetent and amateurish attempts at psychoanalysis based on the assumption that all Poe's stories are about him. It has been further complicated by the fact that a gentleman of Poe's background would not discuss such things in writing. Finally, it has been complicated by the number of dubious memoirs of Poe that tended to proliferate in the last quarter of the nineteenth century, one example of which is the case of Mary Devereaux of Baltimore.

In 1889 *Harper's Magazine* published an article that claimed to be the account of a love affair Poe had with a Baltimore woman before he married Virginia. Mary Phillips repeated the story in her massive biography *Poe the Man*, published in 1926, and Hervey Allen repeated it in his two volume *Israfel*, also published in 1926. Both of these biographies make for lively reading because the authors include every story about Poe that they can find without attending to any effort to verify their authenticity. In his definitive biography of Poe, Arthur Hobson Quinn carefully evaluated each source, and he mentions this story of the Baltimore lover in order to demonstrate basic principles of critical evaluation. Quinn provides a brief summary of the story of Mary Devereaux: "The reminiscences of a woman of seventy-one, who claimed that Poe was passionately in love with her, tried to force his way into her room, and cowhided her uncle who objected to the match."[23]

Quinn then takes the time to explain to the reader how to regard an unsubstantiated account of something that might have happened fifty-five years earlier. Quinn explains: "If there is any form of evidence that is fundamentally unreliable, it is that of an elderly woman concerning her youthful love affair with a man who has since become famous. She dramatizes and magnifies their relations unconsciously, and every desperate act of her lover becomes a tribute to her attractions."[24] He points out the unreliable assertion in the

97

article that Mr. Allan's second wife had been his housekeeper and that she could not continue to take care of the house unless he married her. Quinn argues that when a story disagrees with the proven character of a person, the burden of proof lies with the story. While acknowledging that Poe had his share of failings, Quinn insists that Mary Devereaux's picture of Poe's attitude toward love and honor fly in the face of the reliable record of him. She claimed, "He didn't value the laws of God or man. He was an atheist. He would just as lief have lived with a woman without being married to her as not."[25]

In his romanticized biography of Poe, the novelist Hervey Allen continually refers to the girlishness of Virginia Poe, suggesting that Poe could not have had a passionate attraction to her. Poe had been in love before he met his young cousin and he had courted before. All the visitors to the Poe home who have left a record describe Virginia as a beautiful woman. Some would have her ever as the wasted corpse lying upon her deathbed whose image was preserved in a drawing. Descriptions of her vivacity, however, picture her as anything but a wasted corpse. Though she married days short of her fourteenth birthday, Virginia was not a perpetual child but an early blossoming woman, as the portrait of her preserved by the descendants of her cousin, Elizabeth Poe Herring, bears witness. Perhaps it is not purely coincidental that Virginia was the same age as Juliet when she and Romeo fell in love and married. Some biographers confuse Virginia and Madeline Usher, but when Poe wrote of Madeline Usher, he would have had no such vision of dissipation from his enthusiastic and energetic wife.

William Gowan, a bookseller who boarded with the Poes in New York in 1837, described Virginia as a woman "of matchless beauty and loveliness, her eye could match that of any houri, and her face defy the genius of a Canova to imitate; a temper and disposition of surpassing sweetness."[26] Mayne Reid, the Irish novelist who often visited Poe at home in Philadelphia in 1843, described Virginia as "a lady angelically beautiful in Person and not less beautiful in spirit. No one who remembers that dark-eyed, dark-haired daughter of Virginia . . . her grace, her facial beauty, her demeanour, so modest as to be remarkable—no one who has ever spent an hour in her company but will endorse what I have above said."[27] Poe had a wife to come home to.

If Poe's schoolteacher may be trusted, he wrote his earliest poetry for the pretty girls in Richmond. Love poetry started him on his way. It was not great, but he learned that it could be highly effective. From love poetry, Poe learned the power of poetry and literature in general to have an effect on a person. He did not ascend the heights with his teenage verse, like "Octavia," in which he pled,

> But Octavia, do not strive to rob
> My heart, of all that soothes its pain
> The mournful hope that every throb
>   Will make it break for thee!

His early poetry was all of love and of the lost Elmira, whose highborn kinsmen came and bore her away from him. In the poetry that fills the rare volume of *Tamerlane* (1827), he pours out his anguish for first love's broken heart.[28]

Having reached the solemn age of eighteen and run off to join the army, after Elmira had been pledged to another, Poe writes with ancient wisdom about the days of his lost youth. In "Stanzas" he wrote, "In youth have I known one with whom the Earth / In secret communing held—."[29] In "Imitation" he wrote,

> A dark unfathom'd tide
> Of interminable pride—
> A mystery, and a dream,
> Should my early life seem.[30]

In "Dreams" he wrote of his "young life" and his "young boyhood," but that was all past now that he was eighteen.[31] Even in "Tamerlane," spoken by the voice of an aged conqueror and despot on his deathbed, he speaks of "Young Love's first lesson."[32] With Elmira Royster married off to an old man, no doubt young Poe felt that he would never love again, like Tamerlane who only had memories of youth's love to sustain him:

> But, father, there liv'd on who, then,
> Then—in my boyhood—when their fire

99

> Burn'd with a still intenser glow
> (For passion must, with youth, expire).[33]

Having experienced the glory of romantic love only to have it crushed, Poe must have doubted that anyone could possibly feel that way again about anyone. In "The Happiest Day" Poe expressed the conviction that "the visions of my youth have been" and that his greatest happiness lay in his past.[34] In "The Lake" Poe continues the theme of reflecting on "the spring of youth" now long gone and replaced by the unceasing death of his romance.[35] Thus, virtually the whole of Poe's first book of poetry, published when he was eighteen and just enlisted in the army, is given over to the grief of love lost. From our perspective, it was puppy love, but from his perspective it was all of life, and it was over.[36]

One does not get over a love like that too quickly, and so into *Al Aaraaf, Tamerlane, and Minor Poems* (1829), Poe continues to pour his grief. In "Al Aaraaf" pain is the price one pays for love. In "Mysterious Star" Poe associates love with sadness, sorrow, grief, and the loss of joy. In "Introduction" the intensity of love and the agony of separation have both begun to change:

> But *now* my soul hath too much room—
> Gone are the glory and the gloom—
> The black hath mellow'd into grey,
> And all the fires are fading away.[37]

The dullness that remains when the beloved has died is even worse than the pain, and it feels like it will never go away. But it did go away, or its refusal to go away pushed Poe to find solace, and he fell in love again.[38] The idea that Poe did not feel romantic, passionate love, however, is a very strange notion that can best be explained by the habit some people have of bringing fixed ideas to a study of Poe that tells us more about the critic than it tells us about Poe.[39]

Romantic Love in Fiction

In spite of all the work he did for Graham, Poe also managed to sell a few pieces to other editors. "Eleonora" appeared in *The Gift* of 1842 which went on sale in the fall of 1841. The beautiful woman dies as in so many other stories, but this is not a tale of horror or of terror. "Eleonora" may be one of the very few tales by Poe which may legitimately be called in any sense autobiographical. Eleonora, the matchless beauty, is fifteen when she and her twenty-year-old cousin fall in love. In case there is any doubt about the identity of the two lovers, they live with Eleonora's mother. If the tale has autobiographical elements, as virtually all scholars agree, Poe makes clear that he and Virginia had more than a Platonic relationship:

> Hand in hand about this valley, for fifteen years, roamed I with Eleonora before Love entered within our hearts. It was one evening at the close of the third lustrum of her life, and of the fourth of my own, that we sat, locked in each other's embrace, beneath the serpent-like trees, and looked down within the waters of the River of Silence at our images therein. We spoke no words during the rest of that sweet day; and our words even upon the morrow were tremulous and few. We had drawn the God Eros from that wave, and now we felt that he had enkindled within us the fiery souls of our forefathers. The passions which had for centuries distinguished our race, came thronging with the fancies for which they had been equally noted, and together breathed a delirious bliss over the Valley of the Many-Colored Grass.[40]

101

And with their passion, flowers bloomed, the grass grew greener, asphodels replaced the drab daisy, flamingoes appeared, and even the fish sang. Passionate love has a powerful sensory effect that makes the whole world more glorious.

The tale is a beautiful love story in which the narrator makes a promise to the dying Eleonora never to wed another and binds the promise with an oath to God.[41] Sometime after Eleonora has died, he falls in love again and marries Ermengarde. One would have come to expect of Poe that some grim horror would befall the narrator along the lines of "Morella" or "Ligeia." Instead, he hears a "familiar and sweet voice," saying, "Sleep in peace!—for the Spirit of Love reigneth and ruleth, and, in taking to thy passionate heart her who is Ermengarde, thou art absolved, for reasons which shall be made known to thee in Heaven, of thy vows unto Eleonora."[42] In this story, Poe brings together many of his most cherished themes: Beauty, Death, Justice, and Knowledge beyond what science can reveal. The beauty of the Valley of the Many-Colored Grass where the lovers dwelt spoke "in loud tones, of the love and of the glory of God."[43] Love and Beauty point beyond the physical world. Though death seems to vanquish Beauty, Love vanquishes death.[44] This line of thought would grow stronger in Poe's mind as he tried to understand what kind of universe he inhabited and what kind of God had made it. Poe mused at the beginning of this story that spiritual knowledge is often mistaken for madness in a world of tangible facts. After all, the imagination which makes invention and creativity possible also makes delusion possible. Ironically, Poe would be labeled a madman in 1848 for writing a long essay on this very theme.

"Three Sundays in a Week" can be called a science fiction story for its anticipation of the theory of relativity. It could also be called a comic tale for the farcical tone. Yet, it also is a romantic comedy in the best Shakespearean tradition. The passionate lovers are cousins in "Three Sundays in a Week" just as they were in "Eleonora." In this comic romance, however, the lovers' friendship and the girl's cleverness in outwitting the great-uncle's opposition to the marriage predominate. We have no glimpses of passion in the story, except that the fierce determination of the lovers conveys their urgency for more than a simple continuation of their friendship. What the story conveys about Poe's understanding of passion, however, is the playfulness, joy, and delight that lovers experience together, which was the public hallmark of Poe's relationship with Virginia. Prior to the twentieth century, public displays of passion did not occur among well-mannered ladies and gentlemen, among which number the Poes would have counted themselves.

As mentioned earlier in reference to friendship, one of Poe's funniest stories is "The Spectacles." In addition to friendship, mistaken identity, male vanity, and female cleverness, the story also involves love at first sight, which has nothing to do with an admiration for a person's keen mind or noble spirit. It involves physical attraction. Even a partial view of the beloved's form left the narrator "deeply, madly, and irrevocably in love."[45] This farcical romantic comedy hinges on the fact that the women in the family of the narrator have married by the age of sixteen for generations, like Virginia Poe.

In "The Domain of Arnheim" Poe explores the poetic imagination manifested as landscape gardening. In discussing what brings happiness in life, he refers to romantic love. The narrator describes how his friend Ellison came to inherit a great fortune, but that he did not derive his happiness from his wealth. Of Ellison's four conditions for bliss, the narrator thought the first a strange one: "free exercise in the open air."[46] The second condition is a woman's love. Poe highly prized exercise in the open air. He was noted since childhood for his swimming exploits and for his walks through mountains in college. In the army he had walked across the beaches of Sullivan's Island, and in 1847 when he wrote "The Domain of Arnheim" while grieving Virginia's death, he walked for miles along the river. Poe still would not have counted exercise first in a short list of conditions for bliss. In fact, Ellison's greatest happiness did not come from exercise. The narrator tells us, "Above all, it was in the sympathy of a woman, not unwomanly, whose loveliness and love enveloped his existence in the purple atmosphere of Paradise, that Ellison thought to find, *and found*, exemption from the cares of humanity, with a far greater amount of positive happiness then ever glowed in the rapt of day-dreams of De Staël."[47] Ellison found happiness in the arms of a woman—not a phantom, but a woman. He had no platonic, spiritual relationships in mind, and Poe emphasizes that he not only sought, but found this kind of happiness. Ellison's spirituality came in the contemplation of his artistic goal, but his supreme happiness came with a woman.[48]

In "Landor's Cottage," written in January 1849, Poe's description of the countryside and the simple grace of the little cottage comes to a climax with his description of a woman who steals his heart. Upon entering the cottage of Mr. Landor, the narrator beholds a young woman of grace and enthusiasm from whose eyes there gleamed an intense expression of romance. The narrator described what he meant by romance: " 'Romance' and 'womanliness' seem to me convertible terms:—and, after all, what man truly *loves* in woman is, simply, her *womanhood*."[49] The narrator is not captivated by a platonic ideal. He has fallen in love at first sight with a lively woman of flesh and blood. This bit of prose, that might be

103

called creative nonfiction today, describes Poe's cottage at Fordham, with a few alterations, and the married woman he had fallen in love with—Nancy Richmond, whom he always called "Annie."

The Corruption of Romantic Love

Poe contrasted the healthy, vibrant love between a man and a woman with the perverse aberrations of true love. Contrasting beauty with ugliness created an effect within the readers of his tales of repugnance for corrupt distortions or betrayals of love. In contrast to his personal dependence upon and expressions of love, Poe condemns the betrayal of love in his prose.[50] The corruption of love constitutes a great violence which Poe portrays in the most vivid of terms. The vile imitations and substitutes for love, as well as the betrayal of love, compel the reader to agree with Poe that the betrayal of true love violates the underlying nature of the universe. The literary confrontation with false love confirms the reality of true love.

Poe's foster father, John Allan, had destroyed a once beautiful love in his betrayal of Frances Allan, or perhaps he had never really loved her at all. In the same stroke he had used women for his own lustful purposes, but without love. The narrator of "The Black Cat" killed his wife with an ax in a fit of fury when she tried to prevent him from attacking his pet cat. The greatest depth of affection he had expressed about his wife to this point was that her "disposition [was] not uncongenial" with his.[51] Allan did not kill Frances Allan, but one often misses the point in Poe's work if one forgets that he is a poet. Death does not usually mean death in Poe.

Jane Austen had explored the same ideas in her novels a few years earlier. Wickham represents the true enemy of romantic love in *Pride and Prejudice*. He is interested in his own pleasures in terms of the satisfaction of his will, but he has no interest in the other person. Wickham is a Tamerlane who has abandoned the possibility of love in his pursuit of transient things. At least Tamerlane understood at the end what a devil's bargain he had made, for on his deathbed he laments the lost love he traded for fame, glory, and a temporal crown:

104

Halo of Hell! And with a pain
Not hell shall make me fear again—
O craving heart, for the lost flowers
And sunshine of my summer hours![52]

Elizabeth and Mr. Darcy must each deal with their own perversity that endangers love. For Elizabeth it is her prejudice, and for Mr. Darcy it is his pride.

The American literary tradition has tended to focus on the tales of corruption when thinking of Poe's "love stories," as Allen Tate explained in his famous lecture, "Our Cousin, Mr. Poe":

> His contemporaries could see in the love stories neither the incestuous theme nor what it meant, because it was not represented literally. The Theme and its meaning as I see them are unmistakable: the symbolic compulsion that drives through, and beyond, physical incest moves towards the extinction of the beloved's will in complete possession, not of her body, but of her being; there is the reciprocal force, returning upon the lover, of self-destruction. Lawrence shrewdly perceived the significance of Poe's obsession with incestuous love. Two persons of the least dissimilarity offer the least physical resistance to mutual participation in the *fire* of a common being. Poe's most casual reader perceives that his lovers never do anything but contemplate each other, or pore upon the rigmarole of preposterously erudite, ancient books, most of which never existed. They are living in each other's insides, in the hollows of which burns the fire of will and intellect.[35]

Here Tate describes as clear an antithesis to the Apostle Paul's description of Love in 1 Corinthians 15 as one could hope to find. Yet, it is of only a particular kind of love story that Tate writes—the tale of horror. Tate focused his attention on "The Fall of the House of Usher," but properly speaking, that tale refers to the corruption of affection. By placing this kind of story within a horror, Poe tells us that he does not approve.

In "Berenice," the horror tale that Mr. White feared would offend the subscribers to the *Southern Literary Messenger*, the narrator states bluntly that even before his wife's dissipating illness

105

when she was a radiant beauty, he "had never loved her."[54] Part of the narrator's depravity comes from his inability to perceive Beauty. For Poe, the physical world provides a constantly unfolding vista of beauty in the unity of nature. The narrator, however, cannot see "the big picture." This "disease," as he had been told to call it, involves a fixation on particular objects distinct and isolated from their context. He could not perceive the unity of effect that Poe regarded as critical.

In "The Murders in the Rue Morgue" Dupin made this same criticism of Vidocq, the founder of the Paris police, because "He impaired his vision by holding the object too close."[55] In many ways the narrator represents the Enlightenment mindset that fragments the world and loses the significance, proportion, harmony, and unity of effect that Poe believed was necessary for the perception of Truth, Beauty, and the experience of passionate love.[56] Furthermore, the narrator's fixations never bring him pleasure, the effect of Beauty in all its forms.

The narrator in "Morella" never feels any passionate love for his wife Morella, though he acknowledges the deep affection of *storge*. He also insists that she has always made him happy. As time passes, however, the narrator can "no longer bear the touch of her wan fingers, nor the low tone of her musical language, nor the luster of her melancholy eyes."[57] As Morella grows ill and pines away, the narrator can feel pity for her, but then he feels sickened by her and longs for her death. The horror of "Morella" occurs because the narrator withholds his love from his wife, who pronounces a curse upon him as she dies. The love withheld from Morella would be given to their daughter. The narrator bestows inappropriately intense love upon the daughter, whom he gives Morella's name and in whom he perceives the identity of the wife he failed to love. Only disaster can follow.

The narrator of "Ligeia" regards Ligeia first as a friend, then as a colleague, and finally as the wife received as "a wildly romantic offering on the shrine of the most passionate devotion."[58] He describes her beauty at length as he gives a full inventory of the exquisiteness of every feature of her face. The narrator believes, along with Francis Bacon, that true beauty must have some slight irregularity, some strangeness about it, and he finds this irregularity in Ligeia's unusually large eyes.[59] Furthermore, the narrator claims that his passion for Ligeia is more than returned by her "whose more than passionate devotion amounted to idolatry."[60] Yet, he wonders if that great passion was not directed at him so much as at life itself.

In contrast to his relationship with Ligeia, Lady Rowena has no real love for him, his moodiness, or his temper. In his turn, he takes pleasure in his wife's distance and "loathe[s] her with a hatred belonging more to demon than to man."[61] The marriage descends into mutual destruction as the narrator retreats further into a perpetual state of opium-induced disorientation and the Lady Rowena's disease-ridden body ebbs toward death. The miserable couple betrays each other with their disdain for love—the Lady Rowena marrying for money and the narrator marrying to stop the monotonous emptiness he feels without Ligeia.[62] His second wife is merely a diversion.

Intriguingly, the narrators of "Berenice," "Morella," and "Ligeia" cannot be trusted for their accounts. Those who prove untrustworthy in love are unreliable. They have sinned against the universe, and the punishment is madness.

Conclusion

Like Shakespeare, Poe chose to express romantic love best in comedy with all the delight, joy, and foolishness associated with being in love. For sin against Love, Poe also joined Shakespeare in portraying betrayal and falsehood, as in the horrors of Lady Macbeth, Hamlet, or Othello. Melancholy and sadness, the pain of grief over the death of a *lovely* beautiful woman has such power because it is the substance of something lost: the lost Lenore, the rare and radiant maiden. Sadness is the evidence of the truth of Love. The magnitude of the pain demonstrates the reality of the love. In Poe's tales we find his greatest fear and horror: that Love might not last. On the other hand, the fact of Love which Poe experienced in abundance provided another lesson for Poe. Instead of asking if Love survives the grave, Poe's question turned to the source of Love. Given the perversity of the world, does Love tell us something about God? Given the perversity of the world, does Love have another source beyond ourselves?

THE PROBLEM OF JUSTICE

In April 1841 Edgar Allan Poe published the first detective mystery story ever written. In "The Murders in the Rue Morgue" Poe created a form of literature that illuminates in a profoundly subtle way one of the most intriguing philosophical problems in the universe. By the time he wrote the first mystery story, Poe assumed "the problem of evil." The mystery story, however, suggests a greater mystery. The problem with the problem of evil is that evil does not pose a problem unless some overarching principle of Justice lies behind the universe that judges evil to be a problem.

A. H. Strong, one of the leading Calvinist theologians in America, dealt with Poe in a book on the theology of the major American poets. He condemned Poe for ignoring "all moral issues."[1] This view conformed to the long established tradition founded by Griswold that Poe did not carry into his work a "moral sense," as W. H. Davenport Adams had phrased it in 1880.[2] Strong faulted Poe as "a soured and self-willed unbeliever, esteeming the Bible to be a mere rigmarole."[3] When William Mentzel Forrest, professor of biblical history and literature at the University of Virginia, made a study of *Biblical Allusions in Poe*, however, he found 684 quotations, allusions, and reflections on biblical texts in the body of Poe's work.[4]

Poe quoted the Bible in his stories, his poetry, his criticism, his essays, and his letters. Forrest analyzed fourteen of Poe's biblical quotations and found that all but two of them contained errors in punctuation, capitalization, vocabulary, or all three. He argued that a person not well acquainted with the Bible would copy a text from the page, but a person well acquainted with the Bible would rely upon memory and make minor mistakes.[5] Poe had a profound familiarity with the Bible, in spite of what Strong assumed.[6]

How do we account for the common early critical view that Poe's works had no hint of morality about them? Poe believed that each literary form was best suited to attend to a specific aspect of human experience. Whereas the New England poets in the Calvinist tradition (long after they had abandoned Christianity) believed that poetry should teach a moral lesson, Poe believed that sermons, lectures, and essays were the literary forms that best taught lessons. Poetry and stories best address another aspect of what it means to be human. A. H. Strong represents that strand of Calvinism that encouraged or required Christians to withdraw from the world of Western art that the church had originally helped to create. Strong believed that art must teach a lesson. Poe's conviction that art most touches the aesthetic dimension related to the emotions rather than the intellect offended Strong's brand of Calvinism which strove to expunge the emotional dimension from faith. Strong also applied his own misunderstanding of Poe's *Eureka*, not written until two years before Poe's death, to misconstrue Poe's literary theory.

In spite of the New England tradition that Poe had no moral compass, a powerful sense of right and wrong, good and evil, permeates Poe's stories. Forrest argued that "the idea of judgment stands out with startling clearness in Poe."[7] Justice prevails in story after story, often in the form of some disaster falling upon the perpetrator of evil or injustice. We assume the idea of Justice in Poe's detective stories, but we also find Justice as the compelling universal theme in a variety of other tales, including "The Black Cat," "The Tell-Tale Heart," "The Imp of the Perverse," "William Wilson," "The Man of the Crowd," and "Hop-Frog."[8] Forrest describes Poe's emphasis as "poetic justice," though this term can be misleading as a mere literary device. The success of these stories depends upon something that we call Justice—that sense of right and wrong that people in every culture carry through life. Poe discovered that Justice goes to the heart of the universe and animates all human dealings. The concept of fairness and treating people "right," or righteously, works its way through story after story.[9]

The Power of Stories

Each type of story tells us something about people and the nature of the universe we inhabit. Our stories strike at the very nature of reality. Though the plots and characters may reflect the personalities, concerns, and culture of the storyteller, the form of each type of story goes much deeper than its individual authors.

The love story appeals to a primordial urge of people to reproduce. It involves the nature of sexuality and the desire of humans to have intimate relationship and companionship with members of the opposite sex. The love story represents a ritual or liturgical recital of the continuity of the human race that goes far beyond the talents of individual storytellers. William Shakespeare and Barbara Cartland use the same story type with different levels of skill and with different literary forms. For the stories to work, however, the audience must bring to the story the deeply held belief in romantic love.

The adventure story reminds us of the struggle to survive in a sometimes harsh and competitive environment filled with hostile adversaries. It urges us to master the skills needed to survive—courage, persistence, ingenuity—and conquer what would conquer us. The adventure story reminds us that strength and power alone are not sufficient to ensure success.

The love story and the adventure story reflect the challenges of survival in an evolutionary model of nature. Of course, these kinds of stories have been around for much longer than Darwin's theory of natural selection, which is why they are so revealing. The very act of storytelling emerges from deep within us and tells us something about the universe if we take the time to listen. So it is with the mystery story.

111

The Detective Mystery Story

In 1929 Dorothy L. Sayers edited a collection of the world's great mystery stories. In her introduction she recognized the relationship between the horror story and the detective story. Whereas the horror story appears throughout history in cultures around the world, the detective story was only hinted at until Edgar Allan Poe wrote "The Murders in the Rue Morgue" in 1841.[10] It is not difficult to see Poe's process of creation in retrospect. Poe deplored the horror story but felt obliged to write them as a sure source of income because the public of his day was obsessed with them. The horror story represents only a small percentage of the kind of stories Poe wrote, but his name has become associated with horror for a reason. Though hundreds of authors in the English speaking world produced these lurid tales in massive quantities during the first half of the nineteenth century, few of the authors and their stories are remembered. Poe's horror stories stand alone as though he were the only one writing horror during his age because his horror stories stand on their own as works of literary distinction.

112

Poe's first detective mystery represents the inverse of a horror story. The horror story aims in its effect to make the reader feel horrible or repulsed. The didactic tale of the day relied upon a moral explanation in the narrative to teach the reader the way they ought to think and believe. The horror story, on the other hand, arouses within the reader a feeling toward a particular topic. It does not teach the reader that it is wrong to withhold affection or to nurture ill feelings or to be selfish and cruel. Instead, the horror story aims at rousing within the reader the agreement of feelings about the inappropriateness of withholding affection, nurturing ill feelings, or being selfish and cruel.[11] Whereas the lecture or sermon speaks to the reason or intellect, the horror story speaks to the emotions or passion. While retaining all the emotional appeal of the horror story, the detective mystery story also speaks to reason.

In the horror story Poe found vulgarity and bad taste of a general sort that the public adored. He succeeded in raising the caliber of writing, but the horror story remains a tale of irrational brute force, of gratuitous violence, of meaningless atrocity, and grotesque excess. Poe recognized all of these forces at work in the world and would explore them, but he also recognized a force of order at work in the world. His fascination with science and the remarkable discoveries and technological advancements of his age had taught him that the universe has an underlying principle of order that transcends the periodic displays of irrationality and confusion. Today, physicists refer to this order in the midst of confusion as chaos theory.

The horror story begins on a low key and builds with intensity toward a grand climax. In his satire on horror stories, "How to Write a Blackwood Article," Poe emphasized the extent to which the average horror story could get along perfectly well without a plot, just so long as it had plenty of sensation: "Sensations are the great thing after all. Should you ever be drowned or hung, be sure and make a note of your sensations—they will be worth to you ten guineas a sheet."[12] At the end of the horror story, blood and guts abound. Heads roll through the streets. Bodies are slashed. Gore prevails. The public gets the good scare they have paid for.[13] With the detective mystery story, however, Poe moved the blood and gore to the beginning of the story. Meaningless violence ceases to be the goal of the story; it becomes the beginning of the search for meaning. The apparent meaninglessness occasions the questions that reveal the underlying order.

Poe began "The Murders in the Rue Morgue" with a brief introduction about the nature of imagination (which will require some exploration at the end of this chapter and more expansively in chapter 6).[14] The action of the story begins with a double murder on the fourth floor of a mansion in Paris. The two murdered women have been slashed with a razor and blood gushes everywhere. Screams from the victims and the voice of the assailant were heard by the neighbors who were prevented from intervening because the door to the room was locked from the inside. When the door was finally opened, the dead bodies were eventually found but not the murderer. Furthermore, there was no way the murderer could have escaped from the upper story room. The question arose: Who done it?

113

With the first detective mystery story, Poe transformed the horror story, which embodies the human attempt to grapple with the experience of suffering, into a quest for meaning and for justice. In order for the mystery story to work, however, the reader must bring something to the story. The reader must furnish from within themselves the sense of justice, without which the mystery story cannot work upon the reader. This sense of justice has several dimensions that interact to make the mystery story compelling, for it acts upon the intellect as well as upon the emotions.

First of all, the sense of justice involves a conviction that cuts across intellect and emotion that some things are right and some things are wrong, regardless of the gray areas of life. Right and wrong have implications for virtually every area of life, as Poe observed by peppering his letters with references to actions or situations that he regarded as matters of "injustice." This sense of right and wrong lies at the heart of the horror story, for without the idea of wrongness, no horror can ever occur.

Second, the sense of justice acts upon a person so that they care about the victim of the crime. This caring involves more than mere curiosity, though curiosity forms part of the dynamic. It is one thing for me to care about wrong done to me or to one of my family members or even a friend. For the mystery story to work, however, the reader must care about someone they do not know. The caring must go beyond self-interest and survival as a pure materialist understanding of human motive might suggest. Though Poe wrote before Darwin, he understood Malthus and the "survival of the fittest" argument perfectly well. The mystery story does not depend upon the virtue of the reader or their innocence; it depends merely on their unconscious care that justice has been violated. The reader must care that justice has been violated and that someone has unjustly suffered as a result. If the reader does not care, they will stop reading once the horror has been described.

Third, the sense of caring fostered by justice moves the reader to desire that the innocent accused be set free. In "The Murders in the Rue Morgue" an innocent man has been charged with the crime. The man is not personally known to any reader, yet in this first detective mystery, as in all others that follow in which an innocent person has been charged with a crime, the reader desires the vindication and freedom of the wrongly accused. The story does not make the argument to persuade the reader of the morality of such a position. Instead, the story allows the reader to agree to something that they know at a primordial level of their existence. We see this same dynamic at work in a modern detective mystery, the Harry Potter stories, when the Ministry of Magic falsely imprisons Stan Shunpike for something they know he did not do.

Fourth, the sense of caring also extends to the insistence that the wicked person be caught. Justice demands that wickedness not be allowed to profit. Wrongful behavior cannot be rewarded. This aspect of caring need not extend to the concept of punishment. Justice is primarily concerned with stopping the violation of what is just and right. Again, the appeal of justice comes in a disinterested way that has no benefit for the reader and no effect on how soundly they sleep at night. If the murderer is not caught, it will not affect their survival. It is the disinterested caring that injustice cannot be allowed to continue that compels the reader to continue the story. 115 The action of the murderer is not simply against the victim but against the universe.

Fifth, the sense of justice assumes the basic rationality and order of the universe so that Truth may be discovered. The reader wants to know the truth. The mystery story does not teach truths; it assumes Truth.

When Jill Paton Walsh completed Dorothy L. Sayers' *Thrones, Dominations* (1998), she included a discussion between Lord Peter Wimsey and his wife Harriet Vane, who also wrote detective fiction, about the worth of detective stories. As a new form of literature, the detective story has not been accepted as "serious" literature by professors of English and American literature (ironically, a new discipline in the academy). Harriet tended to accept this verdict of her art form, but Lord Peter dissented:

> "You seem not to appreciate the importance of your special art form," he said. "Detective stories contain a dream of justice. They project a vision of a world in which wrongs are righted, and

villains are betrayed by clues that they did not know they were leaving. A world in which murderers are caught and hanged, and innocent victims are avenged, and future murder is deterred."

"But it is just a vision, Peter. The world we live in is not like that."

"It sometimes is," he said. "Besides, hasn't it occurred to you that to be beneficent, a vision does not have to be true?"

"What benefits could be conferred by falsehood?" she asked.

"Not falsehood, Harriet; idealism. Detective stories keep alive a view of the world which ought to be true. Of course people read them for fun, for diversion, as they do crossword puzzles. But underneath they feed a hunger for justice, and heaven help us if ordinary people cease to feel that."[15]

Mystery stories work because people already know about justice, if only through the experience of injustice. Some standard has been violated that goes beyond any social contract or concern for personal survival. We may not notice it when we do the violating ourselves, but when we have the leisure to sit back and read about it in a story, we recognize it immediately. Without his concept of a story or poem creating an effect upon the reader, Poe might never have conceived of the mystery story, but once created, it cannot but call forth the reader's assent that justice must be done. The form demands the assent of the reader.

P. D. James, who preserves the tradition of horror in her murder mysteries, self-consciously understands the role of justice in the mystery story. Especially when so many real murder cases go unsolved and when so many meaningless acts of violence fill the news headlines, James believes

it leads to a loss of faith not only in life but in goodness. There is no doubt the detective story is popular in times of depression and social unease. It affirms that we live in a morally comprehensible universe, that problems can be resolved, that a kind of justice can be achieved.[16]

In light of the power of the detective story to reveal the transcendent reality of justice, the Nazi decision to ban the detective story in Germany makes perfect sense.[17]

Cryptography and Puzzles

While the idea of justice provides the foundation for the mystery story, Poe had another advantage that helped him create the variety of mystery plots he concocted. He loved riddles, puzzles, and mind twisters of all sorts. Mathematics and logic fascinated him. René van Slooten has argued that Poe's military training in the artillery corps and at West Point provided him with the necessary mathematical tools to undertake *Eureka*.[18] Without this practical mathematical preparation, however, he likely would not have had the material for his imagination to draw upon for the ingenious solutions to his mysteries, especially "The Gold-Bug."

One of Poe's most popular columns dealt with the science of cryptography. He challenged his readers to submit a code that he could not decipher. From December 1839 until May 1840, Poe worked as editor for *Alexander's Weekly Messenger* in which he published his solutions to the cryptograms in a series of fifteen columns with such headlines as "Our Late Puzzles," "Our Puzzles— Again," "More Puzzles," and "Our Puzzles Once More."[19] Over the five-month period, Poe received and solved approximately one hundred ciphers including one that Poe demonstrated was bogus, composed of a collection of meaningless characters.[20] Poe was intrigued that many of his readers believed that he had concocted the ciphers himself, which may have suggested the idea of how people might respond to Dupin when he explained how he solved a crime or deduced any other facts.

Soon after joining *Graham's Magazine* and shortly after the publication of "The Murders in the Rue Morgue," Poe published a column in the July 1841 issue on how cryptic writing works and how secret codes are developed. Poe declared that "it may be roundly asserted that human ingenuity cannot concoct a cipher which human ingenuity cannot resolve."[21] Poe believed that the thought process of deciphering riddles calls analytical ability "forcibly" into action and should be included in academic training. The complexity of the construction of a cipher does not mean that it is necessarily more difficult to "unriddle." The solution rests more with the "general principles of the formation of language" than with the laws of constructing ciphers.[22] Poe's explanation of how to devise codes provides the aspiring mystery writer with a guidebook to the construction of ciphers. In fact, we find detectives from Sherlock Holmes to Lord Peter Wimsey deciphering the kinds of codes that Poe explains in this essay.

The substance of *Eureka* began with a similar puzzle but one of more than pedestrian standing. One of the great scientific puzzles that had perplexed astronomers for centuries was known as Olber's paradox. As we shall see in a later chapter, Poe's solution to Olber's paradox formed the basis for his Big Bang Theory theory. For now it is sufficient to observe how the development of the mystery story depended upon Poe's previous work.

As Dupin began to unravel the mystery of the murders in the Rue Morgue, his solution to how the window might have been the means of escape is given in terms of one of Poe's popular newspaper riddles: "The riddle, so far, was now unriddled."[23] When he comes to the final solution of the murder, Dupin remarks upon the exclamation of *mon Dieu!* heard by the witnesses, "Upon these two words, therefore, I have mainly built my hopes of a full solution of the riddle."[24]

Five Basic Plots

Dorothy L. Sayers declared emphatically that "Poe (himself a past-master of the horrible) produced five tales, in which the general principles of the detective-story were laid down for ever."[25] Not a general principle but certainly an intriguing tradition of the detective story is the formula of associating a brilliant but eccentric amateur sleuth with a "sidekick." Poe's unnamed narrator is the friend who lives with the brilliant impoverished aristocrat, Auguste Dupin. Sherlock Holmes has his Doctor Watson. Hercule Poirot has his Captain Hastings. Even Sayers' Lord Peter Wimsey has his man Bunter, then his friend Inspector Parker, then his beloved Harriet Vane. The sidekick serves an invaluable service to the storyteller by providing a way for explanations and observations to be introduced into the story that would otherwise have seemed too didactic for Poe.

The peculiarities of the detective make the character truly one with the plot, for those traits of the detectives that set them apart from everyone else are the very traits that enable them to solve the mystery. In recognition of Poe as the founder of their literary form, the Mystery Writers of America named their annual award for achievement in mystery writing the Edgar. Furthermore, a tradition has grown up since Sherlock Holmes discussed the methods of Dupin in Sir Arthur Conan Doyle's first mystery story that mystery writers eventually pay tribute to Poe in some way in one of their stories.[26]

In writing five mystery stories, Poe created five plots. While Sayers argued that though Poe's plots are "thin to transparency," they represent virtually all "the deceptions in the mystery-monger's bag of tricks."[27] In other words, Poe constructed the basic plots upon which almost all later mystery stories have been based.[28] At first, this claim may seem grandiose until we consider that the love story has only one plot: boy meets girl; boy falls in love with girl; boy loses girl; boy gets girl. We may also consider the plot of adventure stories: introduction, conflict, crisis, resolution. Poe not only created a new kind of story, but thought of multiple ways to tell the story. As in his science fiction, Poe aimed at an air of realism and incorporated details with which his audience would be familiar.[29]

Several features mark out "The Murders in the Rue Morgue." These elements of the story have become the common stock of detective stories. First, an innocent person has been arrested based on the preponderance of evidence. Second, the crime took place in a room that was locked from the inside and allowed for no means of escape. Third, the detective provides an unexpected and surprising solution to the mystery. Fourth, the detective draws entirely different deductions from the evidence than what the police have deduced. Fifth, the detective recognizes clues that the police do not see. These last two have particular significance for Poe's ultimate exploration of the problem of the universe, for he draws entirely different conclusions about the nature of the universe than the conclusions of the standard physics of his day, and he sees a cosmology that no one else had ever seen before. Poe attributed this capacity of seeing what others cannot see to imagination.

119

Besides the components of plot that Poe introduced with "The Murders in the Rue Morgue," he also introduced the two great aphorisms of detective fiction. Sayers credits Poe for declaring "that when you have eliminated all the impossibilities, then, whatever remains, *however improbable*, must be the truth," and "that the more *outré* a case may appear, the easier it is to solve."[30] Dupin explained his reasoning method this way: "Now, brought to this conclusion in so unequivocal a manner as we are, it is not our part, as reasoners, to reject it on account of apparent impossibilities. It is only left for us to prove that these apparent 'impossibilities' are, in reality, not such."[31] Poe lays down so many fundamental elements of the detective story in his first mystery that Sayers calls it "almost a complete manual of detective theory and practice."[32]

Poe's second mystery story earned special praise from Sayers because it put Poe in a rare class of mystery writers: those who actually investigate crimes themselves. In "The Mystery of Marie Rogêt," Poe brings back Auguste Dupin in an effort to force the New York police to investigate the murder of a young woman who was not socially acceptable enough to warrant attention. Here was the case of injustice that Poe could not abide. Poe transferred the murder of Mary Rogers from New York to Paris and altered her name just enough to be sure the public knew exactly what he was doing. The police claimed that she was the victim of a gang, but Poe believed an individual had killed her. This story introduces another standard feature of detective fiction: every suspect had an airtight alibi. Also in this story, Dupin solves the case from his arm chair without venturing forth to investigate. Poe's solution to the crime proved substantially correct.[33]

Poe's third Dupin story deals with stolen state documents. "The Purloined Letter" represents the prototype of a subcategory of detective fiction that became highly popular during the twentieth century: the espionage or spy thriller. The story involves more than simply the theft of valuable property. The papers have been stolen to destroy someone and possibly cause the collapse of a government and even spark an international crisis. A reputation is at stake.[34] Poe had experienced the injustice of character assassination at the hands

120

of John Allan and William Burton. In this case, as in most James Bond stories of the same type, the authorities know who has the documents. The problem comes with finding the documents. To this basic plot Poe adds a feature of detective fiction that authors have adored since Sir Arthur Conan Doyle first borrowed it.[35] The document is hidden in the one place that the police would never think to look: in plain sight. Again, Poe suggests in a different way that the ability to see the truth is often hindered by the assumptions that people bring to the quest.

Poe's fourth mystery story departs from Paris and has an entirely different tone from the Dupin stories. He chose to tell "Thou Art the Man" with a humorous tone that Dashiell Hammett would follow for *The Thin Man* featuring Nick and Nora Charles. Because of his love of humor, it was inevitable that Poe would attempt a mystery from that perspective. The plot for this story involves three more standard features of mystery plots. First, the murderer has laid a trail of false clues that leads to an innocent person. Second, the murderer turns out to be the most unlikely person. Finally, the detective knows who did it, but cannot prove it; therefore, the detective must trick the murderer into confessing the crime. An interesting feature of this story, however, comes from the title taken from one of the most famous short stories in the Bible. It not only serves to provide the story with a familiar title, but it also demonstrates Poe's thesis about a short story or poem having an effect upon the audience.

121

In the story of the prophet Nathan's confrontation with King David, Nathan must accuse the king of murder without getting himself killed in the bargain. He confronts the king by telling the story of a wealthy man who takes the only lamb of a poor man in order to serve it at a feast for his friends. The story enrages the king's sense of justice. The king declares that the man deserves to die, whereupon Nathan announces, "Thou art the man." The story creates the effect upon the audience that Nathan intended. Justice is ensured, and Poe's theory of the short story is vindicated.

Poe's fifth kind of mystery story differs from the others in that a crime has not been committed. "The Gold-Bug" is a mystery story that requires detection, but the intense issue of justice is not at stake in the same way. Justice operates differently in "The Gold-Bug"—not to punish a wrong, but to right a wrong. Justice does not aim at retribution but at restoration, as in the biblical concept of the Year of Jubilee in which deprived property was to be restored. This story depends upon decoding a treasure map, but the mystery is more complicated than a simple cipher decryption. First the detective must see that a mystery exists before it can be solved—in this case the decoding of a map. "The Gold-Bug" was Poe's most popular story in the nineteenth century. Pirated printings of the story appeared in newspapers and magazines all over the country, and Poe estimated that several hundred thousand copies of the story had circulated within a few years of its appearance. The basic plot has been adapted with great success ever since. Robert Louis Stevenson used it to great effect in *Treasure Island*. It is the basic plot for popular motion pictures like *Pirates of the Caribbean* and *National Treasure*. Every one of the Harry Potter novels requires that Harry first realize that a mystery exists before he can solve it, from the sorcerer's stone to the horcruxes.

122   Sayers described the landscape of detective mysteries as ranging from the Sensational at one end of the continuum to the purely Intellectual at the other end. The Sensational story depends upon thrills and action mixed with bewilderment and confoundment until the last moment when the detective reveals all. The Intellectual story, on the other hand, depends upon the methodology of the solution to the mystery. Sayers says that the Sensational is never dull but sometimes given to nonsense, while the Intellectual is highly ingenious but lacks movement and emotion. Most mystery writers tend toward one extreme or the other, but Poe wrote across the continuum with his five basic plots, illustrating his concern for originality and variety. Having created the five basic plots to the mystery story by 1845, Poe moved on to his other projects, but he did not abandon his concern for justice.

Crime and Justice

Though Poe only wrote the five basic mystery stories, he wrote a number of other stories that we might call "crime stories." In these stories the reader knows exactly who committed the crime and how they did it. They know the details of the horror. The open question in these stories involves whether the guilty shall come to justice. The most dramatic of these crime stories are "The Tell-Tale Heart," "The Black Cat," and "The Cask of Amontillado." These stories have tended to be the ones included in secondary school American literature anthologies.

James Russell Lowell published Poe's "The Tell-Tale Heart" in the first issue of his short-lived magazine, the *Pioneer*, in January 1843. This tale of murder provides an interesting twist to the detective tale since the narrator explains the crime to the reader. Against the backdrop of the final act of cruelty against another person, Poe explores the phenomenon of guilt that operates on a person who finally confesses the wickedness they have done. The theme of justice that permeates Poe's stories brings the crime to light without the help of the police.[36]

In "The Black Cat," which appeared in the *United States Saturday Post* on August 19, 1843, Poe returned to the horrible tale, but the underlying concern for justice and the idea that what is hidden will be revealed form the climax.[37] It is "The Tell-Tale Heart" without the guilt. The story explores the human capacity to indulge and nurture perversity while at the same time insisting that nature itself works toward justice. As with "The Tell-Tale Heart" the police stumble upon the solution to a crime, but it is revealed to them by the screams of a crazed cat. As with "The Tell-Tale Heart," the narrator who commits the horrible murder seems mentally unbalanced, but Poe implies that all acts of cruelty offend against reason. It is not necessary to be insane to sin against reason. This tendency of people lies at the heart of the perversity of human nature that Poe examines.

In "The Pit and the Pendulum" Poe explores the horror of institutionalized injustice.[38] Against the backdrop of the Spanish Inquisition, Poe considers how cultural instruments of justice may offend against a higher justice that apprehends us from beyond a mere social contract. There is nothing wrong with the Spanish Inquisition or the Holocaust if justice is merely a cultural phenomenon based upon a social contract. As in all his stories, however, Poe creates the effect he desires within his audience by relying upon something that he knows we bring to the story.

In "William Wilson" Poe explores how the loss of a sense of right and wrong destroys a person's humanity and their participation in the human race. Having murdered his moral self, William Wilson remains "*dead to the World, to Heaven and to Hope!*"[39] Poe uses one of his favorite literary devices to advance the story—the fragmented dichotomy that destroys essential unity.[40] Poe had an intense dislike for Descartes' dichotomy between mind and body. This doubling and its destructive result appear over and over again in his stories. Without a moral conscience William Wilson loses all connection with creation because justice lies at the very heart of the meaning of the universe.

In "The Cask of Amontillado" and "Hop-Frog" Poe twists the plot. This time the protagonists act out of revenge instead of justice. In "The Cask of Amontillado" Montresor has endured a "thousand injuries" from Fortunato, all of which he bore, but when Fortunato adds insult to injury, Montresor plots murder. Poe has no sympathy with the cowardly act done in secret. This story lays bare the horror of the human heart that nurtures a grudge and reduces a human to less than a beast. The tradition of literary criticism that sees Poe as the subject of all his stories claims that Poe is the murderer and Thomas Dunn English, with whom Poe had carried on a very public literary quarrel, is the victim in this tale of revenge. Poe never sought revenge in the shadows; he always called his opponents by name in public. Ironically, Montresor does behave the way Rufus Griswold behaved toward Poe, but Poe in his continual state of innocent naïveté never realized how deeply Griswold hated him.

In "Hop-Frog," the idea of revenge becomes more ambiguous. One might legitimately see Poe as Hop-Frog. The tale of revenge has a stronger resemblance to the situation in "The Pit and the Pendulum" than to "The Cask of Amontillado." What do we do when the institution for providing protection and insuring justice becomes the instrument of oppression and injustice? The king, the administrator of justice, injures Tripetta, a delicate dwarf ballerina.

Hop-Frog clearly commits murder, but Poe sets up the story in such a way that justice rather than revenge is the operative dynamic in the sympathy of the audience. Whereas the audience is horrified by the act of Montresor, the ghastly carnage of the king and his council burning alive leaves the audience alarmingly satisfied that "they got what was coming to them." Here Poe introduces an element of plot that appears throughout detective fiction in which the sleuth may act against the law in the pursuit of justice, as Hercule Poirot did in his last case. Long before these stories of revenge, however, Poe wrote "Politian."

Poe published the first five scenes of "Politian," his only play, in the *Southern Literary Messenger* in December 1835 and January 1836. Poe wrote the play in blank verse, a rare venture for him. He based the play on an actual murder case in Kentucky that involved revenge. In 1825 Jereboam Beauchamp stabbed Col. Solomon P. Sharp to death in fulfillment of a promise he made to his fiancée in exchange for her promise to marry him. Sharp, a prominent Frankfort lawyer, had seduced Anne Cooke but refused to marry her. Beauchamp and his wife Anne were convicted of the murder and sentenced to be hanged, but she committed suicide before the execution. A number of novelists and playwrights tried their hand at telling the story of betrayal and revenge which was known in the press as the "Kentucky Tragedy."[41] Poe never completed "Politian," but it demonstrates that across the span of his career he had a continuing interest in the delicate and shadowy boundary between justice and revenge. Defending a lady's honor complicated the issue for Poe as his introduction to his review of Elizabeth Barrett's *The Drama of Exile* suggests.

125

Behind the criminal act and the violation of justice lies something without which the crime story, the horror story, and the detective story could not be told: something is wrong with people. Poe examined the frailty of humanity in a variety of ways. He often looked in a humorous way at the petty vanities of people, as in "The Spectacles" and "The Man That Was Used Up." In "The Imp of the Perverse" Poe describes the human propensity to act against the moral law and, thus, against one's own best interests. He wrote, "I am not more certain that I breathe, than that the assurance of the wrong or error of any action is often the one unconquerable *force* which impels us, and alone impels us to its prosecution."[42] With a degree of amazement, Poe observed that this tendency operates against the urge to self-defense and survival for this contrariness inevitably results in self-destruction. Poe called this tendency *perverseness*. He recognized a looming disaster: "If there be no friendly arm to check us, or if we fail in a sudden effort to prostrate ourselves backward from the abyss, we plunge, and are destroyed."[43] In the story justice asserts itself by means of the very perversity that led to the murderous act. Perversity betrays itself. Notably, Poe recognizes the "friendly arm to check us." Our only hope lies outside ourselves.

Criticism and Justice

As we have seen, Poe's creation of the mystery story arose in the context of his broader interest in justice. One could argue that Poe wrote a sixth mystery story when he wrote his review of Charles Dickens' *Barnaby Rudge*. Though *Barnaby Rudge* is a murder story, it is not a mystery story. In his review of the serial novel in progress, however, Poe set out to expose the identity of the murderer before Dickens had completed the story. Poe wrote this review in February 1842 after he had published "The Murders in the Rue Morgue" but before he published "The Mystery of Marie Rogêt."

Apart from this rare piece of literary criticism in which Poe could play the part of a sleuth and solve the crime, the very act of literary criticism for him involved the idea of justice and the judgment of a piece of writing as good or bad. The judgment is made with respect to some given standard. Poe developed criteria for judging literature in the midst of the great critical void of book reviews in America during his career. One may disagree with the criteria that he established, but he understood that justice demands an objective criteria evenly applied. Poe probably could not have created the first mystery story if he had not first developed a theory of literary criticism that he applied to himself more severely than to anyone else. In his writing Poe could not escape the existence of a pervasive sense of justice behind the universe whereby people are compelled to judge behavior, thoughts, and attitudes as good or bad. In order to be aware of the urge to justice, however, some standard must also exist independently of a perverse world.

Suspicion

Where would criminal investigation be without suspicion? At one level suspicion arises from the facts in the case that cast a shadow of suspicion upon someone. At another level, however, suspicion involves feeling as much as thought. Poe is aware of the perception of evil apart from evidence of wrongdoing. This feeling of evil coincides with the idea of justice. People experience it in life, and Poe creates this feeling by his prose. He sets the mood that allows his readers to cooperate as he works to create an effect.

In one of the most perfectly written prose sentences in fiction, Poe sets the mood for the action in "The Fall of the House of Usher":

> During the whole of a dull, dark, and soundless day in the autumn of the year, when the clouds hung oppressively low in the heavens, I had been passing alone, on horseback, through a singularly dreary tract of country; and at length found myself, as the shades of evening drew on, within view of the melancholy House of Usher.[44]

127

The reader has entered into the same atmosphere as the narrator who, upon spying the House of Usher for the first time, informs us that "a sense of insufferable gloom pervaded" his spirit.[45] We feel something is wrong. It is important to note, however, that emotional feelings and sensory perceptions have a vital connection. Feelings do not arise for no good *reason*. Visit any house and notice it. It will tell you about the people who live there and what to expect from them. Observation plays a critical role in how suspicion arises. Yet, Poe achieves this effect without actually describing the details of the scene. He has utilized his reader's imagination to fill out the landscape. The narrator in "The Fall of the House of Usher" is over a year away from Poe's creation of the fictional detective; otherwise, he might understand why he feels the way he does.

In the story Poe published just before his first detective story, he provides us with a case study of observation and criminal investigation that rests entirely upon suspicion. In "The Man of the Crowd" the narrator spends the afternoon "people watching" from the comfortable vantage point of a London coffee house.[46] Once night came on, however,

> There came into view a countenance (that of a decrepit old man, some sixty-five or seventy years of age,)—a countenance which at once arrested and absorbed my whole attention, on account of the absolute idiosyncracy of its expression. Any thing even remotely resembling that expression I had never seen before. I well remember that my first thought, upon beholding it, was that Retzch, had he viewed it, would have greatly preferred it to his own pictural incarnations of the fiend.[47]

The rest of the story tells how the narrator "tailed" the suspicious character throughout London until daybreak when he concluded that the old man "is the type and the genius of deep crime."[48]

Ratiocination: Rationality and Imagination

128

Poe named his detective mystery stories tales of "ratiocination." The name did not stick, but it was far more descriptive than the popular name we now use. The idea of ratiocination indicated Poe's understanding of the vital relationship between rationality and imagination. The modern tendency to create a dichotomy between two ideas by pitting them in opposition to each other had characterized the period of the Enlightenment with its emphasis on the rational and the Romantic period with its emphasis on imagination. Poe realized that all great advances in knowledge came when the two stood in harmony.

The introduction to "The Murders in the Rue Morgue" gave Poe the opportunity to remark briefly on the relationship between intellect and intuition, between rationality and imagination, between the mathematical and the poetic. Descartes' dichotomy of body and spirit coupled with the Enlightenment's exaltation of reason to the exclusion of emotion had only served to heighten the tendency to relegate imagination to poetry and daydreaming. Poe, on the other hand, realized that true analysis could not operate without the imagination. Poe argued that "to calculate is not in itself to analyse."[49]

Poe considered draughts (checkers) a more profound game than chess, which he regarded as merely complicated. The successful chess player need only retain the rules and observe the board in order to do well. Because of the simplicity of checkers, however, the successful player must attend to more than the rules and the board. Modern education places high emphasis on memorization and attention to the "rules" laid down by authorities, but true genius involves another dynamic. Poe elaborated his ideas in a discussion of whist, a popular card game that preceded bridge. In attending to the game the true analyst not only observes but knows what to observe. The great whist player understands that the game involves the players and not just the cards they play. The great analyst compares the face of his partner with those of his opponents. He notices how everyone holds their cards and how they arrange them, perhaps into trumps and honors. He recognizes how different players react to cards played until he knows the normal responses of each player to particular situations. He notices how people pick up tricks and put down cards in relation to their subsequent ability to make another trick in the same suit. Poe piles up the variety of things not covered by the rules of the game that the true analyst might observe until a pattern emerges:

> A casual or inadvertent word; the accidental dropping or turning of a card, with the accompanying anxiety or carelessness in regard to its concealment; the counting of the tricks; with the order of arrangement; embarrassment, hesitation, eagerness or trepidation—all afford, to his apparently intuitive perception, indications of the true state of affairs.[50]

Following this method of observation, the true analyst after two or three rounds of play will know the cards that each player holds in their hands, "and thenceforward puts down his cards with as absolute a precision of purpose as if the rest of the party had turned outward the faces of their own."[51]

True analysis goes beyond ingenuity. Poe claims, "for while the analyst is necessarily ingenious, the ingenious man is often incapable of analysis."[52] Poe then draws the net and makes the grand claim that will become the foundation for the analytic power of the mystery detective and the scientists who are able to understand the operation of the universe:

> Between ingenuity and the analytic ability there exists a difference far greater, indeed, than that between fancy and the imagination, but of a character very strictly analogous. It will be found, in fact, that the ingenious are always fanciful, and the *truly* imaginative never otherwise than analytic.[53]

Poe demonstrated this claim in his explanation of how he constructed "The Raven" as described in "The Philosophy of Composition," and his proposal of the Big Bang Theory theory in *Eureka*. In both cases, however, many critics would claim that he must have been joking. In the same way, a feature of the mystery story is the response of the bystander when the great detective explains how they arrived at their solutions. Merely a parlor trick.

Dupin remarked that the mistake of Vidocq, the real-life Parisian detective who gave some inspiration to the fictional Dupin, lay in "the very intensity of his investigations."[54] Like the good Aristotelian who is an expert at making divisions, Vidocq examined things so closely that he only saw a few things worth noting. His method caused him to lose "sight of the matter as a whole."[55] Imagination allows a person to make connections, see relationships, recognize patterns, and perceive what is otherwise lost to the person who only observes what they have been taught to see. Dupin dismisses the Prefect of Police as a man who is "all head and no body" or perhaps "all head and shoulders, like a cod fish."[56]

Poe's recognition of the organic relationship of reason and creativity accounted not only for the genius of his detective Dupin. He would insist in *Eureka* that this vital dynamic accounts for all great scientific discovery. Perhaps it is not mere coincidence that many of the greatest literary detectives have demonstrated this synthesis of rationality and creativity in their private lives. Sherlock Holmes plays the violin, just as Albert Einstein did. Lord Peter Wimsey plays the piano. Miss Marple chose gardening as her aesthetic outlet. Inspector Dalgliesh wrote poetry.

In his famous review of Rufus Griswold's *Poets and Poetry of America*, Poe argued that it was a mistake to think that the calculating faculties are at war with the ideal; while, in fact, it may be demonstrated that the two divisions of mental power are never to be found in perfection apart. The *highest* order of the imaginative intellect is always preeminently mathematical; and the converse.[57]

About the time Poe wrote these words in a review, he also explored their meaning in "The Mystery of Marie Rogêt." In his introduction to the second mystery story, Poe observed that people sometimes marvel at coincidences that seem too unusual to explain rationally. Such events are typically attributed to chance, or by the term of Poe's day, the calculus of probabilities. Poe remarked, "Now this Calculus is, in its essence, purely mathematical; and thus we have the anomaly of the most rigidly exact in science applied to the shadow and spirituality of the most intangible in speculation."[58] In "The Mystery of Marie Rogêt" Poe anticipates a discussion he would pursue in *Eureka* six years later:

> That Nature and her God are two, no man who thinks, will deny. That the later, creating the former, can, at will, control or modify it, is also unquestionable. I say "at will;" for the question is of will, and not as the insanity of logic has assumed, of power. It is not that the Deity *cannot* modify his laws, but that we insult him in imagining a possible necessity for modification. In their origin these laws were fashioned to embrace *all* contingencies which *could* lie in the Future. With God all is *Now*.[59]

131

In *Eureka* Poe would carry forward his thoughts on "unriddling" perplexing questions by employing the method of utilizing rationalism and empiricism under the banner of imagination to unravel life's biggest mystery and answer the biggest question of justice.

Conclusion

Life experience leads most people to ponder the problem of suffering. It is not an abstract, philosophical question. It is a question that arises as people deal with suffering up close and personally. We may analyze the question from a detached perspective, but it arises when our mother dies or when a friend's mother slowly begins to lose her mind. The question intensifies as we watch a beautiful young wife, who is desperately loved, waste away with a fatal disease. To ask the question of why people suffer, however, we must begin with the assumption that suffering goes against "the code." The question is a question of justice.

The issue with the problem of suffering is that people see it as a problem at all. It is one thing to say, "I do not like to suffer," but it is quite another thing to be concerned about someone else suffering. If the concern were only about a self-centered loss of someone we want to keep the way we always had them, then we might regard the question as another form of "I don't like my situation." Though the problem of suffering may first come to our attention in a personal way, we eventually grow aware as a disinterested person in how pervasive the problem seems to be. Everybody dies.

We catch glimpses of Poe's thoughts about the justice of life and related matters, such as pondering why people do bad things to other people and to themselves. He attributed this trait to an innate perversity. He explored the problem of guilt as well as the idea that the universe itself seems to uphold a standard of justice, even in the face of so much injustice. Related to his life experience that included both Beauty and Love, the problem of why a compelling sense of justice underlies the universe would finally coalesce with his other major philosophical questions as he collected his thoughts from a lifetime of reading and writing and sought to bring some unity to them in *Eureka*.

132

THE PROBLEM OF THE
UNIVERSE

The problem of the universe may be simply stated: Why is there something rather than nothing? In a letter to George Isbell on February 29, 1848, after delivering his lecture on the universe, but before publishing it as *Eureka*, Poe gave his simple answer to this simple question: "Because Nothing was, therefore All Things are."[1]

By far, Poe's most controversial and neglected work is *Eureka*, in which he proposed the original Big Bang theory. Though it is longer than anything else he wrote, except his only novel, the average reader has never heard of it, and the Poe scholar avoids it. Having insisted all his professional life that poetry is "the rhythmical creation of beauty," Poe's full title is *Eureka: A Prose Poem*. What did he mean by calling this extravagant cosmological essay a poem? Though Poe's major scientific proposals in *Eureka* had become the accepted view of physics and cosmology by the end of the twentieth century, his science seemed weird and strange in the nineteenth century and for the greater part of the twentieth century. The science of *Eureka* tended to be dismissed by literary critics who sought to make sense of *Eureka* strictly in terms of symbol and metaphor.[2]

Poe had always taught that the special province of poetry is Beauty, but he argued that *Eureka* deals with Truth. In what sense, then, did he think of it as a poem? He had always seen Truth and Beauty as distinct "Non-overlapping Magisteria," as Stephen Jay Gould would say. Poe provided this cryptic clue in his brief preface:

> To the few who love me and whom I love—to those who feel rather than to those who think—to the dreamers and those who put faith in dreams as in realities—I offer this Book of Truths, not in its character of Truth-Teller, but for the Beauty that abounds in its Truth; constituting it true. To these I present the composition as an Art-Product alone:—let us say as a Romance; or, if I be not urging too lofty a claim, as a Poem.
>
> *What I here propound is true*:—therefore it cannot die:—or if by means it be now trodden down so that it die, it will "rise again to the Life Everlasting."
>
> Nevertheless it is as a Poem only that I wish this work to be judged after I am dead.[3]

On the first page of the text, however, Poe restates the title with a different subtitle: *An Essay on the Material and Spiritual Universe*. In his own writing Poe had always understood that his body of work had a unity that could only be understood in terms of the whole. In working through *Eureka*, Poe believed he had unraveled a mystery that comprehended a unity to the universe. Beauty and Truth, science and religion, mathematics and poetry, matter and spirit all had an intertwining relationship.[4]

Despite the significance of the Big Bang theory for modern cosmology and astrophysics, few people realize that Poe first proposed the theory. Allen Tate, one of the leading poetry critics of the twentieth century, remarked, "I have wondered why the modern proponents of the Big Bang hypothesis of the creation have not condescended to acknowledge Poe as a forerunner."[5] In the modern world of specialization, how could a literary critic or scientist take Poe seriously? Even after his major ideas have been demonstrated, few people can *imagine* how Poe did it. But *imagining* was precisely how Poe did it. Before turning to *Eureka*, however, it will be helpful to see the many steps by which Poe finally arrived at his proposal for the original Big Bang theory of the origin of the universe.

The Long Background

Poe did not suddenly write *Eureka* in 1848. It came at the end of a long consideration of many questions that had dangled independently in his mind.[6] He had always been interested in science and religion. He grew up in an Enlightenment world and attended Mr. Jefferson's university, where students were taught to believe Descartes' view that mind and body, or matter and spirit, were totally unrelated.[7] This Enlightenment way of thinking informed his early view that Beauty and Truth are unrelated spheres and that poetry does not deal in Truth.[8] This same Enlightenment view continues to inform fundamentalist religion in its view that the Bible must deal only with facts in order to be true and the materialist view that what cannot be known through the senses cannot exist. This same Enlightenment view also informs the naturalist philosophy of science for many people who think that the ability to observe and describe a physical phenomenon exhausts its meaning. In *Eureka* Poe repudiates the old Enlightenment thinking as well as the old Enlightenment science.

In "Al Aaraaf," the title poem in his second volume of poetry published in 1829, Edgar Allan Poe addresses the nature of Beauty and the ultimate end of life. He took for his inspiration, however, a scientific phenomenon that occurred at the end of the medieval period and the beginning of the modern period: a supernova observed by Tycho Brahe. Poe was fascinated by astronomy as science and equally with the heavens as Beauty. Poe was a rationalist and a romantic at the same time.[9] The intersection of science and imagination would play an increasingly important role in the development of his poetry, fiction, and understanding of the universe, and of life itself. As an introduction to his *Al Aaraaf* volume of poetry, Poe inserted a poem without a title which he later named "Sonnet—To Science."

> Science! True daughter of Old Time thou art!
>   Who alterest all things with thy peering eyes.
> Why preyest thou thus upon the poet's heart,
>   Vulture, whose wings are dull realities?

How should he love thee? Or how deem thee wise,
　Who wouldst not leave him in his wandering
To seek for treasure in the jeweled skies,
　Albeit he soared with an undaunted wing?
Hast thou not dragged Diana from her car?
　And driven the Hamadryad from the wood
To seek a shelter in some happier star?
　Hast thou not torn the Naiad from her flood,
The Elfin from the green grass, and from me
The summer dream beneath the tamarind tree?[10]

In this poem he calls science a vulture that preys upon the poet's heart. Poe observed that science had robbed the modern world of the ability to experience nature in any way except as brute fact.[11] In "Al Aaraaf," however, Poe utilized the medieval concept of the universe shared by Muslims, Christians, and Jews in which God is not so far removed from natural phenomena as the scientific ability to describe an event supposes. Poe had a growing sense of ambiguity about what could be known and how it could be known. In the end he would not reject science so much as he would reject any philosophy of science or epistemology that made no room for imagination.[12]

Science Fiction

When Poe began experimenting with various forms of stories, he became one of the earliest pioneers in science fiction. This kind of story had no name until the twentieth century, but Poe excelled at it. In 1909 Maurice Renard named Poe the founder of the modern "marvelous-scientific romance" that we now call science fiction.[13] Just as the mystery story builds upon the horror story, science fiction originally built upon the adventure story before branching out. The adventure story is one of the oldest stories on earth and has been used in virtually every culture. The Epic of Gilgamesh, the *Iliad* and the *Odyssey*, the *Aeneid, Beowulf, The Seven Voyages of Sinbad*, and *Gulliver's Travels* all represent ways of telling the adventure story. Science fiction was born when storytellers used imagined forms of technological inventions to go to real places that were otherwise inaccessible. Following Poe, the emphasis in science fiction was placed "on logic, on reason, on coherent forecast and calculation."[14]

Without a name to classify it, science fiction was often thought of as a hoax because it dealt in a realistic way with issues that scientists thought about. Furthermore, this new kind of fiction peppered the narrative with scientific vocabulary and descriptions to lend the air of verisimilitude. These stories did not take place once upon a time. Though Poe's horror stories often took place "Out of SPACE, out of TIME," his science fiction almost always had a physical location and an approximate date.[15] "The Unparalleled Adventures of One Hans Pfaall" commenced in Rotterdam and purports to be recent news. *The Narrative of Arthur Gordon Pym* begins in Nantucket in June 1827, about the time Poe joined the army. The action of "MS. Found in a Bottle" begins on Java in the early nineteenth century. Though Poe gives no time for the action in "A Descent into the Maelström," he gave a precise description of its location in the district of Lofoten in the province of Nordland in the country of Norway. The action of "Three Sundays in a Week" takes place in London on Sunday, October 10, though Poe does not specify the year. The account in "Mesmeric Revelation" is of such immediate concern that Poe dates it as "Wednesday, the fifteenth instant."[16] The transatlantic flight reported in "The Balloon-Hoax" took place between "Saturday, the 6th instant, at 11, A.M., and 2, P.M., on Tuesday, the 9th instant" and involved a flight of seventy-five hours from Penstruthal, Wales, to Charleston, South Carolina. Whether a story was located in a particular time and place depended upon the effect Poe wanted to create in his readers.

137

Contributing to the identification of early science fiction as a hoax was the style Poe used in several of these early stories. Four of his eleven science fiction stories were written in the style of a reporting narrative. "The Balloon-Hoax" first appeared in a newspaper and was taken by many readers to be the actual report of a flight across the Atlantic. It includes a transcript of the journal of one of the aeronauts as well as a technical description of the airship. "Mesmeric Revelation" is written in the style of a case study. Elizabeth Barrett reported to Poe that everyone in London believed it was the actual report of a real case. *The Narrative of Arthur Gordon Pym* was written as a first-person account of a voyage into uncharted waters, the reality of which was accented by Poe's omission of his name from the title page. The preface includes an explanation by "A. G. Pym" of why the early installments of his account had appeared in the *Southern Literary Messenger* as fiction attributed to Edgar Poe.[17] "Von Kempelen and His Discovery" concerns the scientific project that occupied Sir Isaac Newton for his entire life and during which project he postulated the laws of motion, invented calculus, and identified aspects of optics. His lifelong project? The secret of turning lead into gold. Poe wrote this story as a news account in 1849 to coincide with the hysteria over the California gold rush, a topic he also addressed in "Eldorado."

Another reason that the public may have associated science fiction with hoaxes stems from Poe's love of humor. Four of Poe's science fiction stories were humorous tales and he intended them to get a laugh. "Hans Pfaall," "Mellonta Tauta," "Three Sundays in a Week," and "Von Kempelen" all play to the satirical, the farcical, and the ridiculous.[18] Poe's tremendous versatility in storytelling allowed him to tell the science fiction story in a variety of ways, but the idea of a hoax allowed many of his critics to regard *Eureka* as simply an elaborate practical joke when it was published in 1848. This view does not take into account the ethereal science fiction stories he wrote that deal with exalted themes, among them "The Colloquy of Monos and Una," "The Conversation of Eiros and Charmion," "The Island of the Fay," "Mesmeric Revelation," and "The Power of Words."

Poe also dealt with a variety of scientific matters that have since become stock features of science fiction. In "The Unparalleled Adventure of One Hans Pfaall" Poe wrote a humorous tale that involved a trip to the moon. In "MS. Found in a Bottle" the horror version of science fiction involves a ghost ship but the science involves a voyage to the polar regions. The polar regions were a matter of great scientific speculation before they were explored in the twentieth century. In *The Narrative of Arthur Gordon Pym*

Poe repeated the formula of the sea voyage. This time the horror involves a mutiny and a massacre while the science again involves the exploration of the Antarctic.[19] In "The Balloon-Hoax" Poe narrates the adventures of a transatlantic aeronautical passage by means of a cigar-shaped balloon powered by a light engine with a propeller to provide thrust. In "The Conversation of Eiros and Charmion" Poe describes the disaster that ensued when a comet collided with the Earth.[20] In most of these stories Poe explores moral and theological issues while imagining the future direction of scientific discovery and technological development.

Kepler's "Somnium" (ca. 1630) and Voltaire's "Micromégas" (1752) are two of the earliest examples of modern science fiction. Both of these early efforts deal with space travel. Mary Shelley's *Frankenstein* (1818) expanded the possibilities of science fiction to the life sciences. Poe's breadth of topics, however, would have a profound impact on the development and future direction of science fiction largely through his influence on Jules Verne, who took up writing science fiction as a result of reading "The Balloon-Hoax." He promptly wrote *Five Weeks in a Balloon*.[21] Poe's stories inspired a number of other Verne novels, including *From Earth to the Moon*, *Off on a Comet*, *Around the World in Eighty Days*, *Journey to the Centre of the Earth*, and *The Sphinx of the Ice Fields*, a sequel to *The Narrative of Arthur Gordon Pym*.[22]

In terms of understanding *Eureka* and how it relates to the totality of Poe's work, it is important to note that Poe wrote science fiction in every phase of his fiction writing career. In the last year of his life Poe would publish two science fiction stories.

Fascination with Science

In 1838 during the country's first great economic depression, Poe undertook an unusual commission: to write a popular text on seashells at a time when collecting shells was a major pastime. *The Conchologist's First Book* has always been dismissed by literary scholars as a work of mere plagiarism because of Poe's use of the illustrations from an English text. The Harvard biologist Stephen Jay Gould came across the book several years ago, however, and marveled at what Poe had actually done.[23] Though he used the illustrations from another text, he reversed their order, beginning with the simplest life forms and moving to the most complex. Twenty years before *On the Origin of Species*, Poe's book was the first American text to study animals by beginning with the simplest and moving to the simple. Continuing his fascination with science, when Poe became editor of *Burton's Gentleman's Magazine* he wrote a series of columns that he called "A Chapter on Science and Art" that ran from March 1840 until he left *Burton's* later that summer.[24]

Imagination and Knowledge

Poe began his tenure as editor of *Graham's Lady's and Gentleman's Magazine* in the spring of 1841 by publishing a story called "The Murders in the Rue Morgue," and with it he changed the course of literary history. The mystery story allowed Poe to explore some of the biggest questions that faced him, but it also allowed him to consider how we understand the world and discover Truth. The first mystery detective, C. Auguste Dupin, an impoverished aristo-140 crat, used his acute intellect to solve the crime. In the narrator's introduction to the story, Poe explored his growing understanding of the relationship between analytical thought and fancy or between science and imagination:

> The analytical power should not be confounded with simple inge-
> nuity; for while the analyst is necessarily ingenious, the ingenious
> man is often remarkably incapable of analysis. The constructive or
> combining power, by which ingenuity is usually manifested, and
> to which the phrenologists (I believe erroneously) have assigned
> a separate organ, supposing it a primitive faculty, has been so
> frequently seen in those whose intellect bordered otherwise upon
> idiocy, as to have attracted general observation among writers on
> morals. Between ingenuity and the analytic ability there exists a
> difference far greater, indeed, than that between the fancy and
> the imagination, but of a character very strictly analogous. It will
> be found, in fact, that the ingenious are always fanciful, and the
> *truly* imaginative never otherwise than analytic.[25]

Poe rejected the choice between the rational and the intuitive, insisting instead upon a union of the two. Thus, he does not fit easily into the categories of Enlightenment or Romantic.[26] Laura Saltz points out that "Dupin advocates not an escape from the senses but a proper understanding of their functions. Through such comprehension, the human sense of sight can be employed strategically to give a more correct and complete view of the universe."[27] Something greater than either rationalism and empiricism is at work that allows someone to see what no one else has ever seen before, to go to places where no one has ever traveled, to see the sun at the center of the heavens when everyone else using the same data had seen the earth at the center. The scientist and the artist do the same thing and utilize the same profound attribute to do it: imagination.[28]

Poe followed the first mystery story with "A Descent into the Maelström" in the May issue of *Graham's*. The tale of terror relies upon the slow movement toward unavoidable doom, but Poe does not add the final touch of horror that the reader knew must surely come. The giant whirlpool does not snuff out the life of the narrator. Whereas "Ligeia" had depended upon the supernatural (or the irrational) to bring about the preservation of life, this tale of the sea depends upon the forces of nature and the power of creative analysis by the fisherman. The focus of the story shifts from the horror of the brother swallowed by the whirlpool to the ingenious method by which the narrator survives.

141

In April, Poe's story "A Tale of the Ragged Mountains" appeared in *Godey's*. Poe set the story in the Blue Ridge Mountains surrounding Charlottesville, Virginia, where he had attended the University of Virginia. This tale once again brings Poe into science fiction at the intersection of the supernatural. The science of the mind was in its prenatal state during Poe's lifetime if we can regard Freud's work as its infancy.[29] Phrenology and hypnotism stood at the cutting edge of the secrets to the mind, and Poe suggests "that between Doctor Templeton and Bedloe there had grown up, little by little, a very distinct and strongly marked *rapport*, or magnetic relation" through the use of hypnotism to relieve pain.[30] Young Bedloe falls into a dreamlike state while out walking the mountains and experiences the siege of a city in India almost fifty years earlier as the elderly Dr. Templeton writes about the events at home. This arabesque tale is constructed in such a way by Poe, however, that the patient's large daily dose of morphine might explain the dream that merely captured what Bedloe had heard Templeton speak about earlier. In this tale Poe captures a huge philosophical problem that modern science had raised: do natural explanations exhaust all possible knowledge or does some knowledge lie beyond the bounds of scientific explanation? The story is also important, however, for recognizing the many levels at which Poe realized that the imagination operates. The dream or the imagination occurs as rational or irrational, natural or drug-induced, artistic or inventive, utilitarian or fantasy.[31] Hallucination and psychosis occur through the imagination, but so do scientific discovery and artistic creation. Sexual adventure occurs through the imagination, but so does organizational planning. The mistake of reducing "dream" to a single psychological state in Poe's stories and poems will only confuse the reader. The mistake of equating Poe's concept of imagination with that of Coleridge will also cause the reader to miss the comprehensive nature of Poe's view that eliminates the Cartesian mind-body dualism.

142

Time and Space

With "The Colloquy of Monos and Una" in the August 1841 issue of *Graham's* magazine, Poe renewed his exploration of life after death combined with a critique of the problems of earthly existence. Poe relates a conversation between two lovers who have died and experienced new birth. His contemplation of the meaning of time and space when viewed from eternity anticipates issues with which Einstein would grapple sixty years later, while the general tone and subject matter demonstrates that the ideas that blossomed in *Eureka* (1848) were already in the making. His story rejects the idea of absolute time which had been the dogma of physicists for centuries.

In a humorous tale Poe went further in his consideration of time and space. "A Succession of Sundays" (now known as "Three

Sundays in a Week") appeared in the *Saturday Evening Post* on November 27, 1841. The heroine was fifteen and her cousin past twenty, and they wanted to marry. The hero's great uncle would not permit it until three Sundays came together in a week. On Sunday, October 10, the two cousins visit their great uncle when two sea captains also call on him after year-long voyages in which they circled the globe in opposite directions. One captain insists that the previous day was Sunday, the other captain insists that the next day would be Sunday, and the great uncle knew that it was Sunday. Finally, the veil lifts and the sea captains explain how a traveler who circumnavigates the globe across twenty-four hourly divisions of the globe (this insight occurs prior to the establishment of time zones) will either gain or lose time with respect to the point of origin. The imagination allows the players to "see" what was evident, like "The Purloined Letter," always there to see for those who had the imagination to see it. The enlightened captain adds the observation that "it is positively clear that we are *all right*; for there can be no philosophical reason assigned why the idea of one of us should have preference over that of the other."[32] This humorous tale of the relativity of time and space would be taken up a few years later by Jules Verne in *Around the World in Eighty Days*. It would be taken up sixty years later by a Swiss patent office clerk named Einstein in his general theory of relativity. When Poe introduced this clever observation, however, the idea that no place in the universe was privileged with respect to time or space was scientific heresy. With this science fiction tale, however, we do well to note that Poe, like Chaucer, Shakespeare, Benjamin Franklin, and G. K. Chesterton, often presented his most serious ideas while creating a comic effect.

143

The Plot of God

In August 1844 Poe published "Mesmeric Revelation," which dealt with a mortally ill man who had been placed under a hypnotic trance to treat his pain. Having had a growing sense of impressions for which he could not account, the dying man asks his hypnotists to place him in a trance once again and to pose a series of pointed questions. Under hypnosis the dying man describes what his unconscious state has the capacity to perceive and understand about God, life, death, and immortality. When the session ends the patient is in an advanced state of rigor mortis, suggesting that he had been dead throughout most of the session.

This tale allows Poe to expound on his growing interest in how God relates to the physical world, and in particular, how God can allow physical suffering. The hypnotized patient explains everything. God is the universal mind, and all created things are the thoughts of God. For other individual minds, matter is necessary. Mind is incarnated into individual bodies, but people are creatures who will always be embodied, even after death. The body after death, however, is of a different kind that has been changed, "corresponding with the two conditions of the worm and the butterfly."[33] This passage seems to be a gloss on the Apostle Paul's discussion of resurrection in 1 Corinthians 15 in which he discusses the relationship between a physical body and a spiritual body, like the relationship between a seed that is planted and the plant that grows from it. They have continuity with each other, but a great transformation occurs. This view contrasts sharply with the traditional Greek view of Plato and Aristotle that has so influenced Western culture with the idea that the body is an evil to be discarded, like the chambered nautilus of the transcendentalists that Poe so disliked.

In affirming creation Poe has a basis for understanding pain, not merely as a terrible accident, but as part of the divine purpose:

> Through the impediments afforded by the number, complexity, and substantiality of the laws of organic life and matter, the violation of law is rendered, to a certain extent, practicable. Thus pain, which in the inorganic life is impossible, is possible in the organic. *P.* But to what good end is pain thus rendered possible?
> *V.* All things are either good or bad by comparison. A sufficient analysis will show that pleasure, in all cases, is but the contrast of pain. *Positive* pleasure is a mere idea. To be happy at any one point we must have suffered at the same. Never to suffer would have been never to have been blessed. But it has been shown that, in the inorganic life, pain cannot be; thus the necessity for the organic. The pain of the primitive life of Earth, is the sole basis of the bliss of the ultimate life in Heaven.[34]

Poe had come to understand that pain and suffering are the necessary corollaries to Love and Beauty. We also see Poe exploring how the dream state of the imagination provides the bridge of continuity between the physical realm and the spiritual.

In November 1844 Poe began a column he called "Marginalia" in the *Democratic Review*, and he would publish additional episodes in *Graham's*, *Godey's*, and the *Southern Literary Messenger* over the next five years. In his first "Marginalia" column Poe explored the nature of plot. It reflects a continuing interest Poe had in the nature of the universe and the spiritual domain. In his essay "The American Drama" the next year in the *American Review*, he permitted himself to quote extensively from the first "Marginalia." His thought anticipates Charles Darwin's reflections on the adaptation of organisms, but without Darwin's philosophical predisposition to naturalism:

> All the Bridgewater treatises have failed in noticing the *great* idiosyncrasy in the Divine system of adaptation:—that idiosyncrasy which stamps the adaptation as divine, in distinction from that which is the work of merely human constructiveness. I speak of the complete *mutuality* of adaptation. For example:—in human constructions, a particular cause has a particular effect—a particular purpose brings about a particular object; but we see no reciprocity. The effect does not re-act upon the cause—the object does not change relations with the purpose. In Divine constructions, the object is either object or purpose as we choose to regard it, while the purpose is either purpose or object; so that we can never (abstractly—without concretion—without reference to facts of the moment) decide which is which.
>
> For secondary example:—In polar climates, the human frame, to maintain its animal heat, requires, for combustion in the capillary system, an abundant supply of highly azotized food, such as train oil. Again:—in polar climates nearly the sole food afforded man is the oil of abundant seals and whales. Now whether is oil at hand because imperatively demanded? Or whether is it the only thing demanded because the only thing to be obtained? It is impossible to say:—there is an absolute reciprocity of adaptation for which we seek in vain among the works of man.
>
> The Bridgewater tractists may have avoided this point, on account of its apparent tendency to overthrow the idea of *cause*

145

in general—consequently of a First Cause—of God. But it is more probable that they have failed to perceive what no one preceding them has, to my knowledge, perceived.

The pleasure which we derive from any exertion of human ingenuity, is in the direct ratio of the *approach* to this species of reciprocity between cause and effect. In the construction of *plot*, for example, in fictitious literature, we should aim at so arranging the points, or incidents, that we cannot distinctly see, in respect to any one of them, whether that one depends from any one other or upholds it. In this sense, of course, perfection of plot is unattainable *in fact*—because Man is the constructor. The plots of God are perfect. The Universe is a plot of God.[35]

This interesting reflection and analogy suggests the speculative train of Poe's thought during this period of his wife's illness. He would continue to reflect on this theme rationally, empirically, and imaginatively for the rest of his life. With Poe's theory of the unity of effect, he had the basis for understanding the universe in its totality, rather than merely in its fragmented form. The problem of pain can only be understood in relation to the rest of the plot. He would also include this passage on mutual adaptation and the plot of God in *Eureka*.

146

Denouement

Edgar Poe fell deathly ill after Virginia's death in January 1847. Marie Louis Shew, who had nursed Virginia, nursed him now and noted his symptoms, which she reported to Dr. Valentine Mott and later recorded. Poe's "pulse beat only ten regular beats, after which it suspended, or intermitted (as the doctors say)."[36] She suspected that he suffered from a lesion on one side of the brain. He had a fever, but she did not report how high it was. He also had a rapid pulse with the fever accompanied by delirium that subsided once the pulse slowed to eighty beats. When he recovered he learned that the *Saturday Evening Post* had charged him with plagiarism in the case of *The Conchologist's First Book*, which he had edited on contract in 1838. He also learned that he had won his defamation case against Fuller.

Poe published very little in 1847. He rarely left Fordham and the security of the cottage. The lawsuit provided him and Mrs. Clemm enough to live on for a while, and Mrs. Shew proved highly successful in securing gifts from admirers who sought to help Poe in his time of broken health and grief. He wrote a poem "To M. L. S.—" in appreciation of Mrs. Shew which was published by N. P. Willis in the *Home Journal* in March. Also in March, the *Columbian Magazine* published "The Domain of Arnheim," a revised and expanded version of "The Landscape Garden." In December the *American Review* published "To ———. Ulalume, A Ballad," now known simply as "Ulalume," Poe's poem of grief over Virginia after the fact, just as "The Raven" is his poem before the fact. In "The Raven" he anticipates what the loss of Virginia will feel like, but in "Ulalume" he knows.

Instead of writing poetry or pressing forward with his ever present magazine project, Poe devoted his time to working on a problem that had gnawed at the edges of his work for twenty years. He had made a number of observations and conclusions in his essays and critical reviews that now began to come together with his creative imagination and powers of observation. He had speculated about what lay beyond the grave, but now the issue took on new importance because Virginia lay beyond the grave. Poe was not a religious person at this point of his life, in terms of having any personal commitment to a religious tradition, but he was what might be called a spiritual man. He had observed the problems of human behavior and explored what leads people to commit acts of horror against other people. The problem of evil was not a great problem, but the problems of Beauty, Love, and Justice were enormous. He had explored how Beauty, Love, and Justice pointed to something beyond the material world. It is not unusual for someone going through grief to set themselves the task of understanding some deep question. Poe set out to resolve the question of "life, the universe, and everything."

Eureka

On February 3, 1848, Poe gave a public lecture at the Society Library in New York where he read what he considered to be his greatest work, the culmination of ideas that had swirled in his brain for years.[37] He entitled it *Eureka: A Prose Poem.* George Putnam, who had published several of Poe's earlier books, published *Eureka* in July 1848 with a printing of five hundred copies and a fourteen dollar advance to Poe. Poe had asked for an initial run of fifty thousand! This book has generally been regarded as a hoax, a grand metaphysical speculation, or an experimental poem, but few have explored the scientific ideas that Poe proposes as the basis for his metaphysical conclusions. Until the latter part of the twentieth century when an expanding universe finally became the accepted cosmology, the science seemed too weird. In the twenty-first century, however, physicists marvel at how Poe could have conceived the basic ideas of modern physics and cosmology. In Russia *Eureka* was suppressed under the tsars and did not become available in recent times until 1996 with the reprinting of Konstantin Bal'mont's version of 1912. In contrast to the American reading of *Eureka*, the Russians recognized immediately that it has a significant scientific section apart from its philosophical and theological conclusions.[38]

148

In this amazing synthesis of empirical observation and rational analysis through the power of imagination, Poe proposed what science now calls the Big Bang theory.[39] Building upon his solution to Olber's paradox and the nebular hypothesis of Laplace before it had become generally accepted, Poe recognized implications of his theory that Laplace did not see. In short, Laplace proposed that our solar system is part of a much larger galaxy composed of millions, if not billions, of stars like the sun, and that the universe is filled with untold other galaxies. By a series of logical steps that proceed from the observation of the distribution of the stars in the sky and the action of gravity, Poe argues that this vast but finite universe came from one "primordial particle" that God willed into being.[40] In "Three Sundays in a Week" Poe made use of the relativity of time and space for his clever climax. In *Eureka* he anticipated Einstein by arguing that "*Space and Duration* [time] *are one.*"[41] In *Eureka* Poe stresses that with light, "there is a *continuous* outpouring of *ray-streams*, and *with a force which we have at least no right to suppose varies at all.*"[42] He argued for the curvature of space and made the prediction that "It would scarcely be paradoxical to say that a flash of lightning itself, travelling *forever* on the circumference of this unutterable circle, would still, *forever*, be travelling in a straight line."[43] He argued that life has its origin in the stars that expel the matter that became "animate—sensitive—and in the ratio of their heterogeneity; —some reaching a degree of sensitiveness involving what we call *Thought* and thus attaining obviously Conscious Intelligence."[44] The world was not yet ready for these ideas.

The Power of Imagination

How could a modern language major have conceived the basic principles of Big Bang cosmology and relativity, while proposing that some additional forces besides gravity and electromagnetism must be at work? Poe answered this question by resuming a discussion he had begun in the introduction to his first mystery story. At the beginning of *Eureka* Poe uses a satirical science fiction tale set one thousand years in the future to explain the superiority of imagination over either empiricism or rationalism as a basis for new knowledge.[45] He expanded this satire and published it in 1849 as "Mellonta Tauta," a Greek term meaning "things to come," a title borrowed in 1936 for a classic futuristic film with screenplay by H. G. Wells.

149

In his fictional introduction to *Eureka*, Poe explores the limitations of the revered mental exercises of the Enlightenment to conclude that rationalism and empiricism cannot take us to new knowledge. Only imagination, using empiricism and rationalism as tools, has the power to see what has never been seen "by seemingly intuitive leaps."[46] Poe rejected the "inability to conceive" of a thing as a valid criterion for judging any theory, because imagination equips a person to conceive of what no one has ever conceived before. He argued that the only true thinkers were people of "ardent imagination."[47] While the average person of science might refine and apply the great breakthroughs in knowledge, Poe attributed the actual discoveries of new knowledge to people of imagination.[48] Poe pointed to the example of Kepler as one who *guessed* at or *imagined* the laws upon which modern astronomy are based, and then proceeded to dismantle the universe as the science of his day understood it.[49]

Modern physicists readily acknowledge Poe's thesis. Copernicus did not arrive at the sun-centered heaven by calculating Ptolemy's math better (rationalism). He did not see the sun as the center around which the planets move by more advanced astronomical observations (empiricism). He "saw" that the planets move around the sun. Charles Towne imagined that Light Amplification through Stimulation by Radiation (LASER) would result in a concentrated beam of light while he sat on a park bench. Newton famously imagined his laws of gravity while sitting under an apple tree. New knowledge does not come by calculating the old ideas but by seeing what has never been seen before in the same old data. Scientific insight comes in a flash of illumination, often when the scientist least expects it. In "The Philosophy of Composition" Poe did not deny the intuitive or imaginative dimension of poetry. He merely tells us what the poet must go through to turn the idea into a poem. Townes still had a lot of work to do between the flash of imagination on the park bench and the label reader at the grocery store checkout counter. Imagination allowed Einstein to "see" the universe in a new way like Dupin in his arm chair without the need of any additional observations, even though he had to hire someone else to do his mathematic calculations and still others would have to do the hard work of applying his theories.[50]

Poe spoke of the capacity for intuition or imagination as *"the conviction arising from those inductions or deductions of which the processes are so shadowy as to escape our consciousness, elude our reason, or defy our capacity of expression."*[51] Poe argued that a feature of the intuitive power of imagination is its inaccessibility to analysis. Poe argued that Laplace and Newton could not cross boundaries that lay outside physics or mathematics. He thought Leibnitz capable of exploring metaphysics "in search of the treasure:—that he did not find it after all, was, perhaps, because his fairy guide, Imagination, was not sufficiently well-grown, or well-educated, to direct him aright."[52] Imagination was the "gold-bug" that would lead Poe to the treasure, for it allowed him to see and understand the clues that all the other detectives had missed.[53] Poe was on the case as his own Dupin, and what's more, he understood the metaphor. In fact, Poe mentions in *Eureka* that he had earlier laid out the basic process of his method in "The Murders in the Rue Morgue."[54] Indeed, Poe claimed that his understanding of an expanding universe had come to him "in a train of ratiocination"—that term he invented for the detective story to describe the combination of empirical observation, rational thought, and imagination.[55]

Olber's Paradox

In 1848 the world of science was certain that the infinite universe had always existed and that it was composed of an infinite number of stars. With an infinite number of stars, every speck of the night sky should have been filled with a point of light. If we put an infinite number of black dots on a white piece of paper, the paper will be completely black. Olber's paradox simply asked the question, "Why is the night sky dark?" It would seem that the infinite number of stars would give the night sky a dull, luminous glow. Instead, the night sky has a dark background with a general distribution of points of light.

151

When Poe looked at the night sky, he did not see the sky that he had been told to see. He did not see Aristotle's eternal universe or Newton's infinite universe. He saw a pattern of stars spread out the way bird shot spreads out when fired from a shotgun. Inside the gun the shot is tightly packed together, but once fired, it leaves the barrel and spreads outward the farther it travels from its beginning position. Imagination allowed Poe to see in a new way the same data that the human race had viewed since the dawn of time. The reason that the infinite number of stars does not create a luminous night sky is because the universe does not contain an infinite number of stars. The universe is a large but limited place. Reasoning backwards from the general distribution of stars, Poe concluded that the stars had their origin in one tightly compressed point that had expanded outward.

In contrast to the physics of his day, Poe declared that the universe had a beginning and that it had a finite number of stars. When we look at the night sky, we see the stars scattered, but in a universe with an infinite number of stars, we should see something else: "Were the succession of stars endless, then the background of the sky would present us an uniform luminosity . . . *since there could be absolutely no point, in all that background, at which would not exist a star.*"[56] While Poe made several guesses about astrophysics that do not hold, his essential argument corresponds amazingly with what came to be the accepted understanding of the origin of the universe during the last third of the twentieth century. To go against the established scientific understanding in 1848, however, meant that people labeled Poe a madman, completely insane.

The Beginning of the Universe

Poe had long since stopped caring about public opinion. He knew he was right and that one day he would be vindicated. He also recognized, however, that the origin of the universe has profound theological implications. Poe believed that the explanation for everything in the universe is contained in the initial will of God in creating the original primordial particle and causing it continually to divide until it had expanded into the universe.[57] Poe continually borrows from the language of the Bible to discuss his understanding of how the vast universe could have begun with one inconceivably small "primordial Particle."[58] When originally created out of nothing, the original Particle was "*without* form and void."[59] The first cause occurred "in the beginning."[60] Poe invokes "rendering unto Caesar" when he criticizes Laplace for accepting unwarranted assumptions about the universe.[61] At the end of all things Poe believed God would be "all in all."[62]

Out of this original Particle, the constitution of the entire universe of matter was produced from *One* into *Many*. The one Particle "radiated spherically—in all directions—to immeasurable but still to definite distances" as it grew to an "inexpressibly great yet limited

152

number of unimaginably yet not infinite minute atoms."[63] In other words, the universe expanded outward from what physicists now call its "singularity" to its inconceivably large but finite size.

Poe proposed that the universe began with unity but that it then carried out a design: "The design of multiplicity out of unity—diversity out of sameness—heterogeneity out of homogeneity—complexity out of simplicity—in a word, the utmost possible multiplicity of *relation* out of the emphatically irrelative *One*."[64] Poe made several assumptions that the modern Big Bang theory does not corroborate. For instance, he believed that the universe expanded into empty space, whereas the modern theory holds that no empty space exists apart from the material universe that simply expanded. Without the benefit of modern knowledge of strong and weak nuclear forces, Poe also believed that the expansion occurred as a result of the continual division of the primordial particle, rather than through the formation of atoms from the primordial "soup" that emerged as the singularity expanded. Nonetheless, his cosmology was more consistent with the twenty-first-century view than the cosmologies of Ptolemy, Copernicus, Kepler, Newton, or even Einstein.

For Poe, the universe must have begun with a single unity. Modern physics has accepted this proposition in terms of what it calls the "unified field," the original unity of the four fundamental forces: gravitation, electromagnetism, strong nuclear force, and weak nuclear force. In 1848 science only knew of gravity and electromagnetism. Having identified gravitation and electromagnetism, however, Poe chose to speak of attraction and repulsion instead because he had to account for what science had not yet described in the strong and weak nuclear forces that hold atoms and elements together. Poe also recognized that until the primary act of "Radiation from Unity," no principles or laws of nature existed.[65] Poe knew that some force operates at the atomic level, just as Darwin knew that some mechanism for heredity must exist even though his theory could not explain it.

Because Poe asks his readers to reject everything that science taught about the nature of the universe, he had to make a case for the nature of axioms and how people apply them. As great

153

as Newton's achievements in describing the action of gravity, Poe pointed out that Newton had given no adequate explanation for what gravity actually is. Einstein would go where Newton had not ventured, but his work would come more than fifty years after Poe had died. Long before Heisenberg stated his uncertainty principle and made physics a much more humble and tentative discipline, Poe described the mutability of the assumed axioms of science:

> Now, it is clear, not only that what is obvious to one mind may not be obvious to another, but that what is obvious to one mind at one epoch, may be anything but obvious, at another epoch, to the same mind. It is clear, moreover, that what, to-day, is obvious even to the majority of mankind, or to the majority of the best intellects of mankind, may tomorrow be, to either majority, more or less obvious, or in no respect obvious at all. It is seen, then, that the *axiomatic principle* itself is susceptible of variation, and of course that axioms are susceptible of similar change. Being mutable, the "truths" which grow out of them are necessarily mutable too; or, in other words, are never to be positively depended on as truths at all—since Truth and Immutability are one.[66]

154

Poe stated his view on the uncertainty of Enlightenment science in more specific terms in a letter to Charles Fenno Hoffman, who had ridiculed *Eureka*: "What I *really* say is this:—That there is no absolute *certainty* either in the Aristotelian or Baconian process" and that neither philosophy has the right to sneer at the imaginative power of intuition.[67] Several of Poe's stories reflect his modern understanding of the limitations of empiricism and rationalism. "The Spectacles" and "The Sphinx" illustrate how all sense data requires proper interpretation. His expanding universe resulted from interpreting the old data in a new way through the insight of imagination. Stories like "The Tell-Tale Heart" and "The Fall of the House of Usher" remind us of the frailty of rationalism.

The cardinal scientific axiom of the universe during the time of Poe, which had prevailed since Aristotle had laid it down 2,300 years earlier, states that the universe had always existed. The corollary axiom to the eternity of the universe was its infinite size.

This view continued to be held and taught until the last third of the twentieth century. Einstein so fervently believed in the "steady state" or static universe that he altered the math of his relativity theory to add a "cosmological constant" to prevent the impression that the universe was expanding.

Poe argued that gravity came about as a result of the beginning of the universe and did not exist prior to the beginning. Current scientific research hopes to find grounds for the existence of a grand unified field from which the four fundamental forces began to separate after the Big Bang. String theory and M-theory are efforts in this direction, but so far these approaches have no experimental method to support them. Poe also argued that the force which caused the primordial particle to begin to radiate, or expand in every direction, had a determinate rather than a continuing quality; otherwise, the force of attraction could never commence.

In accounting for the diffusion of the primordial particle through the universe while also allowing for the diffusion to gather together as the various elements, Poe argued that an "effort at Unity" would have commenced that resulted in a condensation of matter. Poe explained:

> The development of Repulsion (Electricity) must have commenced, of course, with the very earliest particular efforts at Unity, and must have proceeded constantly in the ratio of cöalescence—that is to say, *in that of Condensation*, or, again, of Heterogeneity.
>
> Thus the two Principles Proper, *Attraction* and *Repulsion*— the Material and the Spiritual—accompany each other, in the strictest fellowship, forever. Thus *The Body and The Soul walk hand in hand*.[68]

With this phrase that affirms the unity of body and soul, Poe embraced a biblical view of matter and spirit while rejecting the Greek and Cartesian dualistic models. We may also recognize a theme in Poe's stories that almost amounted to a preoccupation over the startling number of opposites, polarities, mirror images, and doublings in the world.[69] Poe found that science suggested a reason why this phenomenon might occur with such ubiquity.

155

Gravity (attraction), or the tendency of matter to seek unity, appears when the initial act of creation ceases, but electricity (repulsion) also appears, which prevents the immediate return of matter to a single unity. Poe argued that matter is nothing more than attraction and repulsion.[70] Because of the interrelatedness of the universe by attraction and repulsion, Poe had "no patience" with the idea that God placed individual stars and planets in particular places by separate and individual acts of creation. Building on an idea he had discussed at the conclusion of "The Mystery of Marie Rogêt,"[71] he argued

> that Nature and the God of Nature are distinct, no thinking being can long doubt. By the former we imply merely the laws of the latter. But with the very idea of God, omnipotent, omniscient, we entertain, also, the idea of *the infallibility* of his laws. With Him there being neither Past nor Future—with Him all being *Now*—do we not insult him in supposing his laws so contrived as not to provide for every possible contingency?—or, rather, what idea *can* we have of *any* possible contingency, except that it is at once a result and a manifestation of his laws? He who, divesting himself of prejudice, shall have the rare courage to think absolutely for himself, cannot fail to arrive, in the end, at the condensation of *laws* into *Law*—cannot fail of reaching the conclusion that *each law of Nature is dependent at all points upon all other laws*, and that all are but consequences of one primary exercise of the Divine Volition.[72]

Instead of thinking of God as the divine watchmaker as the deists and most of the natural philosophers had done, Poe spoke of God as an artist writing a story.[73] Poe included in *Eureka* a section from his 1845 essay about the reciprocity of divine creativity that explored the difficulty of identifying cause and effect in adaptation and repeated: "The Universe is a plot of God."[74] Reflecting upon the universe as a plot of God, Poe reasoned:

> Creation would have affected us as an imperfect *plot* in a romance, where the *dénoûment* is awkwardly brought about by interposed incidents external and foreign to the main subject; instead of springing out of the bosom of the thesis—out of the heart of the

ruling idea—instead of arising as a result of the primary proposition—as an inseparable and inevitable part and parcel of the
fundamental conception of the book.[75]

With his early grasp of the concept of the mutuality of adaptation,
Poe avoided Darwin's assumption that natural observation excluded
divine involvement. He observed, "The clearness with which even
material phenomena are presented to the understanding, depends
very little, I have long since learned to perceive, upon a merely
natural, and almost altogether upon a moral, arrangement."[76]

In response to Napoleon's question about how God fits into
the universe, Laplace famously replied that he had no need of that
hypothesis. Charles Darwin concluded that his observation of natural
processes at work left no place for God to work. Poe drew entirely
different conclusions and severely criticized the kind of thinking
that confused scientific observation with philosophical conclusions.

Poe rejected the notion of ether, the invisible, indetectable
substance that physicists believed connected all matter, allowing
light to travel and gravity to operate upon objects at a distance.
Physicists would not finally lose faith in ether until the end of the
nineteenth century, but Poe saw no need for it in his universe with
attraction and repulsion. It spoiled the plot as an unnecessary addition. On the other hand, he posited a different kind of ether which
permeated the Universe that involved "vitality, consciousness, and
thought—in a word, of spirituality."[77] The ether of science offended
Poe's aesthetic standard that science should be beautiful in order to
be true. The ether corresponded to "an unnecessarily complex work
of human art," which Poe would have judged as bad art. In his "Philosophy of Furniture" and his essay on "American Drama" he had
argued for simplicity as a hallmark of Beauty. The ether complicated
physics the way that Ptolemy's epicycles complicated the motion of
the heavenly bodies before Copernicus and Kepler simplified matters with their orbits of the planets around the sun.

Poe accepted the nebular hypothesis of Laplace on aesthetic
grounds as we might suppose from a poet who always strove for
Beauty. Poe said that he found the nebular hypothesis "*beautifully
true*. It is by far too beautiful, indeed, *not* to possess Truth as its

essentiality—and here I am very profoundly serious in what I say."[78] At this point we begin to see how a modern language major and a poet could conceive of the principal ideas of Big Bang cosmology, relativity theory, and the evolution of the species from stardust. Poe recognized the essential similarity of the activity of true science, mathematics, and poetry. He had suggested this relationship in "The Purloined Letter" in 1844.[79] In the twentieth century, with fabulous breakthroughs in relativity theory, quantum theory, chaos theory, and so many related discoveries, physicists now speak of theories as elegant or beautiful rather than merely true. Poe declared:

> It is the poetical essence of the Universe—*of the Universe* which, in the supremeness of its symmetry, is but the most sublime of poems. Now symmetry and consistency are convertible terms: —thus Poetry and Truth are one. A thing is consistent in the ratio of its truth—true in the ratio of its consistency. *A perfect consistency, I repeat, can be nothing but an absolute truth.* We may take it for granted, then, that Man cannot long or widely err, if he suffer himself to be guided by his poetical, which I have maintained to be his truthful, in being his symmetrical, instinct. He must have a care, however, lest, in pursuing too heedlessly the superficial symmetry of forms and motions, he leave out of sight the really essential symmetry of the principles which determine and control them.[80]

The standard for acceptance of a new idea in mathematics, chemistry, and physics is not "Is it true?" but "Does it have Beauty, symmetry, simplicity?" Poe's concept of Beauty as he argued it in *Eureka* has become the standard for evaluation.

Poe's biggest scientific error in *Eureka* came because of his reliance on the new nebular hypothesis of Laplace. According to the nebular hypothesis, the solar system came about through the rotation of a gigantic gaseous cloud that coalesced at its center to form the sun while the outer bands of the rotating cloud formed the planets. Contemplation of the nebular hypothesis was not a recent enterprise for Poe, who had mentioned it in "The Murders in the Rue Morgue" seven years earlier.[81] For Poe, the nebular hypothesis signified a reversal of the expansion of the universe toward a reunification. Poe believed that not only our solar system, but the entire universe of stars represented this process of movement toward unity. Poe argued that the Milky Way was rotating like the solar system toward a reunion of the matter within it, and by extension, he believed that the entire universe was in the process of moving toward a unity through the force of attraction. The modern formulation of the Big Bang theory remained uncertain about the fate of the universe until the latter half of the first decade of the twenty-first century when observations suggested that the universe is continuing to expand at an accelerated rate such that the force of gravity cannot reverse the expansion. Until these observations, however, scientists remained divided over whether the universe would end with a "big crunch" as the universe collapsed, or with a "big freeze" as the universe expanded forever.

The nebular hypothesis as postulated by Laplace has long since been discredited, but a new version of it continues as the standard understanding of how the solar system developed. Because of his commitment to the nebular hypothesis, however, Poe reflected on the implications of his Big Bang in terms of a final reunion of all things. Until this point, Poe's "prose poem" sounds like conventional natural theology, except that his nineteenth-century audience would have thought him crazy for postulating a finite universe that began from a primordial particle. In the conclusion of *Eureka*, however, Poe made a startling proposal.

Poe's Solution to the Problem of Suffering

The materialist regards matter as the sum total of all things. Only matter exists. Poe, on the other hand, regarded matter as a means to an end. By the creation of matter "is *Spirit Individualized.*"[82] The material universe is only a temporary structure that will cease once its purpose has been accomplished. Poe argued that "Matter *exists* only as Attraction and Repulsion."[83] With this definition Poe anticipated the strong and weak nuclear forces. Attraction implies for Poe a plurality of "parts, particles, or atoms" that might be attracted or related to each other. Poe's understanding of the expanding universe included the idea that the physical universe would eventually collapse in on itself as everything returned to a complete unity without individual differentiation. In such a condition, attraction and repulsion would lose all meaning and matter would cease to exist. The physical universe will cease to exist, and "God will remain all in all."[84]

The end of the universe need not imply the end of all universes. Poe proposed that, just as God had created this universe for eventual destruction once its purpose had been met in bringing about conscious intelligence, the process of creating universes might go on "forever, and forever, and forever" with "a novel Universe swelling into existence, and then subsiding into nothingness, at every throb of the Heart Divine."[85] With this phrase we return to the question of what Poe meant by calling *Eureka* a "prose poem" in defiance of all he had written about poetic theory. The "throb of the Heart Divine" returns us to Poe's idea of poetry as the "rhythmic creation of Beauty." The universe itself manifests the source of rhythmic beauty, for Poe conceived the universe as a regularly expanding and contracting creation.[86] The beating of the heart has long been suspected as the origin of the use of rhythm in music and poetry. Poe interposed the beating heart in several of his works, most probably to heighten the excitement, as in "The Tell-Tale Heart" and in "The Raven" where the narrator recounts, "So that now, to still the beating of my heart, I stood repeating." And with the repetition, the rhythm continues. We also see a similar dynamic at work in "Domain of Arnheim," in which landscape gardening represents the finest expression of poetic art, for in the garden, the rhythm of the seasons creates the beauty. Finally, *Eureka* does not satisfy Poe's condition for the length of a poem. One of Poe's major points in *Eureka*, however, is that the universe has not existed forever but has had a very brief duration in comparison with eternity. The content of *Eureka* is not a hoax, but the title is a grand riddle that the content solves. Science is poetry and the universe is a poem.

160

In the last few paragraphs of this 143-page book, Poe made his most dramatic suggestion.[87] Against the backdrop of Poe's fierce sense of justice, he argued that the human rebellion against the idea that a thinking soul might be inferior to another provides us with proof that "no soul *is* inferior to another."[88] In contemplating the relationship between the spiritual and the material, Poe concluded that each person is in part its own Creator because the God who created matter "now exists solely in the diffused Matter and Spirit of the Universe: and that the regathering of this diffused Matter and Spirit will be but the reconstitution of the *purely Spiritual* and Individual God."[89]

Poe concluded that in creating the primordial particle and dividing it throughout what became the universe, God dispersed himself throughout the whole and that what we call his creatures are actually "infinite individualizations of Himself."[90] By multiplying himself through division, God maximized his experience of happiness but also subjected himself to pain. In the end, the force of attraction will draw the whole universe back into the one.[91] Poe reached a pantheistic conclusion in which all is God and all individual identity becomes lost in the one.[92] Almost lost in the last few phrases of what he considered his most important work is the little word "pain." It is impossible to understand what Poe was trying to find in *Eureka* (Greek for "I have found it!") apart from the little word "pain."

Poe's critical statement comes in the next to the last paragraph of *Eureka* in which he makes clear that he had been looking for a solution to the problem of pain:

> In this view, and in this view alone, we comprehend the riddles of Divine Injustice—of Inexorable Fate. In this view alone the existence of Evil becomes intelligible; but in this view it becomes more—it becomes endurable. Our souls no longer rebel at a *Sorrow* which we ourselves have imposed upon ourselves, in furtherance of our own purposes—with a view—if even with a futile view—to the extension of our own *Joy.*[93]

In the back of his mind, Poe had been dealing with "the problem of pain" for all his adult life. The problem can be briefly stated: "If there is a good, all powerful God, then why is there suffering in the world?" This was the question that occupied the Buddha, who concluded that the world of sensory experience is an illusion. The same question plagued Charles Darwin, born the same year as Poe, whose little daughter died. He resolved the problem by concluding that God plays no role in the physical world which is "red in tooth and claw." This same issue settled C. S. Lewis into atheism when his mother died when he was nine years old. Poe and Lewis had similar experiences and similar responses of skepticism toward organized religion. On the other hand, both felt a profound sense of "the beautiful" and of "the imagination" that pointed them beyond the world to something else. They followed similar paths of exploring what kinds of knowledge are possible. As we have seen with Poe and his creation of the mystery story, the intuitive domain of knowledge was one he could not escape, and it suggested something beyond the mere physical.

Poe joined Lewis, Darwin, and Buddha in resolving that some sort of deity existed, but not one who stood too close or could actually make any difference. Poe could make the most of his own share of the divine spark until his time to sink into oblivion. As we shall see, however, Poe never left a poem, a story, or an idea alone for long.

162

Conclusion

Almost every scholar who has touched on Poe's metaphysics or commented on *Eureka* has suggested that Poe embraced the idea of annihilation. It was not a prospect, however, that he embraced joyfully. A God who only created for the purpose of maximization of his own pleasure, only to repeat the process eternally without any particular interest in the individual self-conscious beings who live and suffer annihilation might be the creative source of Beauty, but it certainly provided no grounds for Love, much less justice. This vision of God may have an internal philosophical coherence that Poe found consistent with his understanding of an expanding universe that was doomed to collapse because of the force of attraction, but this vision of God remains somehow incompatible with Poe's experiential knowledge of Love and justice.

Poe appears to have remained unwavering in his view that the universe had a beginning. On the other hand, he appears to have continued to revise his view of the nature of God and the continuity of human consciousness beyond death. In the end, the problem of

Love seems to have overcome the problem of evil. In the letters he wrote between the publication of *Eureka* and his death a year later, Poe seems to settle his mind that individual identity continues so that people may know and love each other, for without individual identity, Love does not occur. Love requires relationship, even for God.[94]

EX POE'S FACTO

For many people, the great mystery of Poe's life surrounds the cause of his death. Dozens of theories have been proposed to explain the circumstances under which he was discovered at a polling place in a state of delirium after several days during which his whereabouts remain unknown. For me, however, the great mystery of Poe's life surrounds the circumstances under which he went forward at a Sons of Temperance meeting in the late summer of 1849 in Richmond during his courtship of Elmira Royster Shelton. While Poe's death resembles "The Mystery of Marie Rogêt," his experience with the Sons of Temperance resembles more "The Gold-Bug" because an observer from the twenty-first century must first realize that a mystery exists, and few do.

Like the piece of paper from the story that seemed completely ordinary, but was in fact the key to a treasure, Poe's act of "signing the pledge" at a Sons of Temperance meeting seems common enough, but it is full of meaning that is lost to the eyes of the twenty-first-century observer. The Sons of Temperance was one of many evangelical Christian parachurch ministries of the nineteenth century devoted to social reform. In every age evangelical Christians have had a two-prong concern in the expression of their faith: to make Jesus Christ known as savior and to address the social ills of the world. In the English-speaking world, the social concerns they addressed changed as society changed. In the seventeenth century they sought to abolish blood sports like bear baiting, dog fighting, and cock fighting. In the eighteenth century they opposed slavery, established orphanages, promoted education for the masses, and promoted political reform. In the early nineteenth century they opposed slavery, established schools and colleges, and fought the use of alcohol as a beverage. Their assault on demon rum was tireless. Today, various twelve-step programs, but notably Alcoholics Anonymous, recognize the importance of acknowledging a higher power and a person's dependence upon that power as a critical aspect in gaining mastery over an addiction. The Sons of Temperance were not so vaguely religious. They were an evangelical Christian parachurch ministry like the Young Men's Christian Association or the Christian Women's Temperance League.

The nineteenth-century context in which Edgar Allan Poe went to the Sons of Temperance meeting and went forward to "take the pledge" was a religious meeting. These were the kinds of meetings that evangelical ministries conducted in the slums of the great cities of America in what were called for many years "Rescue Missions," the kinds of meetings conducted by the Salvation Army, the kinds of meetings conducted by Charles Finney across New York and Ohio that came to be called "revival meetings." Finney championed the use of the public invitation as a means to challenge those in the audience to make a public decision. The international evangelistic ministry of Billy Graham in the second half of the twentieth century stands in this religious tradition.

The public invitation at one of these evangelical meetings always involved giving up self-destructive behavior, but the invitation was to accept the help of Jesus Christ in doing it. Instead of the one-dimensional, legalistic view of sin with which Poe seems to have been acquainted since his childhood with the dour, Calvinistic Scotsman, John Allan, the evangelicals also stressed that sin operated like a chain from which one needs to be set free. They presented Jesus Christ, not as a condemning judge, but as one who came to free people from whatever bound them. As far as we know, Poe had not been acquainted with this stream of Christianity earlier.

From all accounts we have of Poe, he was shy in public. He did not seek center stage in a crowd and required encouragement to recite his work at social gatherings outside the intimacy of his own home. Going forward at a Sons of Temperance meeting was not the thing that Edgar Allan Poe would be expected to do. It did not fit with his social background or temperament. To a great extent, such a public display would have constituted public humiliation for Poe. Indeed, the event was reported in newspapers all over the country. Tongues would have wagged. Men would have laughed. Ladies would have shot knowing glances at one another. Walking "the sawdust trail," as termed by the urban evangelistic meetings for the sawdust strewn on the muddy ground when the meeting took place in a tent, seems uncharacteristic for Edgar Allan Poe.

It seems to me that we have two options for why Poe embraced the public symbolism of the Sons of Temperance. First, he was the charlatan and scoundrel that Griswold said he was. By this account he would have done anything to persuade Elmira Shelton to marry him so that he could get her money. Second, he had a conversion experience. By this account he changed his mind about the collapse of all individuality into God and accepted the story of Jesus Christ as consistent with his view of the universe.

With respect to the first view, the readers must make up their own minds, though one would hope that they would base their judgment on the best evidence we have of the character of Poe and not on the Griswold tradition. It might be helpful to recall, however, that under the terms of her late husband's will, Elmira would lose most of the inheritance if she remarried. She would bring a small bit of money with her, but not what a celebrity like Poe could have gotten as the stories of women chasing him would suggest. A scoundrel most likely would have gone after a larger fortune that was secure. Of course, I am a cousin and am prone to see him in the best light.

With respect to the second view, Poe would have had to change his mind in a major way. The view he expressed in *Eureka* about

167

the end of all things would involve the loss of all individual identity into God. We should note, however, that Poe's understanding of the beginning of all things is a separate question than the end. His Big Bang theory is based on his observation of the general distribution of stars that suggested a common point of origin. His theory of the collapse of all things into God is based on his interpretation of the nebular hypothesis.

Poe's primary consideration, however, had to do with the principles of attraction and repulsion. He reasoned that the force of *expansion* was exercised only once and that the principle of *attraction* would finally draw all things together again. He also had the idea that God had diffused himself throughout the universe and that the experience of pleasure and the experience of suffering somehow involve God's participation in the physical universe. He thought that the physical world served a utilitarian purpose toward a great end. He rejected the view of science that an invisible physical substance permeated the universe and provided the mechanical means by which gravity works. Instead, he believed that gravity works at a distance, but that a spiritual ether permeates the universe. In his eschatology, or his view of the end of all things, God draws all things to himself in order to become all in all. How could Poe reconcile these ideas with classical Christian faith in a way that allowed him to go forward at a Sons of Temperance meeting with integrity?

168

For Poe, it would only take a brief "aha" moment to see that the story of Jesus fulfills his basic design. The idea of a beginning to the universe with the expansion from a primordial particle is perfectly consistent with the biblical concept of the creation of all things. The diffusion of God through the universe is not necessary for this first part of his view to stand and addresses a different question for Poe that involves justice, Beauty, and Love. The Christian faith understands that God is diffused throughout the universe as Holy Spirit, the spiritual ether of Poe. The notions of justice, Beauty, and Love come from God, whose spirit has immediate access to people through their spiritual being. Biblical faith involves believing that people bear the image of God that expresses itself through imagination and the creative impulse.

Poe believed that the creation of the universe somehow increased the pleasure of God. As an artist he understood that the creative impulse brings pleasure, but that it also bestows pleasure when done well. Thus, his entire philosophy of creativity aimed at the effect upon the audience. He also believed and repeated that the creation of the universe occurred as an act of volition. God willed it into existence. Both of these ideas are completely consistent with biblical faith. In the last book of the Bible, the mysterious and often misunderstood book of Revelation that describes the end of all things, we are told that God has created all things for his "pleasure" in the King James translation, but modern translations say by his "will." The Greek word behind "pleasure" and "will" is the same word (Rev 4:11). Perhaps a more illuminating passage comes from Paul's Letter to the Ephesians in which we are told in the first chapter that God's plan in creation was to unite people into him through Christ Jesus in keeping with the pleasure of his will (Eph 1:5).

The importance of the passage is that the first chapter of Ephesians continually speaks of God having a plan that he conceived before creation, and that it will not be completed until the end, when he brings all things together in Christ Jesus. Poe had assumed in *Eureka* that if everything and everyone came together in God, that it would mean the loss of all individual identity. According to the Christian faith, coming together in Christ actually preserves individual identity. In the brief three-page speculation at the end of *Eureka*, Poe has not worked out several important matters. He seems to hold to the idea of an intermediate state of continuing identity beyond the grave until everything comes together in God, which means that spiritual life beyond the physical world continues without a physical connection. The collapse of the physical universe as God draws all things to himself, however, involves the physical property of attraction, or gravitation. Once people are separate from their physical bodies, Poe does not have a vision worked out for how their spiritual bodies relate to the physical universe. Thus, his understanding of the ultimate fate of people remains a work in process at the end of *Eureka*.

Poe's solution to the problem of suffering involves the necessity of God sharing the experience of suffering. It also involves the idea that the possibility of suffering is necessary in order for pleasure and free will to exist. Suffering is the cost of Beauty and Love. In order to maintain justice, also referred to in the Bible as righteousness and on the playing field as fairness, God must also be subjected to what humans endure. In *Eureka* God participates in the physical world at the beginning. In the Christian faith God steps into time and space, as Poe termed it, in the middle. Jesus Christ did not simply claim to be a close relation to God, like the Prince of Wales, who is son of the monarch and destined to reign. In referring to himself, Jesus used the term *Son of Man*, whom the world would see "coming on the clouds of heaven." *Son of Man* was an ancient Hebrew term that could mean *person*, but with the phrase "coming on the clouds of heaven" and related phrases used by Jesus, it means the manifestation of God in human likeness at the end of time when the great judgment of all things occurs, as prophesized by Daniel in his vision of the four world empires (Dan 7:1-14).

170   The Christian story is every bit as weird as *Eureka*, for it tells of a God who became fully human: he entered the world the way all humans do, by being born, and he left the only way humans do, by dying. While becoming fully human as the Son, however, God did not cease to continue in eternity outside of time and space as the Father, nor did he cease being diffused throughout the physical universe as Holy Spirit. Christians believe in only one God, but a God who exists in three ways at the same time: Father, Son, and Holy Spirit. In this way God can fully experience suffering as well as human delight. He can experience Love and Beauty as well as the effects of hatred, ugliness, and injustice. He not only knows what suffering is, he knows how it feels. The resurrection of Jesus involved the preservation of his individual identity beyond death. This story satisfies Poe's concern that God belong to earth as well as to heaven.

The preservation of individual identity beyond death may have been the critical question for Poe if he went down the path of faith instead of the way claimed by Griswold. In his handwritten addendum to *Eureka*, written some time before his last visit to Richmond, Poe wrote,

> The pain of the consideration that we shall lose our individual identity, ceases at once when we further reflect that the process, as above described, is, neither more nor less than that of the absorption by each individual intelligence, of all other intelligences (that is, of the Universe) into its own. That God may be all in all, each must become God.[1]

The thought shows us that Poe was still thinking about the problem of loss of identity, a concern that arises in many of his stories, though this study has not pursued the issue.

In his letters to Annie Richmond, Poe betrayed a continuing belief in the continuation of personal identity beyond death. He hoped that their relationship would endure "hereafter & forever in the Heavens."[2] He renewed this way of thinking as he recalled, "As I clasped you to my heart, I said to myself—'it is for the last time, until we meet in Heaven.'"[3] The intensity of this belief was bound up with his experience of Love. Love requires self-conscious, personal identity, for Love involves relationship with another. In October 1848 Poe wrote to Sarah Helen Whitman, to whom he was engaged, "She whom the great Giver of all Good had preordained to be mine—mine only—if not now, alas! then at least hereafter and *forever*, in the Heavens."[4] Wishful thinking and the desire to be with someone forever would still not have been a satisfying reason to overturn the concept of everyone losing their identity when drawn into God. The resurrection, however, presents a different picture of how it could happen.

In "Annabel Lee," written after *Eureka* during the last year of Poe's life, Poe relies on the basis of Hebrew poetry to carry the verse. Auden had criticized Poe for the modern sin of redundancy, but ancient Hebrew poetry depended upon repetition and saying one thing in at least two ways: "Create in me a clean heart, O God, and renew a right spirit within me" (Ps 51:10). The phrase "kingdom by the sea" is repeated too much for modern verse, but it is in keeping with Hebrew poetry. The redundancy we find in "Of those who were older than we— / Of many far wiser than we—"

171

represents a positive feature of Hebrew poetry. Poe uses this same parallel structure at the close of the poem:

> And so, all the night-tide, I lie down by the side
> Of my darling—my darling—my life and my bride,
>   In the sepulcher there by the sea—
>   In her tomb by the sounding sea.

We find that in the King James Version of the Bible that Poe would have known, the New Testament accounts of the resurrection of Jesus use the term "sepulchre" for the tomb where Jesus was laid (Matt 28:1, 8; Mark 16:2, 5, 8; Luke 24:1-2, 9, 12; John 20:1-3, 6, 11). Matthew, the most Hebrew of the four gospels, uses both "tomb" and "sepulchre" in parallel form to describe the burial of Jesus (Matt 27:60).

Given the eschatological ponderings of Poe in *Eureka* and the unending contemplations of the final destiny of humanity throughout his works, it is evident that Poe has set "Annabel Lee" in the context of these musings. Given the other imagery, the image of "the sea" takes on particular significance. In the visions of eternity and the throne of God among the Hebrew prophets, the image of the sea has a striking place. The Hebrews dreaded the sea and viewed it as a place of death and chaos, from the primordial waters of the deep in Genesis to the Red Sea that blocked the way of escape from pharaoh's army in Exodus to the raging waves that terrified the disciples of Jesus. In Ezekiel's vision the sea is transformed at the end of time by the water that flows from the temple of God (Ezek 47). In John's vision of the end of time in Revelation, the sea gives up its dead and the river of the water of life flows from the throne of God to form "what looked like a sea of glass, clear as crystal" (Rev 20:13, 21:1, 4:6). Among the Hebrews, water was a favorite metaphor for the Spirit of God and the gift of life he brings.

The frequent references to seraphs, angels, and demons provides an imagery that littered the pages of nineteenth-century poetry, so these figures need not carry the poem into a biblical frame of reference. Taken with the rest, however, Poe appears to be appealing to things he had heard long ago. His most dogmatic statement in the poem comes with

172

And neither the angels in heaven above,
  Nor the demons down under the sea,
Can ever dissever my soul from the soul
  Of the beautiful ANNABEL LEE:

This passage bears a striking similarity to the Apostle Paul's equally dogmatic statement about the surety of eternal continuity based upon the love of God: "For I am persuaded, that neither death, nor life, nor angels, nor principalities, nor powers, nor things present, nor things to come, nor Height, nor depth, nor any other creature, shall be able to separate us from the love of God, which is in Christ Jesus our Lord" (Rom 8:38-39). The allusion seems unmistakable. The poem does not celebrate necrophilia; it celebrates hope and the eternal power of Love to prevail over death.

In his Letter to the Romans, the Apostle Paul explained that everyone who is baptized is baptized, or immersed, by the Holy Spirit into Christ Jesus (Rom 6:1-7). Just as God participates in the physical universe through Jesus Christ, people participate in God through Jesus Christ. Poe was concerned with the increase of God's pleasure. The pleasure of God is increased by the preservation of those God loves. The two symbols of Christianity, baptism and the Lord's Supper, signify this union with God through Christ. Baptism represents immersion into Christ in which the water signifies the Holy Spirit and the motion of going under the water and coming out again signifies a person's sharing in Christ's death, burial, and resurrection. The image of water and the tomb is the imagery of Christian baptism, as Paul explained:

173

> We died to sin; how can we live in it any longer? Or don't you know that all of us who were baptized into Christ Jesus were baptized into his death? We were therefore buried with him through baptism into death in order that, just as Christ was raised from the dead through the glory of the Father, we too may live a new life.If we have been united with him like this in his death, we will certainly also be united with him in his resurrection. (Rom 6:2-5)

In baptism, the water represents burial in the tomb and incorporation by the Spirit of God. The Lord's Supper, whereby Christians eat the bread as the body of Christ and drink the wine as the blood of Christ, represents participation in Christ or "communion" together with him.

The perversity that so perplexed Poe about humans, in spite of the glorious achievements they had accomplished, also found its solution in the faith of Jesus Christ. As God participates in humanity by stepping into the world, humans participate in God when the Holy Spirit steps into them. The solution to perversity can only come about by an act of the volition of God to change people. When the Holy Spirit enters into a person, in a sense, they die. At last their perversity is gradually wrung out of them. This last matter would have been extremely important to Poe, who had spent fifteen years making promises to amend his ways, but finding that in spite of his great intellect, he could not control himself by an act of his own will. He needed help, and no human help would avail. It would have been humiliating for Poe to face such a situation and confess his need, even if it were only a matter between him and God. But that was the context in which he went forward at a Sons of Temper-
174   ance meeting.

Finally, we come to the problem of Love. If all individual identity is absorbed into God, then Love dies. Love requires someone to love. If God only created the universe for a short fling in time, then Love never existed because he never cared about what he made. He only cared about his own good pleasure. But how could perverse humanity have come up with a sentiment like Love on its own? God must be the source of Love. Yet, how could God be the source of Love before creation if there was only God? At the beginning and at the end of all things, Love poses a problem.

With the Christian God, however, Poe could have found a faith consistent with the cardinal points of *Eureka*. In the Christian faith, God does not let people kill Jesus. Instead, God takes on flesh and lets people kill him while he does not lift a finger from his continuing existence in eternity to stop them because "God was in Christ reconciling the world unto himself" (2 Cor 5:19). A God who exists in three persons as Father, Son, and Spirit has a perfect unity that *is* Love. The very being of God in a communal nature means that Love is perfect within God. Thus, God has more beings to love as a result of creation, but creation gives him nothing which he did not already have. God did not create Love; God *is* Love (1 John 4:8). This kind of God may draw everyone to himself as Poe supposed, but not to annihilate them. With this God, Poe has the hope of spending eternity with all the people he loves.

Having rejected the physical ether of nineteenth-century science in favor of a spiritual ether, Poe would eventually have realized that the principle of attraction whereby God draws people to himself could not be gravity but must be something else. Poe realized that Love, Beauty, and justice all point beyond themselves in the physical world to their eternal origin, and by these means, God draws people toward him. Because of the nebular hypothesis, Poe had assumed the great drawing together stood in the future at the end of all things, but with God coming into the world, the great drawing together begins now. The principle of repulsion that Poe also regarded as undeniable for spirit as well as for matter was perversity, that human trait which pushes away from God. Through *Eureka* Poe would have gained an understanding of the significance 175 of Jesus Christ coming to break the power of perversity.

Whether this is what happened, I cannot say. Poe's cosmological vision in *Eureka* expresses philosophical and theological concerns that are satisfied in Jesus Christ in such a way that Poe could have, in good conscience, affiliated with an evangelical Christian organization. I don't know if he made this connection, but he had all the information he needed about Christianity to have made the connection if he could free himself from the Calvinistic interpretation of Christianity that he would have learned from John Allan. Whether Poe found the help of a different interpretation of Christianity, I cannot say. I do know that when he first called on Elmira Shelton when he returned to Richmond that last summer of his life on a Sunday, she asked him to return later, for she was on her way to St. John's Episcopal Church, just across the street from her house, where Poe's mother was buried.

Poe discovered that the things that interested him (science, religion, and art) lay at the intersection of the rational, the empirical, and the imaginative. As he explored these matters, he found that justice, Love, and Beauty pointed beyond themselves toward something eternal from whence they had come. In the midst of striving to be a poet and to raise the standard of American literature, he managed to affect the course of world literature and to provide a philosophy of art that film directors would follow without having any idea that it came from Poe. Yet such a public figure and popular icon remains a mystery.

NOTES

Chapter One

1   For an alternative, and certainly more conventional reading of Poe, Kenneth Silverman has summarized the critical identification of Poe's core preoccupations in his tales as "their study of incest, doubling, and other aspects of human psychology; their satire of Romantic and Gothic convention; their formalist manner and self-reflexive interest in the process of reading and writing; their fascination with illusion and deception; and not least in their creation of horror and disgust." See Kenneth Silverman, introduction to *New Essays on Poe's Major Tales* (New York: Cambridge University Press, 1993), 15. Surely Poe utilizes all that Silverman mentions, but they are the means by which he pursues his questions. Such a wide spectrum of diverse matters seems to cut against the idea of a "preoccupation" which, by its very nature, suggests a more narrow focus.

2   Barbara Cantalupo, "Interview with Benjamin Franklin Fisher IV," *The Edgar Allan Poe Review* 8, no. 1 (2007): 60.

3   For a discussion of the literary relationship between Poe and Dickens, see Fernando Galván, "Plagiarism in Poe: Revisiting the Poe-Dickens Relationship," *The Edgar Allan Poe Review*, 10, no. 2 (2009): 11–24.

4   See *The Poe Log*, which refers to letters in 1842 concerning Dickens' efforts to find a publisher for Poe in London. Dwight Thomas and David K. Jackson, *The Poe Log: A Documentary Life of Edgar Allan Poe, 1809–1849* (Boston: G. K. Hall, 1987), 370, 385, 387–88.

5   I am indebted to Rebecca Whitten Poe Hays for pointing out this continuing problem in Dickens studies.

6   Rufus Wilmot Griswold, "The 'Ludwig' Article," in *The Recognition of Edgar Allan Poe*, ed. Eric W. Carlson (Ann Arbor: University of Michigan Press, 1970), 32–33. The famous "Ludwig" obituary has been reprinted many places, but this volume also contains reprints of some of the most significant criticisms of Poe from 1829 until 1963.

7   Arthur Hobson Quinn has included the text of the power of attorney in an appendix to his biography of Poe. See Arthur Hobson Quinn, *Edgar Allan Poe: A Critical Biography* (New York: Cooper Square, 1969), 754.

8   Daniel Hoffman, *Poe Poe Poe Poe Poe Poe Poe* (Garden City, N.Y.: Doubleday, 1972), 15. Stanton Garner has laid blame at the feet of Hoffman for continuing an American critical tradition of not taking Poe seriously "by patronizing him, referring to him by frivolous names such as "Edgar," "Edgarpoe," and "Hoaxiepoe" as Hoffman had done. See Stanton Garner, "Emerson, Thoreau, and Poe's 'Double Dupin,'" in *Poe and His Times*, ed. Benjamin Franklin Fisher IV (Baltimore: The Edgar Allan Poe Society, 1990), 131.

9   W. H. Auden, introduction to *Edgar Allan Poe: Selected Prose and Poetry*, in *Recognition* (see n. 6), 228.

178   10   "Edgar Allan Poe," *The Leisure Hour: A Family Journal of Instruction and Recreation* 132 (1854): 427.

11   "Edgar Allan Poe," *The Leisure Hour*, 427.

12   Augustus Hopkins Strong, *American Poets and Their Theology* (Philadelphia: Griffith and Rowland Press, 1916), 163.

13   Griswold, "The 'Ludwig' Article," in *Recognition* (see n. 6), 33.

14   Richard Wilbur wrote, " *The Fall of the House of Usher* is a journey into the depths of the self. I have said that all journeys in Poe are allegories of the process of dreaming, and we must understand *The Fall of the House of Usher* as a dream of the narrator's, in which he leaves behind him the waking, physical world and journeys inward toward his *moi intérieur*, toward his inner and spiritual self. That inner and spiritual self is Roderick Usher." See Richard Wilbur, "The House of Poe," in *Recognition* (see n. 6), 265. Prince Prospero's cry of despair is Poe's cry of despair (277). Like so many others who explain Poe's stories in terms of Poe's mental illness, Wilbur only discusses the horror stories. They fit his theory.

15   Hoffman, *Poe Poe Poe*, 16. D. H. Lawrence assumed that Poe tried "any drug he could lay his hands on" and "any human being he could lay his hands on" in an effort to achieve an ecstasy of experience. See D. H. Lawrence, "Edgar Allan Poe," in *Recognition* (see n. 6), 113.

16 Strong, *American Poets*, 176, 201.

17 Strong, *American Poets*, 175.

18 Basil Ashmore, introduction to *The Mystery of Arthur Gordon Pym* (London: Panther, 1964), 7.

19 Wolf Mankowitz, *The Extraordinary Mr. Poe* (New York: Summit Books, 1978), 124.

20 Thomas R. Slicer, *From Poet to Premier, The Centennial Cycle 1809–1909: Poe, Lincoln, Holmes, Darwin, Tennyson, Gladstone* (London: The Grolier Society, 1909), 32–33.

21 Slicer, *Poet to Premier*, 7.

22 Slicer, *Poet to Premier*, 33.

23 George R. Graham, "The Late Edgar Allan Poe," *Graham's Magazine* 36, no. 3 (1850): 224.

24 Graham, "The Late Edgar Allan Poe," 224. Unless otherwise stated all emphasis in this book is from the original.

25 Graham, "The Late Edgar Allan Poe," 224.

26 Graham, "The Late Edgar Allan Poe," 225.

27 Sarah Helen Whitman, *Edgar Allan Poe and His Critics* (New York: Rudd & Carleton, 1860), 26.

28 See John J. Moran, *A Defense of Edgar Allan Poe* (Washington, D.C.: William F. Boogher, 1885).

29 Susan Talley Archer, "Last Days of Edgar A. Poe," *Scribner's Magazine* 15, no. 5 (1878): 715.

30 The Harrison edition contains several pieces attributed to Poe that have since been discredited. It also lacks several pieces now regarded as by Poe.

31 Two fine recent studies provide excellent guides to the history of Poe criticism. Benjamin Fisher provides a topical introduction to works in *The Cambridge Introduction to Edgar Allan Poe* (Cambridge: Cambridge University Press, 2008). Scott Peeples takes a chronological approach to the history of Poe criticism in *The Afterlife of Edgar Allan Poe* (Rochester: Camden House, 2007).

32 R. H. Stoddard, "Edgar Allan Poe." *Lippincott's Monthly Magazine* (1889): 107–15.

33 Hervey Allen, *Israfel: The Life and Times of Edgar Allan Poe* (New York: Farrar & Rinehart, 1934): 322n489.

34 From James' review of Baudelaire's *Les Fleurs du Mal*, in *Recognition* (see n. 6), 66–67.

35 James, review of *Les Fleurs*, in *Recognition* (see n. 6), 66–67.

36 James, review of *Les Fleurs*, in *Recognition* (see n. 6), 66–67; and James, *Hawthorne* (New York: Harper, 1879).

37 "The Best Ten American Books," *The Critic* 20, no. 597 (1893): 78.

38 From the translation by Lois and Francis Hyslop of Baudelaire's preface to *Nouvelles histoires extraordinaires par Edgar Poe* (Paris: Michel Levy, 1857), in *Recognition* (see n. 6), 45.

39 Lois and Hyslop, Baudelaire's preface, in *Recognition* (see n. 6), 46–47.

40 Lois and Hyslop, Baudelaire's preface, in *Recognition* (see n. 6), 52.

41 Lois and Hyslop, Baudelaire's preface, in *Recognition* (see n. 6), 54.

42 Lois and Hyslop, Baudelaire's preface, in *Recognition* (see n. 6), 59.

43 In his assessment of Poe's reception in France, Henri Justin reasoned, "In fact, it seems to me, Poe kept coupling opposites, pitting them against each other in the arena of the text, sharpening their antagonism while yoking them to create an effect of totality, of unity—a very paradoxical unity. It was a unity that was forcibly maintained by the sheer genius of its conceiver, a unity that few readers, even admirers of Poe, could actually grasp. This is why the history of its reception is very much the history of a splitting apart, the history of a literary *big bang*." See Henri Justin, "The Paradoxes of Poe's Reception in France," *The Edgar Allan Poe Review* 11, no. 1 (2010): 80. For an important earlier study, see Patrick F. Quinn, *The French Face of Edgar Poe* (Carbondale, Ill.: Southern Illinois University Press, 1957).

44 From Vladimir Astrov's translation of Dostoevsky's prefatory essay to Poe's "The Tell-Tale Heart," "The Black Cat," and "The Devil in the Belfry" printed in *Time* (Wremia, 1861), in *Recognition* (see n. 6), 61.

45 I had the pleasure of speaking at eight Russian universities in four cities during Poe's bicentennial in September 2009 and found a deep appreciation for Poe among Russian students.

46 Burtin Pollin includes Melville, James, Hemingway, Kipling, Stevenson, de la Mare, James Thurber, Allen Ginsberg, Saul Bellow, and Terry Southern in *Poe's Seductive Influence on Great Writers* (New York: IUniverse, 2004). To this list can be added D. W. Griffith, Alfred Hitchcock, Roger Corman, and Tim Burton.

47 William Aspenwall Bradley, "Edgar Allan Poe's Place in Literature," *The Book News Monthly* 25, no. 12 (1907): 790.

48 Carlson, *Recognition* (see n. 6), 83, reprinting J. Brander Matthews, "Poe and the Detective Story," *Scribner's Magazine* 42 (1907): 287–93.

49 I am indebted to Alexandra Urakova, who provided me with a synopsis in English of her paper "The Polemics around Poe's Centennial Celebration at the University of Virginia: Barrett Wendell vs. Eugene Didier" (presentation, International Poe Conference, St. Petersburg, Russia, September 10, 2009).

50 C. Alphonso Smith, "Edgar Allan Poe," *The Mentor* 10, no. 8 (1922): 4.

51   Smith, "Edgar Allan Poe," 4.

52   Smith, "Edgar Allan Poe," 6.

53   Smith, "Edgar Allan Poe," 7. More recently, April Selley has argued that Poe should be introduced to students as "distinctly American and indeed part of the mainstream of American literature." See April Selley, "Poe and the Will," in *Poe and His Times* (see n. 8), 94. Specifically, Selley regards Poe's attention to free will as a hallmark of his position. Bonnie Shannon McMullen has argued that as a person born in Boston and reared in Richmond, Poe belonged to both the North and the South. Thus, Poe saw "himself as an American writer and wished to define and help to create an American literary tradition." See Bonnie Shannon McMullen, "'A Desert Ebony': Poe, *Blackwood's*, and Tales of the Sea," *The Edgar Allan Poe Review* 11, no. 1 (2010): 75.

54   Killis Cambell also wrote a number of valuable essays on Poe that brought some scholarly rationality to the academy's understanding of Poe in the first third of the twentieth century. One of his more valuable essays provided the title for a collection of his studies. See Killis Campbell, *The Mind of Poe and Other Studies* (Cambridge, Mass.: Harvard University Press, 1933).

55   For an example of this kind of unhelpful work, see Harold Bloom, introduction to *The Tales of Poe*, Modern Critical Interpretations (New York: Chelsea House, 1987). Despite Bloom's introduction, the volume contains several constructive contributions to Poe studies, including Gerald Kennedy's "Phantasms of Death in Poe's Fiction," in *The Tales of Poe*, ed. Harold Bloom (New York: Chelsea House, 1987).

56   For an anecdotal summary of the formation of the Poe Studies Association and its early guiding lights (including Lasley Dameron, Eric Carlson, James Gargano, Burton Pollin, Alice Moser Caudel, and Benjamin Fisher), see Barbara Cantalupo, "Interview with Benjamin Fisher" (see n. 2), 63–65. Eric Carlson also gave his memories of the founding of the PSA and the initiation of the *PSA Newsletter* in Barbara Cantalupo, "Interviews with Poe Scholars: Eric W. Carlson," *The Edgar Allan Poe Review* 1, no. 1 (2000): 57–58.

57   Claude Richard declared in a lecture at the University of Iowa on December 6, 1980, "What is perhaps difficult to realize, here in America, is that in the list of contemporary writers and critics who write about or around Poe, we find practically all the major names: Poulet, Bachelard, Ricardou, Todorov, Genette, Barthes, Lacan and Derrida." See Claude Richard, "Destin, Design, Dasein: Lacan, Derrida and 'The Purloined Letter,'" *The Iowa Review* 12, no. 4 (1981): 1.

58   John Ward Ostrom, Burton R. Pollin, and Jeffrey A. Savoye, eds.,

The Collected Letters of Edgar Allan Poe, Volume I: 1824–1846, 3rd ed. (Staten Island, N.Y.: Gordian Press, 2008), 595–96. W. H. Auden began his introduction to a selection of Poe's prose and poetry by observing, "What every author hopes to receive from posterity—a hope usually disappointed—is justice. Next to oblivion, the two fates which he most fears are becoming the name attached to two or three famous pieces while the rest of his work is unread and becoming the idol of a small circle which reads every word he wrote with the same uncritical reverence." Auden argued that both fates have befallen Poe. See W. H. Auden, introduction to *Poe: Selected,* in *Recognition* (see n. 6), 220.

59 Even a great critic like Allen Tate tended to think of Poe in terms of one kind of story so that he could claim that Poe's heroines are ill-disguised vampires. He can make this claim because he limits Poe's heroines (Berenice, Ligeia, Madeline, and Morella) to those found in a small handful of his tales. See Allen Tate, "The Angelic Imagination," in *Recognition* (see n. 6), 238. Richard Wilbur committed the same error when speaking of Poe's heroes, who never "breathe the air that others breathe." See Wilbur, "The House of Poe," in *Recognition* (see n. 6), 260. See also Elisabete Lopes, "Unburying the Wife: A Reflection Upon the Female Uncanny in Poe's 'Ligeia,'" *The Edgar Allan Poe Review* 11, no. 1 (2010): 40–47. Lopes suggests that Ligeia embodies the typical female heroine of Poe's stories, though she actually focuses on Poe's horror stories.

60 [George R. Graham], "The Genius and Characteristics of the Late Edgar Allan Poe," *Graham's Magazine* 44, no. 2 (1854): 224.

61 Many of the most significant and substantial Poe scholars of the twentieth century have held that a comic element runs throughout Poe's fiction, especially T. O. Mabbott, James Southall Wilson, Walter Fuller Taylor, James W. Gargano, James M. Cox, Richard P. Benton, G. R. Thompson, Alexander Hammond, J. Gerald Kennedy, Kent Ljungquist, and Benjamin Fisher. See Fisher, *Cambridge Introduction,* 120.

62 Benjamin Fisher offers an informed and helpful picture of Poe's breadth in storytelling "of varied characteristics and qualities, a spectrum ranging from ghastly horrors in 'The Pit and the Pendulum' or 'The Murders in the Rue Morgue' to light comedy in 'Three Sundays in a Week,' or from the serious, but not terrifying, landscape visions in 'The Island of the Fay' and 'The Domain of Arnheim' to the extravagantly satiric mode in 'Loss of Breath.'" See Fisher, *Cambridge Introduction,* 48.

63   Yvor Winters serves in this connection, as in most assessments of Poe, as the prime example of someone who seemed not to pay attention to what Poe did or said. Despite the wide variety of stories that Poe wrote, with their wide variety of types of characters, Winters wrote, "It is significant in this connection that most of his heroes are mad or on the verge of madness; a datum which settles his action firmly in the realm of inexplicable feeling from the outset." See Yvor Winters, "Edgar Allan Poe: A Crisis in the History of American Obscurantism," in *Recognition* (see n. 6), 195.

64   Allen Tate, "Our Cousin, Mr. Poe," *Partisan Review* 16, no. 12 (1949): 1217.

65   Justin, "Paradoxes," 81–82. Justin argues that though Baudelaire recognized the unity of Poe's corpus, his editorial decisions had the effect of dismembering the corpus.

66   T. S. Eliot, "From Poe to Valéry," in *Recognition* (see n. 6), 205.

67   Eliot, "From Poe to Valéry," in *Recognition* (see n. 6), 213–14.

68   Eliot, "From Poe to Valéry," in *Recognition* (see n. 6), 218.

69   Eliot, "From Poe to Valéry," in *Recognition* (see n. 6), 211.

70   Eliot, "From Poe to Valéry," in *Recognition* (see n. 6), 206. While dismissing Poe's work as lacking perfection in any detail, he had to admit that his poetry was as well known to as large a number of people as any poems ever written. T. O. Mabbott went much further, of course, and called "The Raven" "one of the very few works in English verse which all English-speaking people seem ready to discuss." See T. O. Mabbott, introduction to *Selected Poetry and Prose of Edgar Allan Poe* (New York: The Modern Library, 1951), xiv.

71   W. H. Auden remarked of Poe's popularity with the young, "Doomed to be used in school textbooks as a bait to interest the young in good literature, to be a respectable rival to the pulps." See Auden, introduction to *Poe: Selected*, in *Recognition* (see n. 6), 230. Paul C. Jones has observed that "we probably have to admit that these myths about Poe—however, offensive to scholars of his work—are in some way connected to the avid interest that our students bring to Poe's work, an appetite that they do not demonstrate for much of the literature of Poe's contemporaries." See Paul C. Jones, "Matthew Pearl: *The Poe Shadow*," *The Edgar Allan Poe Review* 7, no. 2 (2006): 79.

72   Jeffrey Weinstock has observed, "A peculiarly modern aspect of Poe's fiction is the way in which, through its persistent thematization of the impossibility of being alone, it anticipates contemporary discussions of the constitution of subjectivity." See Jeffrey Andrew Weinstock, "The Crowd Within: Poe's Impossible Aloneness," *The Edgar Allan Poe Review* 7, no. 2 (2006): 50.

183

Chapter Two

1   This story was repeated in the obituary notice for Dr. Creed Thomas, one of Poe's classmates, in the *Richmond Dispatch*, February 24, 1899, in Dwight Thomas and David K. Jackson, *The Poe Log: A Documentary Life of Edgar Allan Poe, 1809–1849* (Boston: G. K. Hall, 1987), 56–57.

2   Eugene L. Didier, *The Life and Poems of Edgar A. Poe, A New Memoir by E. L. Didier, and Additional Poems* (New York: W. J. Widdleton, 1877), 34.

3   Sara Sigourney Rice, ed., *Edgar Allan Poe: A Memorial Volume* (Baltimore: Turnbull Brothers, 1877), 37–42.

4   This story was mentioned by Poe in *The Southern Literary Messenger* in confirmation of the oral tradition, which circulated in Richmond and which continued to be handed down in the Stanard family. See Hervey Allen, *Israfel: The Life and Times of Edgar Allan Poe* (New York: Farrar & Rinehart, 1934), 87. Allen interviewed Robert Stanard's cousin in the preparation of his biography.

5   Rice, *Poe: A Memorial*, 40–41.

6   "Dr. Thomas Creed," *Richmond Dispatch*, February 24, 1899, in Thomas and Jackson, *The Poe Log*, 57.

7   Edgar Allan Poe, *Broadway Journal* 2 (July 19, 1845): 29. Quoted by Arthur Hobson Quinn in *Edgar Allan Poe: A Critical Biography* (New York: CooperSquare, 1969), 50.

8   Edward V. Valentine, "Conversation with Mrs. Shelton at Mr Smith's Corner 8th and Leigh Streets Nov. 19th 1875," in Thomas and Jackson, *The Poe Log*, 65.

9   John Ward Ostrom, Burton R. Pollin, and Jeffrey A. Savoye, eds., *The Collected Letters of Edgar Allan Poe, Volume I: 1824–1846*, 3rd ed. (Staten Island, N.Y.: Gordian Press, 2008), 1:100.

10   The land alone amounted to something over six thousand acres, in addition to which Allan also inherited commercial and residential rental property in Richmond. Hervey Allen has included the text of Allan's and Galt's wills in the appendix to *Israfel*, 687–98.

11   Hervey Allen, *Israfel*, 95n161; and Arthur Hobson Quinn, *Edgar Allan Poe: A Critical Biography* (New York: Cooper Square, 1969), 61, 113.

12   Most of Allan's papers, including correspondence with Edgar, have been preserved at the Valentine Museum in Richmond. See Edgar Allan Poe and Mary Newton Stanard, *Edgar Allan Poe Letters Till Now Unpublished: in the Valentine Museum, Richmond, Virginia* (Philadelphia: J. B. Lippincott, 1925).

13 Drinking has proven to be a gamble for the family. My grandfather's generation included three alcoholics among five children, plus several of his first cousins who were alcoholic. Only one child in the previous generation ever drank, and he was an alcoholic. My great-great-grandfather William Poe wrote to Edgar, warning him of the family curse. For an alcoholic, the warning comes too late once the drinking has begun.

14 Allan's family put out the story that Poe had a gambling debt of $2,500, but Quinn gives the story no credence since it was told years later by an executor and contingent beneficiary of Allan's estate. See Quinn, *Poe: A Critical Biography*, 109.

15 Quinn, *Poe: A Critical Biography*, 91. Quinn provides an extensive portion from the interview with Mrs. Shelton.

16 Interestingly, Jesus does the same thing in the Sermon on the Mount when he argues that the commandment not to kill involves much more than simply stopping the heart of another person. See Matt 5:21-26.

17 Quinn, *Poe: A Critical Biography*, 35.

18 Some years ago, I established the Edgar Allan Poe Young Writers' Conference as an educational program of the Poe Museum in Richmond. It was a great pleasure to spend a week each summer with budding young poets who wrote reams and reams of poetry about death and unrequited love.

19 Ostrom et al., *Collected Letters*, 1:26–27.

20 Edgar Allan Poe, *Al Aaraaf, Tamerlane, and Minor Poems* (Baltimore: Hatch & Dunning, 1829): 11. Poe refined this poem, and in its final version, his dreams would not come beneath the shrubbery, but beneath the tamarind tree.

21 Poe and Stanard, *Letters Unpublished*, 171.

22 Poe and Stanard, *Letters Unpublished*, 258.

23 Edgar Allan Poe, *Poems: Reproduced from the Edition of 1831* (New York: Columbia University Press, 1936), 28–29.

24 Thomas and Jackson, *The Poe Log*, 134.

25 Ostrom et al., *Collected Letters*, 1:84–85.

26 See Stephen Jay Gould, *Dinosaur in a Haystack* (New York: Harmony Books, 1995).

27 Duncan Faherty has interpreted all of the tales in *Tales of the Grotesque and Arabesque* as statements about the terrors of Jacksonian democracy that led to the great depression of 1837. See Duncan Faherty, "'A Certain Unity of Design': Edgar Allan Poe's *Tales of the Grotesque and Arabesque* and the Terrors of Jacksonian Democracy," *The Edgar Allan Poe Review* 6, no. 2 (2005): 4–21.

28 John Ward Ostrom, Burton R. Pollin, and Jeffrey A. Savoye, eds., *The Collected Letters of Edgar Allan Poe, Volume II: 1847–1849*, 3rd ed. (Staten Island, N.Y.: Gordian Press, 2008), 2:356.

29 Edgar Allan Poe, *Eureka, a Prose Poem by Edgar A. Poe* (New York: G. P. Putnam, 1848), 30.

30 Poe, *Eureka*, 117.

31 Poe, *Eureka*, 120.

32 Richard Harwell, *Lee An Abridgment in One Volume of the Four-Volume R. E. Lee by Douglas Southlall Freeman* (New York: Scribner, 1961), 5. Freeman served for many years on the board of the Poe Museum in Richmond, Virginia.

33 John. J. Moran, *A Defense of Edgar Allan Poe* (Washington: William F. Boogher, 1885), 18–21. Moran wrote his memoir at the request of Elmira Royster Shelton after J. E. Snodgrass became a temperance speaker and found Poe highly useful as an object lesson. As a result, it is difficult to sort out exactly what happened based on the recollections of these two players in Poe's death. Their remarks in letters immediately following Poe's death, therefore, are generally regarded as more reliable than their melodramatic accounts given years after Poe's death.

186   *Chapter Three*

1 Gerald Kennedy has contributed a valuable study of Poe's treatment of death. Kennedy's study brings a sense of rationality to a topic that had suffered from its overly melodramatic treatment in earlier decades. See J. Gerald Kennedy, *Poe, Death, and the Life of Writing* (New Haven: Yale University Press, 1987). Thirty years earlier, Edward Davidson remarked on the idea of death in Poe's writings, "However strange and exotic his treatment may be to us, it offered no bafflement to his contemporaries; he was for his age a historian whose reports of death might well be regarded as generally recognized and applicable to his time and as rather suggestive of his own special artistic aims and limitations." See Edward H. Davidson, *Poe: A Critical Study* (Cambridge, Mass.: Belknap Press, 1957), 106.

2 For an excellent study of how Poe's views on taste in decoration weave their way through his stories, see C. T. Walters, "'The Philosophy of Furniture' and Poe's Aesthetics of Fictional Design," *The Edgar Allan Poe Review* 5, no. 1 (2004): 57–79.

3 Edgar Allan Poe, "The Philosophy of Furniture," in *Poetry and Tales* (New York: Literary Classics of the United States, 1984), 382–83.

4 Poe, "Philosophy of Furniture," in *Poetry and Tales*, 383.

5 Poe, "Philosophy of Furniture," in *Poetry and Tales*, 384.

6   Poe, "Philosophy of Furniture," in *Poetry and Tales*, 385.

7   Charles May has argued that Poe's theory of the short story "derives from his earlier discussions of the relationship between aesthetic unity and the concept of plot and looks forward to the ultimate implications of pattern and design presented in *Eureka*." See Charles E. May, *Edgar Allan Poe: A Study of the Short Fiction*, Twayne's Studies in Short Fiction (Boston: Twayne, 1991), 14–15.

8   Edgar Allan Poe, "Nathaniel Hawthorne," *Essays and Reviews* (New York: The Library of America, 1984), 582. Despite Poe's distaste for allegory, some Poe critics insist that Poe's short stories should be read as allegories. Edward Davidson argued that Poe attacked allegory because he could not write allegory, yet his tales were all allegories nonetheless. See Davidson, *Poe: A Critical Study*, 182. After agreeing that modern literary criticism seemed to find symbolism were there were no symbols, Richard Wilbur insisted, "I think we can make no sense about him until we consider his work—and in particular his prose fiction—as deliberate and often brilliant allegory." See Richard Wilbur, "The House of Poe," in *The Recognition of Edgar Allan Poe*, ed. Eric W. Carlson (Ann Arbor: University of Michigan Press, 1970), 255. Jeremy Cagle summarizes the symbolic tradition of interpreting Poe's tales: "In Poe's tales, borders *are* erected and abstractions formalized in symbolic representation: underground tombs or underneath spaces such as basements become representations of the unconscious mind or irrationality; houses become heads with various rooms representing emotions, passions, or fears; ships or brigs become representations of human psyche with its various subdivisions (long before Freud, it should be noted)." See Jeremy Cagle, "Reading Well: Transcendental Hermeneutics in Poe's 'The Man of the Crowd,'" *The Edgar Allan Poe Review* 11, no. 2 (2008): 17. Tim Bryant argues that "The Man of the Crowd" is an allegory about the professional's relationship to a mass audience and particularly of Poe's own standing within the democratic stream of mid-nineteenth-century America. See Tim Bryant, "Poe's Aristocratic Decryptions: Professional Authority in Democratic America," *The Edgar Allan Poe Review* 9, no. 1 (2008): 25.

187

9   Poe, "Hawthorne," in *Essays and Reviews* (New York: The Library of America, 1984), 582–83. Richard Wilbur argued that Poe's stories must be read as allegories, even though Poe despised allegorical writing, because meaning belongs not on the surface as brute fact, "but below the surface as a dark undercurrent." See Wilbur, "House of Poe," in *Recognition* (see n. 8), 256. See also Liliane Weissberg, "In Search of Truth and Beauty: Allegory in 'Berenice' and 'The Domain of Arnheim,'" in *Poe and His Times*, ed. Benjamin Franklin Fisher IV

(Baltimore: The Edgar Allan Poe Society, 1990), 66–75. Weissburg argues effectively that Poe did not reject allegory so much as its misapplication and that he made use of it strategically.

10   Poe, "Hawthorne," in *Essays and Reviews*, 584.

11   Poe, "Hawthorne," in *Essays and Reviews*, 584.

12   Poe, "Hawthorne," in *Essays and Reviews*, 584.

13   Yvor Winters took strong exception to Poe's theory of poetry and mounted perhaps the longest sustained attack on Poe's ability as a writer ever attempted. In challenging Poe's view of the "long poem," he insisted that "we understand and remember *Paradise Lost* as a whole, seize the whole intention with intellect and with memory, and, plunging into any passage, experience that passage in relationship to the whole." His critique recapitulates much that others had said, but he systematically works his way through several of Poe's critical essays on writing; including, "The Poetic Principle," "The Philosophy of Composition," and "The Rationale of Verse." See Yvor Winters, "Edgar Allan Poe: A Crisis in the History of American Obscurantism," in *Recognition* (see n. 8), 178, 180. In his treatment of Winters, Scott Peeples observed, "Winters combines a new critical reverence for the text with a neo-humanist insistence on moral edification through literature." See Scott Peeples, *The Afterlife of Edgar Allan Poe* (Rochester, N.Y.: Camden House, 2007), 65. T. S. Eliot also took Poe to task over the idea of a "long poem" in "From Poe to Valéry," in *Recognition* (see n. 8), 211. Eliot, whose *Murder in the Cathedral* may be his finest work, wrote long poems and defended all that Poe identified as the defect of long poems. W. H. Auden, on the other hand, defended Poe as a man of his time: "Poe was forced to attack all long poems on principle, to be unfair, for example, to *Paradise Lost* or *An Essay on Criticism*, in order to shake the preconceived notions of poets and public that to be important a poet must write long poems and give bardic advice." See W. H. Auden, introduction to *Edgar Allan Poe: Selected Prose and Poetry*, in *Recognition* (see n. 8), 227.

14   Poe, "Hawthorne," in *Essays and Reviews*, 585.

15   Poe, "Hawthorne," in *Essays and Reviews*, 585.

16   Henri Justin has argued that Arthur Conan Doyle became the master of the detective story because he returned to the short story form that Poe advocated. See Henri Justin, "The Paradoxes of Poe's Reception in France," *The Edgar Allan Poe Review* 11, no. 1 (2010): 84.

17   Poe, "Hawthorne," *Essays and Reviews*, 572.

18   Poe, "Hawthorne," in *Essays and Reviews*, 586.

19   Poe, "Hawthorne," in *Essays and Reviews*, 586. Critics like Yvor Winters completely misunderstood Poe's concern for the creation of an

effect. Winters went so far us to conclude that Poe meant that "the tale of effect" was a genre of story like the mystery story or the humorous tale. See Winters, "Poe: A Crisis," in *Recognition* (see n. 8), 196. Poe meant that every story that could be called a good story succeeded as such precisely because it created the effect toward which it aimed. If a story succeeded in conveying Truth, it did so by creating its desired effect, rather than by preaching a sermon. From another perspective, Ruijuan Hao has declared, "The construction of 'effect' in unity and the 'horror of the soul' have become the cornerstone of the Chinese writing philosophy" in the last twenty years. See Ruijuan Hao, "Edgar Allan Poe in Contemporary China," *The Edgar Allan Poe Review* 10, no. 3 (2009): 118–19.

20 After dismissing social allegory or hoax as the key to understanding "King Pest," Elvira Osipova concluded that it must be understood as Poe's use of "unusual and morbid images bound to produce a strong effect on the reader rather than having the story insinuate a 'moral precept.'" See Elvira Osipova, "Aesthetic Effects of 'King Pest' and 'The Masque of the Red Death,'" *The Edgar Allan Poe Review* 8, no. 2 (2007): 28.

21 Edgar Allan Poe, "The Philosophy of Composition," in *Essays and Reviews* (New York: The Library of America, 1984), 16.

22 Dennis Pahl has argued that "the aesthetic pleasure Poe associates with 'the beautiful' cannot help but correspond with the Burkean sublime" in "Poe's Sublimity: The Role of Burkean Aesthetics," *The Edgar Allan Poe Review* 7, no. 2 (2006): 33. In order to reach this conclusion, however, Pahl must first conclude that "the perceiving subject, forever alienated, is left without chance of moving to a state of Reason or of preserving a unified identity" (31). Poe's understanding of Beauty, however, seems to depend upon the unity of body and mind, reason and imagination, character and senses, as he moves toward the conclusions of *Eureka*.

23 Allen Tate commended Poe for recognizing "that poetry must be centered in the disciplined sense-perception which he inadequately calls taste; and he thus quite rightly opposes the 'heresy of the didactic' and the 'mathematical reasoning of the schools.'" See Allen Tate, "The Angelic Imagination," in *Recognition* (see n. 8), 247.

24 This paragraph may seem harsh, irresponsible, or ignorant by many; nonetheless, poetry was a popular art form at the beginning of the twentieth century and at the end of the century it was not. It went from being a common form of entertainment, as it is in every culture, to being a rare literary form appreciated and enjoyed by a tiny elite. Though poetry had not died to some, it had died to the culture and

189

no longer represented an art form of the culture. Allegory died to the culture four hundred years ago. Whether poetry can experience a revival, as allegory did not, is yet to be seen.

25   Poe, "Philosophy of Composition," in *Essays and Reviews*, 15. Winters insisted that Poe had little or no taste himself, largely because Winters can perceive no "paraphraseable theme" in Poe's writings. See Winters, "Poe: A Crisis," in *Recognition* (see n. 8), 197–98. This book pursues some of the themes that cut across Poe's works, and others would identify more, such as the frailty of humanity, the challenges of modern urban life, the human body, the human mind, and more.

26   Poe, "Philosophy of Composition," in *Essays and Reviews*, 15.

27   Poe, "Philosophy of Composition," in *Essays and Reviews*, 15.

28   Poe, "Philosophy of Composition," in *Essays and Reviews*, 16.

29   Winters and many of Poe's critics misunderstood him at some points in his estimation of Beauty, but at other points they have simply disagreed. At a certain level, Winters both misunderstood and disagreed, as he argued, "Poe appears never to have grasped the simple and traditional distinction between matter (truth) and manner (beauty); he does not see that beauty is a quality of style instead of its subject-matter, that it is merely the most complete communication possible, through connotation as well as denotation, of the poet's personal realization of a moral (or human) truth, whether the truth be of very great importance or very little, a truth that must be understood in conceptual terms, regardless of whether the poem ultimately embodies it in form of description, of narration, or of exposition." See Winters, "Poe: A Crisis," in *Recognition* (see n. 8), 182.

30   Poe, "Philosophy of Composition," in *Essays and Reviews*, 16.

31   Rudolf Otto, *The Idea of the Holy*, trans. John W. Harvey (New York: Oxford University Press, 1979). Otto argued that the numenal experience may be described as *mysterium, tremendum, et fascinans*, that mysterious experience that presents itself powerfully yet fascinates and attracts.

32   This feature of art separates the World War II army training film from art. The evangelistic films produced by the Billy Graham Evangelistic Association in the 1960s and early 1970s suffered from the same problem. The art form was asked to perform a task it was ill suited to perform.

33   Poe, "Philosophy of Composition," in *Essays and Reviews*, 17.

34   Poe, "Philosophy of Composition," in *Essays and Reviews*, 17.

35   Poe, "Philosophy of Composition," in *Essays and Reviews*, 18.

36   Poe, "Philosophy of Composition," in *Essays and Reviews*, 19.

37   No one represents this confusion better than Yvor Winters. In this

famous passage about the topic of "The Raven," Poe has not claimed that the death of a beautiful woman is a beautiful subject, but that the fact of the woman's beauty heightens the sense of sadness. Yet, Winter concludes that Poe has said, "beauty is the subject of poetry." See Winters, "Poe: A Crisis," in *Recognition* (see n. 8), 187. Winters also claimed that Poe had said, "Truth is not poetry; truth should therefore be eliminated from poetry, in the interests of a purer poetry." See Winters, "Poe: A Crisis," in *Recognition* (see n. 8), 183. His long denunciation of Poe's poetry continues in this vein as he assumed that Poe's commitment to Beauty as the standard for judging the quality of a poem precluded Poe from allowing content other than Beauty. After quoting Poe's discussion of how the musical quality of true poetry has a powerful impact on people, Winters again asserted, "Briefly, Poe implies something like this: the proper subject-matter of poetry is Beauty." See Winters, "Poe: A Crisis," in *Recognition* (see n. 8), 186.

38   Pat Conroy, *My Reading Life* (New York: Nan A. Talese/Doubleday, 2010), 282.

39   R. H. Stoddard, "Oblivion," *The Union Magazine*, 2 (1848): 238.

40   Gerald Kennedy contrasted Poe's view of death with that of Bryant: "Those still influenced by a deistic or pantheistic saw death as Bryant had painted in 'Thanatopsis': a beatific return to the bosom of nature, that 'mighty sepulchre' of humanity." See Kennedy, "Phantasms of Death," in *The Tales of Poe*, ed. Harold Bloom (New York: Chelsea House, 1987), 116.

41   Poe, "Philosophy of Composition," in *Essays and Reviews*, 20.

42   Poe, "Philosophy of Composition," in *Essays and Reviews*, 21.

43   Poe, "Philosophy of Composition," in *Essays and Reviews*, 21.

44   W. H. Auden attributed Poe's faults as a poet to his attempt at originality. Auden explained, "His difficulty as a poet was that he was interested in too many poetic problems and experiments at once for the time he had to give to them." See Auden, introduction to *Poe: Selected*, in *Recognition* (see n. 8), 224.

45   Poe, "Philosophy of Composition," in *Essays and Reviews*, 25.

46   Yvor Winters emphatically rejected Poe's understanding of rhythm and meter. He argued, "Read three times, his rhythms disgust, because they are untrained and insensitive and have no individual life within their surprising mechanical frames." See Winters, "Poe: A Crisis," in *Recognition* (see n. 8), 189. Rather than beautiful and musical, Winters regarded Poe's poetry as "rigid" and "mechanical." Winters even refused to discuss "The Raven" in his lengthy essay because he regarded its meter as "so thoroughly bad" that it did not deserve consideration. Surely, the striking feature of the meter and rhythm of

"The Raven," however, lies in its unforced flow. The consistency of its beat continue within the syntax of normal English sentence structure without the awkward rearrangement of normal word order to which most poets resort in order to make the meter work. Except for "Let me see, then, what thereat is," Poe's words flow like prose.

47 Poe, "The Rationale of Verse," in *Essays and Reviews*, 26.

48 Poe, "The Rationale of Verse," in *Essays and Reviews*, 33.

49 Poe, "The Rationale of Verse," in *Essays and Reviews*, 34

50 Huxley argued that Poe's attention to his meters and rhythms was as vulgar as a man wearing "diamond rings on every finger." Of course perfect attention to meter, rhythm, and rhyme can create a musical quality, Huxley acknowledged, but it is too musical and too poetic. Huxley preferred a poem driven by "meaning" that did not succeed so much at poetry. See Aldous Huxley, "Vulgarity in Literature," in *Recognition* (see n. 8), 161–64.

51 Poe, "The Rationale of Verse," in *Essays and Reviews*, 34.

52 Poe, "The Rationale of Verse," in *Essays and Reviews*, 29–31, 36.

53 Poe, "The Rationale of Verse," in *Essays and Reviews*, 37.

54 Poe, "The Rationale of Verse," in *Essays and Reviews*, 39.

55 Poe, "The Rationale of Verse," in *Essays and Reviews*, 44. W. H. Auden applauded Poe because he "put so much energy and insight into trying to make his contemporary poets take their craft seriously, know what they were doing prosodically, and avoid faults of slovenly diction and inappropriate imagery that can be avoided by vigilance and hard work." See Auden, introduction to *Poe: Selected*, in *Recognition* (see n. 8), 227.

56 In his defense of Poe's poetry, George Saintsbury of the University of Edinburgh concluded, "A poet of the first order must be able to satisfy both the ears and the eyes of the mind; and beyond, though through, this satisfaction he must give the indefinable but by the right recipients unmistakable poetic 'effluence,' 'emanation,' or whatever you like to call it. For me and for my house Poe does this." See George E. B. Saintsbury, "Edgar Allan Poe," in *Recognition* (see n. 8), 159.

57 Poe, "The Rationale of Verse," in *Essays and Reviews* (see n. 8), 44.

58 Poe, "The Rationale of Verse," in *Essays and Reviews*, 47.

59 Poe, "The Rationale of Verse," in *Essays and Reviews*, 47.

60 W. H. Auden found fault with Poe's meter, a difficulty resulting in artificiality. He argued, "Here it is the meter alone and nothing in the speaker or the situation which is responsible for the redundant alternatives of 'stopped or stayed he' and 'lord or lady.'" See Auden, introduction to *Poe: Selected*, in *Recognition* (see n. 8), 225. Auden supposes that stopping and staying represent the same action, but

they do not. A car may stop at a traffic light before moving on, but if it stays, it must park. I will not bore the reader with the differences between a man and a woman. Dennis Eddings has argued that the faults in "The Raven" do not come from Poe, but from the narrator. In other words, Poe has intentionally violated his own principles in order to be faithful to the state of mind of the narrator in the poem, just as we find him doing with the form and diction of characters in his humorous tales. See Dennis W. Eddings, "Theme and Parody in 'The Raven,'" in *Poe and His Times* (see n. 9), 209–17.

61 Poe, "The Rationale of Verse," in *Essays and Reviews*, 50.

62 Poe, "The Rationale of Verse," in *Essays and Reviews*, 56.

63 Poe, "The Rationale of Verse," in *Essays and Reviews*, 63–64.

64 Poe, "The Mystery of Marie Rogêt," in *Poetry and Tales*, 523–24.

65 Poe, "The Domain of Arnheim," in *Poetry and Tales*, 858.

66 Poe, "The Domain of Arnheim," in *Poetry and Tales*, 859. Laura Saltz has observed of "Domain of Arnheim," "Although Poe does not explain why landscape gardening is a 'peculiar' medium for the expression of the poetic sentiment, the reason is implicit in his view that poetic sentiment is manifested in the ethereal and immaterial." See Laura Saltz, "'Eyes which Behold': Poe's 'Domain of Arnheim' and the Science of Vision," *The Edgar Allan Poe Review* 7, no. 1 (2006): 4.

67 Poe, "The Domain of Arnheim," in *Poetry and Tales*, 859.

68 Poe, "The Domain of Arnheim," in *Poetry and Tales*, 863.

69 Poe, "The Fall of the House of Usher," in *Poetry and Tales*, 317–18.

70 Poe, "The Domain of Arnheim," in *Poetry and Tales*, 863.

71 First published in "Gods," *Proceedings of the Aristotelian Society* (London, 1944–1945) and reprinted many times in philosophical texts since then. Cited in John Hick, *Philosophy of Religion*, 2nd ed. (Englewood Cliffs, N.J.: Prentice-Hall, 1973), 86.

72 Poe, "William Wilson," in *Poetry and Tales*, 338.

73 Poe, "The Poetic Principle," in *Essays and Reviews*, 78–79.

74 Poe, "The Poetic Principle," in *Essays and Reviews*, 76.

75 Poe, "The Poetic Principle," in *Essays and Reviews*, 76.

76 Poe, "The Poetic Principle," in *Essays and Reviews*, 77.

77 Poe, "The Poetic Principle," in *Essays and Reviews*, 77.

78 Poe, "The Poetic Principle," in *Essays and Reviews*, 77.

79 Poe, "The Poetic Principle," in *Essays and Reviews*, 80.

80 The Honorable Benjamin Warthen, member of the bar in the Commonwealth of Virginia and sometime city councilman of Richmond, has served on the board of trustees for the Poe Museum for many years and has played a key role in the continuing recognition of Edgar Allan Poe at his alma mater, the University of Virginia.

81 Edward Davidson argued, "The poem is, therefore, not about *a* woman, Mrs. Stanard, Mrs. Allan, nor even Helen of Troy. Its subject is the way the mind can move toward the past and, in some such symbol as the indefinable beauty of woman, is able to comprehend a world and culture long vanished from this earth." See Davidson, *Poe: A Critical Study*, 33. Surely, the poem does comprehend a world and culture long vanished from this earth, but it is not *about* the mind's ability to do such a thing.

82 Richard Wilbur argued that Poe's understanding of Beauty related to his understanding of God: "Not to worship beauty, not to regard poetic knowledge as divine, would be to turn one's back on God and fall from grace." See Wilbur, "House of Poe," in *Recognition* (see n. 8), 258.

83 Edgar Allan Poe, "[review of *Ballads and Other Poems*. By Henry Wadsworth Longfellow. Author of "Voices of the Night," "Hyperion," &c. Second Edition. John Owen: Cambridge]," in *Essays and Reviews*, 685–86.

Chapter Four

1 Gerald Kennedy has observed of the death of a beautiful woman in Poe's poetry, "Although grief and mourning are necessary processes of accommodation to death, Poe's poems suggest that because the male protagonist has staked his entire being on the love of a beautiful woman, her absence leaves him not only bereaved but prostrated by melancholy." See J. Gerald Kennedy, "Poe, 'Ligeia,' and the Problem of Dying Women," *New Essays on Poe's Major Tales*, ed. Kenneth Silverman (New York: Cambridge University Press, 1993), 117.

2 Stephen Post identifies no less than eight Greek words for Love: *eunoia, physike, xenike, eroike, eros, philia, storge*, and *agape* in *Unlimited Love: Altruism, Compassion, and Service* (Philadelphia: Templeton Foundation Press, 2003), 17. Thomas Jay Oord only identifies *eros, philia*, and *agape* in *Science of Love* (Radnor, Pa.: Templeton Foundation Press, 2004), 7–8. C. S. Lewis argued for *storge, philia, eros*, and *agape* in *The Four Loves* (London: Geoffrey Bles, 1960), 42, 69–70, 106, 150–53.

3 Edgar Allan Poe, "To My Mother," in *Poetry and Tales* (New York: Literary Classics of the United States, 1984), 101–2.

4 Kopley explores the source material behind the Dupin stories to develop this view in a highly convincing manner. See Richard Kopley, *Edgar Allan Poe and the Dupin Mysteries* (New York: Palgrave Macmillan, 2008), 76–85.

5   Poe, "The Gold-Bug," in *Poetry and Tales*, 562.
6   Poe, "Landor's Cottage," in *Poetry and Tales*, 896.
7   Poe, "Instinct vs. Reason—A Black Cat," in *Poetry and Tales*, 372.
8   Poe, "The Black Cat," in *Poetry and Tales*, 597.
9   Poe, "Metzengerstein," in *Poetry and Tales*, 140.
10 Poe, "Ligeia," in *Poetry and Tales*, 270. In the face of the Abolitionist charge that slaveholders had children by their slaves that they then sold, Poe pointed out the common practice in the North as well as the South, which he regarded as "the infinitely worse crime of making matrimonial merchandise—or even less legitimate merchandise—of one's daughter." See Edgar Allan Poe, *Essays and Reviews* (New York: The Library of America, 1984), 763.
11 Lord Peter Wimsey, the aristocratic detective in Dorothy L. Sayers' stories, shared an interest in collecting rare books.
12 Poe, "The Murders in the Rue Morgue," in *Poetry and Tales*, 400.
13 Poe, "The Murders in the Rue Morgue," in *Poetry and Tales*, 401.
14 Poe, "The Murders in the Rue Morgue," in *Poetry and Tales*, 401.
15 Poe, "The Purloined Letter," in *Poetry and Tales*, 680.
16 Poe, "The Gold-Bug," in *Poetry and Tales*, 560.
17 Poe, "The Spectacles," in *Poetry and Tales*, 619.
18 Poe, "The Fall of the House of Usher," in *Poetry and Tales*, 619.
19 Poe, "The Cask of Amontillado," in *Poetry and Tales*, 848, 849.
20 Poe, "The Cask of Amontillado," in *Poetry and Tales*, 848.
21 Poe, "William Wilson," in *Poetry and Tales*, 341.
22 Poe, "William Wilson," in *Poetry and Tales*, 342.
23 Quinn, *Poe: A Critical Biography*, 196.
24 Quinn, *Poe: A Critical Biography*, 196.
25 Quinn, *Poe: A Critical Biography*, 196–97.
26 William Gowan quoted in Quinn, *Poe: A Critical Biography*, 267.
27 Quinn, *Poe: A Critical Biography*, 347.
28 Edward Davidson has argued, "As in love and life, the woman could be appealed to and wooed all over again in death. Poe's poems and tales are ritual incantations to the erotically desirable young woman who is forever white, aloof, reserved, virginal, bridal, whether she lies on the wedding bed or the funeral bier." See Edward H. Davidson, *Poe: A Critical Study* (Cambridge, Mass.: Belknap Press, 1957), 111. Perhaps Davidson stretches the point of the Romantics a bit far, because Poe was powerfully aware that death poses a real barrier to a romantic relationship.
29 Poe, "Stanzas," in *Poetry and Tales*, 35.
30 Poe, "Imitation," in *Poetry and Tales*, 34.

31 Poe, "Dreams," in *Poetry and Tales*, 31.

32 Poe, "Tamerlane," in *Poetry and Tales*, 27.

33 Poe, "Tamerlane," in *Poetry and Tales*, 26.

34 Poe, "The Happiest Day," in *Poetry and Tales*, 36.

35 Poe, "The Lake—To—," in *Poetry and Tales*, 37.

36 Edward Davidson made a great deal over Poe's adolescent love poetry
    and carries the idea throughout all of Poe's works, interpreting Poe as
    someone who regarded himself as his own God: "The mood of a poet
    who is his own God and prophet marks one salient feature of Poe and
    of nearly all his poetry: Poe feels himself the scapegoat, the innocent
    wronged one, the outcast. If there really is a God, He is on *their* side;
    therefore, the poet must be his own god or else find another one."
    See Davidson, *Poe: A Critical Study*, 13. Though Davidson gives more
    attention to *Eureka* than most critics, he tends to read all of Poe's
    works as though they were written *after* Poe wrote *Eureka* in 1848,
    rather than recognizing how themes and topics touched on in his
    earlier work formed part of the path that eventually led to *Eureka*.

37 Poe, introduction to *Poetry and Tales*, 55.

38 Gerald Kennedy has argued that Poe hedged his bet by pursuing mul-
    tiple women at once. See Kennedy, "Poe, 'Ligeia,' and the Problem of
    Dying Women," in *New Essays* (see n. 1), 117–18.

196 39 Glen A. Omans argues concerning the place of the beautiful woman
     in Poe's work, "The woman, however, must be seen as symbol rather
     than as human being—not as a lover but as a revelation in material
     form of ideal beauty." See Glen A. Omans, "Poe and Washington
     Allston: Visionary Kin," in *Poe and His Times*, ed. Benjamin Franklin
     Fisher IV (Baltimore: The Edgar Allan Poe Society, 1990), 8.

40 Poe, "Eleonora," in *Poetry and Tales*, 470.

41 Benjamin Fisher has argued that "Eleonora" is a tale of madness in
    which the references to madness do not mean an impassioned, roman-
    tic state, but actual mental illness. Fisher argues, "[The narrator's]
    outspoken direction of our attention to madness is couched in terms
    that place the burden of deciding for or against his madness with us."
    See Fisher, "'Eleonora': Poe and Madness," in *Poe and His Times* (see
    n. 39), 186.

42 Poe, "Eleonora," in *Poetry and Tales*, 473.

43 Poe, "Eleonora," in *Poetry and Tales*, 469.

44 Charles May suggests that the only explanation for Eleonora's forgive-
    ness "is that Eleonora's whispered exoneration of his transgression
    suggests that the 'Spirit of Love' transcends any individual manifesta-
    tion of love—an idealization that indeed can only be made known to
    the narrator in Heaven, as it was made known to Eleonora herself

after her death." See Charles E. May, *Edgar Allan Poe: A Study of the Short Fiction,* Twayne's Studies in Short Fiction (Boston, Mass.: Twayne, 1991), 67–68.

45 Poe, "The Spectacles," in *Poetry and Tales,* 621.
46 Poe, "The Domain of Arnheim," in *Poetry and Tales,* 856.
47 Poe, "The Domain of Arnheim," in *Poetry and Tales,* 864.
48 Liliane Weissberg reads the story as an allegorical version of "Berenice," in which the landscape is laid out before Ellison for his use, as a woman offers herself or perhaps is taken. See Liliane Weissberg, "In Search of Truth and Beauty: Allegory in 'Berenice' and 'The Domain of Arnheim,'" in *Poe and His Times* (see n. 39), 72.
49 Poe, "Landor's Cottage," in *Poetry and Tales,* 896.
50 Gerald Kennedy has noted this contrast: "Poe's personal dependence on woman's love and his poetic evocations of the beloved's blissful presence or agonizing absence stand in contrast to the sheer malevolence in his prose versions of a beautiful woman's death." See Kennedy, "Problem of Dying Women," in *New Essays* (see n. 1), 118.
51 Poe, "The Black Cat," in *Poetry and Tales,* 597.
52 Poe, "Tamerlane," in *Poetry and Tales,* 24.
53 Allen Tate, "Our Cousin, Mr. Poe," 1212.
54 Poe, "Berenice," in *Poetry and Tales,* 229.
55 Poe, "The Murders in the Rue Morgue," in *Poetry and Tales,* 412.
56 Joan Dayan observes of the tales by Poe that treat corrupted love, "While using his narrator to disincarnate the lady (reducing her either to teeth in 'Berenice' or to no more than eyes in 'Ligeia' or to the syllables of the name in 'Morella'), Poe puts his reader in the position of dismantling the prose connected with her." See Joan Dayan, "Poe, Locke and Kant," in *Poe and His Times* (see n. 39), 43.
57 Poe, "Morella," in *Poetry and Tales,* 235.
58 Poe, "Ligeia," in *Poetry and Tales,* 262.
59 Elisabete Lopes has suggested that the eyes of Ligeia represent both heightened sexuality and death. See Elisabete Lopes, "Unburying the Wife: A Reflection Upon the Female Uncanny in Poe's 'Ligeia,'" *The Edgar Allan Poe Review* 11, no. 1 (2010): 42.
60 Poe, "Ligeia," in *Poetry and Tales,* 267.
61 Poe, "Ligeia," in *Poetry and Tales,* 272.
62 Jerry Herndon reminds us of an interpretive tradition that presents an even stronger offense against Love—that the narrator has murdered his second wife. See Jerry A. Herndon, "Poe's 'Ligeia': Debts to Irving and Emerson," in *Poe and His Times* (see n. 39), 113. Herndon goes on to argue that "Ligeia" is a satirical portrait of Emerson's transcendentalism.

197

Chapter Five

1   Strong, *American Poets and Their Theology* (Philadelphia: Griffith & Rowland Press, 1916), 161.

2   W. H. Davenport Adams, *Wrecked Lives; or Men Who Have Failed* (London: Society for Promoting Christian Knowledge, 1880), 305.

3   Adams, *Wrecked Lives*, 162.

4   William Mentzel Forrest, *Biblical Allusions in Poe* (New York: Macmillan, 1928), 151–96. In the appendix Forrest provides a 45-page table that lists each Poe work, its location in Harrison's edition of Poe's works, a portion of the biblical phrase Poe quotes, and the biblical reference by book, chapter, and verse.

5   Forrest, *Biblical Allusions in Poe*, 147.

6   Richard Kopley discusses Poe's use of the Bible in *Pym* and "Ragged Mountains" in "Poe's *Pym*-esque 'A Tale of the Ragged Mountains,'" in *Poe and His Times*, ed. Benjamin Franklin Fisher IV (Baltimore: The Edgar Allan Poe Society, 1990), 172–74.

7   Forrest, *Biblical Allusions in Poe*, 78.

8   David Halliburton argues that Poe has tried "to get God, or a god-figure, or a godly power, into his stories." See David Halliburton, "The Tales," in *Critical Essays on Edgar Allan Poe*, ed. Eric W. Carlson (Boston: G. K. Hall, 1987), 136. While Halliburton and Robert Daniel would see Dupin as a god created by Poe, he seems to be more the mystic who "sees." While this reading is not as controversial as Halliburton's reading, it corresponds more to Poe's understanding of humans and God, and the faculty of imagination. As the creator of a rational universe, God is already in Poe's stories before he puts pen to paper. The notion of justice is his rational base.

9   T. O. Mabbott argued that Poe rejected the didactic theories of Wordsworth not because of some aversion to morality, but because he believed "sensible people were not much influenced by fictions: 'Why should a man be deterred from murder because a fictional George Barnwell was hanged for killing a fictional uncle?'" On the other hand, Mabbott insisted that Poe wrote moral stories rather than stories that attempted to teach morality. See T. O. Mabbott, introduction to *Selected Poetry and Prose of Edgar Allan Poe* (New York: The Modern Library, 1951), xiii.

10 The finest study of Poe's creation of the mystery story must surely be the treatment by Richard Kopley. Kopley becomes Dupin as he follows every lead and discovers the rich background out of which Poe created his mysteries in order to give them a compelling air of realism. See Richard Kopley, *Edgar Allan Poe and the Dupin Mysteries* (New

York: Palgrave Macmillan, 2008). For an intriguing discussion of the interplay between Poe and Baudelaire that influenced the development of crime fiction, see Kathryn Oliver Mills, "Painting Modern Life: Baudelaire and Crime Fiction," *Nineteenth Century Studies* 22 (2008): 31–40.

11   T. S. Eliot observed of the proximity of horror to mystery, "Conan Doyle owes much to Poe, and not merely to Monsieur Dupin of *The Murders in the Rue Morgue*. Sherlock Holmes was deceiving Watson when he told him that he had bought his Stradivarius violin for a few shillings at a second-hand shop in the Tottenham Court Road. He found that violin in the ruins of the house of Usher." See T. S. Eliot, "From Poe to Valéry," in *The Recognition of Edgar Allan Poe*, ed. Eric W. Carlson (Ann Arbor: University of Michigan Press, 1970), 208.

12   Poe, "How to Write a Blackwood Article," in *Poetry and Tales* (New York: Literary Classics of the United States, 1984), 281.

13   Bruce Weiner has argued that Poe actually had a personal attraction to the sensational tale of horror that he called a Blackwood tale, for it allowed him to explore states of abnormal psychology. See Bruce I. Weiner, "Poe and the *Blackwood's* Tale of Sensation," in *Poe and His Times* (see n. 6), 43–65.

14   Stanton Garner stresses that as he developed the mystery story, Poe came to understand that in addition to the calculating and the analytic aspects of the mind, the imagination operates as a combining capacity. See Stanton Garner, "Poe's 'Double Dupin,'" in *Poe and His Times* (see n. 6), 141. In contrast to Poe's discussion of imagination that became so important to him in *Eureka*, Paul Grimstad sought to ground Dupin's method in the logic theories of Charles S. Peirce (b. 1839). See Paul Grimstad, "C. Auguste Dupin and Charles S. Peirce: An Abductive Affinity," *The Edgar Allan Poe Review* 6, no. 2 (2005): 22–30.

15   Dorothy L. Sayers and Jill Paton Walsh, *Thrones, Dominations* (New York: St. Martin's Press, 1998), 151.

16   Margarette Driscoll, "Murders That Paint a Picture of Our Times," *The Sunday Times*, London, September 12, 2004, 5.

17   I am indebted to Mary Ellen Whitten Poe for calling this bit of Nazi history to my attention. See "Sidelights of the War," *Time* 17, no. 9 (1941), 29.

18   René van Slooten has led an international team of scientists in the creation of a website devoted to *Eureka*. The site contains the text of *Eureka* with heavy annotations together with articles about the essay. See The Eureka Project, "The Eureka Project: A Place Devoted to Edgar Allan Poe's Masterpiece Eureka," http://www.poe-eureka.com.

19 Susan Jaffe Tane, *Nevermore: The Edgar Allan Poe Collection of Susan Jaffe Tane* (Ithaca, N.Y.: Cornell University Library, 2006), 68.

20 Edgar Allan Poe, "A Few Words on Secret Writing," *Graham's Magazine* 19, no. 1 (1841): 34.

21 Poe, "A Few Words on Secret Writing," 33.

22 Poe, "A Few Words on Secret Writing," 34.

23 Poe, "The Murders in the Rue Morgue," in *Poetry and Tales*, 419.

24 Poe, "The Murders in the Rue Morgue," in *Poetry and Tales*, 424.

25 Dorothy L. Sayers, ed., *The Omnibus of Crime* (New York: Payson and Clarke, 1929), 9–10.

26 Benjamin Fisher has catalogued some of these Poe references in "Poe and Detection [Again]," *The Edgar Allan Poe Review* 1, no. 1 (2000): 17–23. Fisher had written earlier pieces for the Poe Studies Association newsletter [*PSA Newsletter* 24, no. 1, pp. 4–7; 24, no. 2, pp. 3–6].

27 Sayers, *Omnibus of Crime*, 17.

28 In his creation of the mystery story, Poe first invented and then reinvented this form, according to John Gruesser in his analysis of the three Dupin stories. See John Gruesser, "Never Bet the Detective (or His Creator) Your Head: Character Rivalry, Authorial Sleight of Hand, and Generic Fluidity in Detective Fiction," *The Edgar Allan Poe Review* 9, no. 1 (2008): 5.

29 Richard Kopley has identified a number of intriguing elements in Poe's mystery stories for which he has traced an original source through a careful examination of the newspapers Poe would have read. For instance, an orangutan had been on exhibit in Philadelphia and created quite a sensation just prior to the writing of "The Murders in the Rue Morgue." See Kopley, *Edgar Allan Poe and the Dupin Mysteries*, 3, 32. In contrast to Kopley's discoveries of Poe's sources through methodical research, William Carlos Williams sought some explanation for the image of the ape in Poe's subconscious. See William Carlos Williams, "Edgar Allan Poe," in *Recognition* (see n. 11), 139. As Kopley discovered, Poe actually chose the ape quite intentionally because he knew what effect the ape would have upon the public from actual experience. Given Poe's continually repeated aim in writing to create an effect upon his audience, the argument of Hop Frog for orangutan costumes is all the more compelling: "Your majesty cannot conceive of the *effect* produced."

30 Sayers, *Omnibus of Crime*, 17. In her second assertion, Sayers' choice of words comes from Dupin who remarked, "It appears to me that this mystery is considered insoluble, for the very reason which should cause it to be regarded as easy of solution—I mean for the *outré*

character of its features." See Poe, "The Murders in the Rue Morgue," in *Poetry and Tales*, 414.

31 Poe, "The Murders in the Rue Morgue," in *Poetry and Tales*, 417. Dupin also remarks "that all apparent impossibilities *must* be proved to be not such in reality" (418).

32 Poe, "The Murders in the Rue Morgue," in *Poetry and Tales*, 417.

33 The case of Mary Rogers and Poe's interest in justice on her behalf has been the subject of several important books, including Daniel Stashower's *The Beautiful Cigar Girl: Mary Rogers, Edgar Allan Poe, and the Invention of Murder* (New York: Dutton, 2006), which won the coveted Edgar Award; and Raymond Paul, *Who Murdered Mary Rogers?* (Englewood Cliffs, N.J.: Prentice-Hall, 1971).

34 Stanton Garner points out that though Poe is not usually thought of as a moralist, Dupin's victory "is won on specifically moral grounds." See Garner, "Poe's 'Double Dupin,'" in *Poe and His Times* (see n. 6), 141.

35 For a helpful discussion of the origin and extent of Poe's influence on Doyle, see Beatriz González-Moreno, "Sir Arthur Conan Doyle and the Hauntings of 'American Blood-Curdler,'" *The Edgar Allan Poe Review* 10, no. 2 (2009): 25–35.

36 Edward Davidson suggested that Poe had abandoned all social and religious constraints in his tales as he set himself up as his own god and made his characters godlike. Davidson argues that when punishment comes, it does not come "from a church, a law, or even from society: it comes from some inner compulsion of the evil-doer himself who suffers from what Poe otherwise terms 'perversity': he must do evil, and yet he wants to be punished and to suffer." See Edward H. Davidson, *Poe: A Critical Study* (Cambridge, Mass.: Belknap Press, 1957), 189. This conclusion relates to Davidson's insistence on reading Poe's tales as allegory and essentially as tales about Poe. Instead, we see Poe exploring the presence of justice in the universe, in spite of the failure of church and society to exercise it. He has constructed the classic moral argument for the existence of God, similar to that proposed by C. S. Lewis in *Mere Christianity*, but he has not done it allegorically or didactically, but through a narrative that compels the reader to agree, "This is wrong; this man must be punished."

37 James W. Gargano suggests that "certain comments by the narrator imply that his behavior can perhaps be reduced to ordinary psychological and moral laws." See James W. Gargano, "'The Black Cat': Perverseness Reconsidered," *Twentieth Century Interpretations of Poe's Tales*, ed. William L. Howarth (Englewood Cliffs, N.J.: Prentice-Hall, 1971), 87.

38 Alexander Hammond proposes that Poe also embedded this story with clues to a grand geometrical puzzle that readers have long overlooked. See Alexander Hammond, "Subverting Interpretation: Poe's Geometry in 'The Pit and the Pendulum,'" *The Edgar Allan Poe Review* 9, no. 2 (2008): 5–16.

39 Poe, "William Wilson," in *Poetry and Tales*, 357.

40 Choosing a Jungian reading of the text, D. J. Moores offers a helpful overview of the major psychological readings. See D. J. Moores, "'Oh Gigantic Paradox': Poe's 'William Wilson' and the Jungian Self," *The Edgar Allan Poe Review* 7, no. 1 (2006): 31–48.

41 In my private collection I have a copy of the *Essex Register* of Salem, Massachusetts, from February 26, 1827, with the entire front page devoted to the story. William Gilmore Simms wrote a two-volume novel, which he named *Beauchamp*. Thomas Chivers also wrote a version.

42 Poe, "The Imp of the Perverse," in *Poetry and Tales*, 827.

43 Poe, "The Imp of the Perverse," in *Poetry and Tales*, 829.

44 Poe, "The Fall of the House of Usher," in *Poetry and Tales*, 317.

45 Poe, "The Fall of the House of Usher," in *Poetry and Tales*, 317.

46 Jeffrey Weinstock, in his reading of this tale, assumes that the man of the crowd is a hallucination of the narrator. See Jeffrey Andrew Weinstock, "The Crowd Within: Poe's Impossible Aloneness," *The Edgar Allan Poe Review* 7, no. 2 (2006): 5. "The Man of the Crowd" has received a great deal of fascinating critical attention in recent years. A number of fine papers about this tale were presented at the Third International Poe Conference in 2009 during the bicentennial of Poe's birth. Among these were Alexandra Urakova on "Poe's 'The Man of the Crowd' vs. Gogol's 'The Portrait': Two Models of Social Representation," Steven Fink on "Who Is Poe's 'Man of the Crowd'?," and Satwick Dasgupta on "Surveillance Camera Players and Discontent: Anonymous Role-Playing in 'The Man of the Crowd.'"

47 Poe, "The Man of the Crowd," *Poetry and Tales*, 392. Jeremy Cagle argues that Poe presents in this tale what Alan Lloyd-Smith calls a "Higher Reason" that is only accessible "through imagination, intuition, and introspection." See Jeremy Cagle, "Reading Well: The Transcendental Hermeneutics in Poe's 'The Man of the Crowd,'" *The Edgar Allan Poe Review* 9, no. 2 (2008): 30.

48 Poe, "The Man of the Crowd," *Poetry and Tales*, 396. As the immediate antecedent to Dupin, this tale has been dubbed a "metaphyscial detective story." See Patricia Merivale and Susan Elizabeth Sweeney, eds., *Detecting Texts: The Metaphysical Detective Story from Poe to Postmodernism* (Philadelphia: University of Pennsylvania Press, 1999).

49 Poe, "The Murders in the Rue Morgue," in *Poetry and Tales*, 397.
50 Poe, "The Murders in the Rue Morgue," in *Poetry and Tales*, 399.
51 Poe, "The Murders in the Rue Morgue," in *Poetry and Tales*, 399.
52 Poe, "The Murders in the Rue Morgue," in *Poetry and Tales*, 399.
53 Poe, "The Murders in the Rue Morgue," in *Poetry and Tales*, 399–400.
54 Poe, "The Murders in the Rue Morgue," in *Poetry and Tales*, 412.
55 Poe, "The Murders in the Rue Morgue," in *Poetry and Tales*, 412.
56 Poe, "The Murders in the Rue Morgue," in *Poetry and Tales*, 431.
57 Edgar Allan Poe, "Griswold's American Poetry," *Boston Miscellany* 2 (1842): 218.
58 Poe, "The Mystery of Marie Rogêt," in *Poetry and Tales*, 507.
59 Poe, "The Mystery of Marie Rogêt," in *Poetry and Tales*, 553.

Chapter Six

1 John Ward Ostrom, Burton R. Pollin, and Jeffrey A. Savoye, eds., *The Collected Letters of Edgar Allan Poe, Volume II: 1847–1849*, 3rd ed. (Staten Island, N.Y.: Gordian Press, 2008), 2:659.

2 Allen Tate regarded *Eureka* as true science when he was a boy, but when he became a man, he discounted Arthur Hobson Quinn's examination of the scientific merit of the piece with the remark, "But even if Professor Quinn is right, the claim is irrelevant, and is only another version of the attempt today to make religion and the arts respectable by showing that they are semi-scientific." See Allen Tate, "Our Cousin, Mr. Poe," 1214–15. The title startled W. H. Auden who remarked, "The man who had flatly asserted that no poem should much exceed a hundred lines in length—'that music (in its modifications of rhythm and rhyme) is so vast a moment to Poesy as never to be neglected by him who is truly poetical,' that neither Truth, the satisfaction of the Intellect, nor Passion, the excitement of the Heart, are the province of Poetry but only Beauty, and that the most poetical topic in the world is the death of a beautiful woman—this man produces at the end of his life a work which he insists is a poem and commends to posterity as his crowning achievement, though it violates every article in his critical creed." See W. H. Auden, introduction to *Edgar Allan Poe: Selected Prose and Poetry*, in *The Recognition of Edgar Allan Poe*, ed. Eric W. Carlson (Ann Arbor: University of Michigan Press, 1970), 225. Accepting T. S. Eliot's view that *Eureka* cannot be read as science, philosophy, or theology since Poe was not a specialist in any of those areas, and accepting the view that *Eureka* is intended as a poem in the same sense that "The Raven" is a poem, and agreeing that Poe has violated his theory of verse in *Eureka*, Seo-Young Jennie Chu proposes a solution involving a distinct form of consciousness called "hypnotic

203

ratiocination." See Seo-Young Jennie Chu, "Hypnotic Ratiocination," *The Edgar Allan Poe Review* 6, no. 1 (2005): 5–19.

3   Edgar Allan Poe, preface to *Eureka* in *Poetry and Tales* (New York: Literary Classics of the United States, 1984).

4   James V. Werner calls attention to this conjunction of Truth and Beauty in " 'Ground-Moles' and Cosmic Flaneurs: Poe Humboldt, and Nineteenth-Century Science," *The Edgar Allan Poe Review* 3, no. 1 (2002): 64–65.

5   Allen Tate, ed., *The Complete Poetry and Selected Criticism of Edgar Allan Poe* (New York: New American Library, 1981): viii. In another essay, Tate accuses Arthur Hobson Quinn of searching for scientists who might bolster Poe's scientific understanding. See Allen Tate, "The Angelic Imagination," in *Recognition* (see n. 2), 253.

6   Edward H. Davidson, in what Benjamin Fisher has argued was the first "critical book of any value for Poe studies," declared that *Eureka* was "a summary and climax of all that had gone before." See Edward H. Davidson, *Poe: A Critical Study* (Cambridge, Mass.: Belknap Press, 1957), vii. Fisher disagreed with Davidson's assessment of *Eureka* as "the culmination of [Poe's] other critical thoughts." See Fisher, *The Cambridge Introduction to Edgar Allan Poe* (Cambridge: Cambridge University Press, 2008), 99. In his study of Poe criticism Scott Peeples includes a number of important critics in the camp of Davidson in viewing *Eureka* as the key to or the culmination of Poe's work, including David Halliburton in *Edgar Allan Poe: A Phenomenological View* (1973), John Lynen in *Design of the Present* (1969), and Richard Wilbur in his introduction to the Laurel Poetry Series paperback collection of Poe's poems, among others. See Scott Peeples, *The Afterlife of Edgar Allan Poe* (Rochester, N.Y.: Camden House, 2007), 78–80. Elvira Osipova concludes her essay on *Eureka* with the declaration that "he depicted a consistent view of the Universe, which he had been building during the last ten years of his life." See Elvira Osipova, "The Reception of *Eureka* in Russia," *The Edgar Allan Poe Review* 5, no. 1 (2004): 25. David Ketterer regarded "*Eureka* as a position to which Poe's work evolves." See David Ketterer, *Edgar Allan Poe: Life, Work, and Criticism* (Fredericton, New Brunswick: York Press, 1989): 28. Ketterer views Richard Wilbur's reading of all of Poe's tales as allegories on *Eureka* as chronologically misguided.

7   Allen Tate asked rhetorically, "Had he not been bred in a society committed to the rationalism of Descartes and Locke by that eminent angel of the rationalistic Enlightenment, Thomas Jefferson?" See Tate, "The Angelic Imagination," in *Recognition* (see n. 2), 248.

8   Allen Tate pondered the religious depths of Poe and wondered about Poe's religious struggles: "He was a religious man whose Christianity, for reasons that nobody knows anything about, had got short-circuited; he lived among fragments of provincial theologies, in the midst of which 'coordination,' for a man of intensity, was difficult if not impossible." See Tate, "The Angelic Imagination," in *Recognition* (see n. 2), 237.

9   Critics have debated over Poe's correct position as rationalist or romantic. Edmund Wilson argued that Poe can only be properly understood as part of the romantic tradition: "Poe was, then, a typical romantic. But he was something more. He contained the germs of a further development," which Wilson argued would lead to symbolism. See Edmund Wilson, "Poe at Home and Abroad," in *Recognition* (see n. 2), 142–52. D. H. Lawrence, on the other hand, argued that Poe was "more a scientist than an artist." See D. H. Lawrence, "Edgar Allan Poe," in *Recognition* (see n. 2), 111.

10   *Poetry and Tales* (New York: Literary Classics of the United States, 1984).

11   Elizabeth Vincelette observes that "the poem can be seen as an early attempt at marrying the false dichotomy between poetry and science, a trend Poe sets forth in 'Al Aaraaf.'" See Elizabeth Vincelette, "Beauty, Truth, and the Word: The Prophecy and Theology of Poe's *Eureka*," *The Edgar Allan Poe Review* 9, no. 2 (2008): 38. Richard Wilbur argued that in Poe's myth of the universe, the exaltation of scientific knowledge above visionary knowledge resulted in the fall away from God. See Wilbur, "The House of Poe," in *Recognition* (see n. 2), 258. Whatever fall has taken place to account for the perversity of humanity that Poe found everywhere, it would have occurred long before the advent of modern science. Nonetheless, Poe abhorred the Enlightenment's neglect of the poetic imagination. At the same time, this awareness of human perversity separated Poe from the transcendentalists who had a much more sunny view of human nature. See Garner, "Poe's 'Double Dupin,'" in *Poe and His Times*, ed. Benjamin Franklin Fisher IV (Baltimore: The Edgar Allan Poe Society, 1990), 142.

12   Edward Davidson observed that "in 'Al Aaraaf' Poe had an early glimpse of this view of the lost centrality of things; in *Eureka* he tried to expand the whole concept in order to demonstrate that, while empirical science and the rational mind of man drive toward diffusion and the comprehension of itself in particles, the imagination is compelled toward a unitary determination." See Davidson, *Poe: A Critical Study*, 250. For another reading, see Christopher Kearns,

"Poe's Peering Eyes of Science," *The Edgar Allan Poe Review* 3, no. 2 (2002): 73–77.

13   Harold Beaver, ed., *The Science Fiction of Edgar Allan Poe* (London: Penguin, 1976), ix, n. 4.

14   Beaver, *Science Fiction of Poe,* x.

15   The quotation comes from Poe's poem, "Dream-Land," in *Poetry and Tales,* 79.

16   Edgar Allan Poe, "Mesmeric Revelation," in *Poetry and Tales* (New York: Literary Classics of the United States, 1984), 717.

17   It has become a tradition among modern critics to speak of *Pym* as a hoax. See Darryl Jones, "Ultima Thule: *Arthur Gordon Pym,* the Polar Imaginary, and the Hollow Earth," *The Edgar Allan Poe Review* 11, no. 1 (2010): 54. Jones argues, however, that Poe was well acquainted with the literature of his day about the polar regions.

18   Maurice J. Bennett has argued that "Hans Pfaall" (and possibly other tales of this sort) should be read "as neither hoax nor science fiction nor a curiously unsuccessful hybrid of the two, but as a fictionalization of Poe's serious aesthetic and metaphysical preoccupations." One might easily argue that all of Poe's tales are fictionalizations of his serious aesthetic and metaphysical preoccupations, but this assertion does not deal with the form of fiction. Bennett seems to exclude the idea of science fiction from Poe's plan because it does not fit the romantic paradigm into which he has placed Poe. See Maurice J. Bennett, "'Visionary Wings': Art and Metaphysics in Edgar Allan Poe's 'Hans Pfaall,'" in *Poe and His Times* (see n. 10), 76–77.

19   Captain James Cook had definitively declared in 1775 that no southern continent existed in the Antarctic Ocean, and Poe's tale suggests that Cook might be wrong. In *Eureka* he would also challenge the best science of his day. See Johan Wijkmark, "Poe's *Pym* and the Discourse of Antarctic Exploration," *The Edgar Allan Poe Review* 10, no. 3 (2009): 84.

20   At the end of the twentieth century, this plot became highly popular among moviemakers because it addressed a theme of great interest to the public. In his theological critique of Poe's work, written in 1952, Allen Tate remarked, "It is not only a serious possibility, it is a moral and logical necessity of the condition to which man has perversely brought himself." See Tate, "The Angelic Imagination," in *Recognition* (see n. 2), 242.

21   Long before science fiction had a name, Jules Verne referred to it simply as the "Poe genre." See Henri Justin, "The Paradoxes of Poe's Reception in France," *The Edgar Allan Poe Review* 11, no. 1 (2010): 82–83. Poe's influence on science fiction and its development did not

end with Verne. For a discussion of Poe's influence on Ray Bradbury, see Burtin Pollin, "Poe and Ray Bradbury: A persistent Influence and Interest," *The Edgar Allan Poe Review* 6, no. 2 (2005): 31–38, and Barbara Cantalupo, "Interview with Ray Bradbury," *The Edgar Allan Poe Review* 10, no. 3 (2009): 133–36.

22 For a discussion of Verne's treatment of the polar regions and the hollow earth in relation to Poe's stories, see Jones, "Ultima Thule," 57–58, 62.

23 Stephen Jay Gould, *Dinosaur in a Haystack*.

24 With his usual attention to detail in the scholarship of primary sources related to Poe, Jeffrey Savoye has tracked down the identity of Count Decuppis, an Italian mathematician and astronomer who claimed to have discovered a new planet, to whom Poe referred in his science column in *Burton's* in 1839 and then again in "Fifty Suggestions" in *Graham's* in 1849. See Jeffrey A. Savoye, "Who Was M. Decuppis?" *The Edgar Allan Poe Review* 7, no. 2 (2007): 65–70.

25 Poe, "The Murders in the Rue Morgue," in *Poetry and Tales*, 399–400.

26 Though he insisted upon reading Poe as a member in good standing of the Romantic movement, Edward Davidson had to admit that "Poe, unlike Whitman, always remained half-rationalist and half-organicist." See Davidson, *Poe: A Critical Study*, 44. Because he interprets Poe only as a romanticist, however, Davidson misses much of Poe. Mab-   207
bott, on the other hand, recognized that Poe did not fit easily into a single literary or philosophical movement: "Poe made fun of classifying poets by schools, but, if we must indulge in this, we may recall that Saintsbury agreed with a critic who pointed out that Poe belonged to that group that came between the romantics and the Victorians, of whom the only other writer now much read is Tom Hood." See T. O. Mabbott, introduction to *Selected Poetry and Prose of Edgar Allan Poe* (New York: The Modern Library, 1951), xii.

27 Laura Saltz, " 'Eyes which Behold': Poe's 'Domain of Arnheim' and the Science of Vision," *The Edgar Allan Poe Review* 7, no. 1 (2006): 13.

28 Coleridge had begun a conversation about imagination, but according to Mabbott, "Poe disagreed with Coleridge on imagination and fancy and insisted that no artist really creates in the sense that God creates. The artist, said Poe, merely combines elements: the combination of things rightly belonging together is imagination; fancy is possible through an improbable combination; and absurd combinations produce humor." See Mabbott, introduction to *Selected Poetry and Prose*, xiii. Poe's real contribution came when he realized that the imagination also lay at the heart of all scientific discovery, as he proposed in *Eureka*.

29   The science of medicine as well as of the mind appears in several of Poe's stories, as David E. E. Sloane makes clear in "Usher's Nervous Fever: The Meaning of Medicine in Poe's 'The Fall of the House of Usher,'" in *Poe and His Times* (see n. 10), 146–53. Benjamin Fisher reminds us that Poe had gained a fair knowledge of the scientific view of mental states in his day through the work of the Philadelphia doctor, Benjamin Rush. See Fisher, "'Eleonora': Poe and Madness," in *Poe and His Times* (see n. 10), 178.

30   Poe, "A Tale of the Ragged Mountains," in *Poetry and Tales*, 656.

31   In dismissing Poe's exploration of the role of imagination in scientific discovery in her discredited psychological study of Poe, Marie Bonaparte remarks, "True, intuition may also lead to dream states and, as we know, these can be thoroughly *consistent* in certain delusional conditions." See Marie Bonaparte, *The Life and Works of Edgar Allan Poe: A Psycho-Analytical Interpretation* (London: Imago Publishing, 1949), 598.

32   Poe, "Three Sundays in a Week," in *Poetry and Tales*, 480.

33   Poe, "Mesmeric Revelation," in *Poetry and Tales*, 723. This passage illustrates a point that Poe clings to across his writing. He does not seek for a way to sever the bonds between body and spirit. Instead, he seeks to understand how body and spirit are eternally related.

208   34   Poe, "Mesmeric Revelation," in *Poetry and Tales*, 726.

35   Edgar Allan Poe, "The American Drama," *The American Review* 2, no. 2 (1845): 121. The Bridgewater Tracts were a series of publications in Britain designed to promote natural theology and to demonstrate the existence of God through science. Unlike the fundamentalist "Scientific Creationism" of today, the tracts were written by leading scientists of the day.

36   Quinn, *Poe: A Critical Biography*, 528. Quinn quotes from John Henry Ingram's *Edgar Allan Poe, His Life, Letters, and Opinions*, vol. 2 (London: John Hogg, 1880), 115–16.

37   Allen Tate traced the trajectory of several of these streams of thought in "The Angelic Imagination," in which he analyzes "The Conversation of Eiros and Charmion," "The Colloquy of Monos and Una," "The Power of Words," and *Eureka*. See Tate, "The Angelic Imagination," in *Recognition* (see n. 2), 236–54.

38   Osipova, "*Eureka* in Russia," 16–17.

39   James Werner has argued that this combination of empiricism, rationalism, and imagination characterized the method of Humboldt as well as Poe. See Werner, "Ground-Moles," 45–69.

40   Poe, *Eureka*, in *Poetry and Tales*, 1289, 1297, 1300–1301, 1305, 1312–14, 1320, 1323.

41 Poe, *Eureka,* in *Poetry and Tales,* 1340.
42 Poe, *Eureka,* in *Poetry and Tales,* 1294.
43 Poe, *Eureka,* in *Poetry and Tales,* 1345.
44 Poe, *Eureka,* in *Poetry and Tales,* 1354.
45 On account of Poe's satirical critique of the philosophy of science
     current in his day, Benjamin Fisher has argued that "there are far
     too many comic insinuations throughout the book for us to deem it
     a major contribution to scientific thought." See Benjamin Fisher, *The
     Cambridge Introduction to Edgar Allan Poe,* 99. Elizabeth Vincelette
     has argued effectively that *Eureka* needs to be taken seriously as a
     work of philosophical theology that remythologizes religion through
     the poem. See Vincelette, "Beauty, Truth, and Word," 36–54.
46 Poe, *Eureka,* in *Poetry and Tales,* 1264.
47 Poe, *Eureka,* in *Poetry and Tales,* 1269. Davidson argued, "The imag-
     ination is, for Poe, the one truly creative or discovering faculty of the
     mind." See Davidson, *Poe: A Critical Study,* 61.
48 Richard Wilbur imagined a struggle within Poe between the physi-
     cal and the spiritual in which Poe rejects the physical world. Wilbur
     argues, "For all these reasons it is not easy for the poet to detach his
     soul from earthly things, and regain his lost imaginative power." See
     Wilbur, "House of Poe," in *Recognition* (see n. 2), 259. Wilbur misses
     Poe's actual struggle. He does not want to detach the physical from   209
     the spiritual. The intellectual climate of his day had done that horror
     already. He sought to bring the two back together, and he recognized
     that imagination united body and spirit. Wilbur's interpretation of
     Poe depends upon a war that Poe was not fighting, and his resulting
     discovery of symbols reflects only what Wilbur wanted to find. Like so
     many others, Wilbur's symbolic method assigned meaning to elements
     of Poe's stories that fit his theory of Poe.
49 Richard Wilbur assumes Poe must be understood as a romantic, and
     thus, he assumes Poe had a romantic understanding of imagination, as
     he explained, "Like many romantic poets, Poe identified imagination
     with dream." See Wilbur, "House of Poe," in *Recognition* (see n. 2),
     259. To the contrary, Poe conceived imagination as coming out of a
     dream. Imagination involved clear understanding. It involved rational
     coherence and the apprehension of relationships and principles never
     understood before. Imagination drove science and mathematics the
     same way it drove art. Charles May has explained, "Indeed, for Poe,
     who earlier rejected Coleridge's assertion that imagination was con-
     structive, the one who creates is he who discovers that pattern that
     is already there." See Charles E. May, *Edgar Allan Poe: A Study of*

the Short Fiction, Twayne's Studies in Short Fiction (Boston: Twayne, 1991), 87.

50 Harold Beaver declared, "At their broadest synthesis, Poe's Universe and Einstein's cohere." See Beaver, *Science Fiction of Poe*, 402. For the person inclined to regard *Eureka* as an allegory or symbolic metaphor for something other than an exploration of cosmology, Beaver's introduction and commentary provide a most helpful introduction to the major scientific issues that Poe explored and how his ideas correspond to the accepted theories of today.

51 Poe, *Eureka*, in *Poetry and Tales*, 1276–77.

52 Poe, *Eureka*, in *Poetry and Tales*, 1290.

53 Allen Tate discussed Poe's concept of imagination in the context of "The Colloquy of Monos and Una" where Poe had made preliminary excursions as he had in "The Murders in the Rue Morgue." Tate argued that "analogy" must be perceptible to other mental domains than the imagination; it must be accessible to reason and cognition. See Tate, "The Angelic Imagination," in *Recognition* (see n. 2), 246. Poe's theory of knowledge, and how he came to alter his earlier view of the mutual exclusion of Beauty, Truth, and Goodness, lay in his recognition that Imagination represents the highest order of mental activity, the bridge between the physical and the spiritual, the bridge between the arts and the sciences, the bridge between humans and God. Reason and cognition were merely the means of applying what imagination had discovered.

54 Poe, *Eureka*, in *Poetry and Tales*, 1293n.

55 Poe, *Eureka*, in *Poetry and Tales*, 1301.

56 Poe, *Eureka*, in *Poetry and Tales*, 1328.

57 In one of the few theological treatments of *Eureka*, Elizabeth Vincelette concludes that, in spite of the apparent "blasphemy" and pantheism, "Poe's tone indicates his sincere belief in the Judeo-Christian God." See Vincelette, "Beauty, Truth, and Word," 49.

58 Maurice J. Bennett has suggested that the primordial particle is the latest manifestation of Poe's star Al Aaraaf, finally transformed as symbol for imaginative vision. This allegorical reading of *Eureka* leaves no room for actual scientific insight as it clings to a romantic notion of imagination. See Bennett, "Visionary Wings," in *Poe and His Times* (see n. 10), 80.

59 Poe, *Eureka*, in *Poetry and Tales*, 1277. This phrase comes from Gen 1:2.

60 Poe, *Eureka*, in *Poetry and Tales*, 1300.

61 Poe, *Eureka*, in *Poetry and Tales*, 1322.

62 Poe, *Eureka,* in *Poetry and Tales,* 1354, 1356. These references come from 1 Cor 15:28.
63 Poe, *Eureka,* in *Poetry and Tales,* 1278.
64 Poe, *Eureka,* in *Poetry and Tales,* 1278.
65 Poe, *Eureka,* in *Poetry and Tales,* 1300.
66 Poe, *Eureka,* in *Poetry and Tales,* 1303.
67 Ostrom et al., *Collected Letters,* 2:688.
68 Poe, *Eureka,* in *Poetry and Tales,* 1306.
69 Gerald Kennedy observed that Poe's stories frequently deal with "the interpretration of life and death, the mingling of metaphysical opposites" which "constitute an esoteric ideography and inscribe a parallel text concerned exclusively with final questions." See Kennedy, "Phantasms of Death," in *The Tales of Poe,* 111–12.
70 Poe, *Eureka,* in *Poetry and Tales,* 1308.
71 Poe, "The Mystery of Marie Rogêt," in *Poetry and Tales,* 553.
72 Poe, *Eureka,* in *Poetry and Tales,* 1313–14.
73 In a profound misunderstanding of Poe, Davidson declared, "The basic hypothesis to account for that universe is, in *Eureka,* a machine." See Davidson, *Poe: A Critical Study,* 227. Poe actually has a personal model for the universe which went quite against the mechanical model associated with the old science that Poe rejected.
74 Poe, *Eureka,* in *Poetry and Tales,* 1342.
75 Poe, *Eureka,* in *Poetry and Tales,* 1352. Richard Wilbur observed of Poe's developing understanding of the whole of the universe, "Poe conceived of God as a poet. The universe, therefore, was an artistic creation, a poem composed by God. Now, if the universe is a poem, it follows that the one proper response to it is aesthetic, and that God's creatures are attuned to Him in proportion as their imaginations are ravished by the beauty and harmony of creation." See Wilbur, "House of Poe," in *Recognition* (see n. 2), 257–58.
76 Poe, *Eureka,* in *Poetry and Tales,* 1330.
77 Poe, *Eureka,* in *Poetry and Tales,* 1352.
78 Poe, *Eureka,* in *Poetry and Tales,* 1312.
79 Poe, "The Purloined Letter," in *Poetry and Tales,* 691–93.
80 Poe, *Eureka,* in *Poetry and Tales,* 1349. Edward H. Davidson argued that "Poe was seeking some way of avoiding the admission that there was, after all, a final rift between science and art and between the world of things and the artist. He conjured up the known pluralisms of the universe—scientific and philosophic—and then posited an ultimate monism. So too art must be, in this term, regarded as but another extension and demonstration of 'the plot of God' and the artist as a god-player." See Davidson, *Poe: A Critical Study,* 240.

81   Poe, "The Murders in the Rue Morgue," in *Poetry and Tales*, 404.

82   Poe, *Eureka*, in *Poetry and Tales*, 1354.

83   Poe, *Eureka*, in *Poetry and Tales*, 1355.

84   Poe, *Eureka*, in *Poetry and Tales*, 1356.

85   Poe, *Eureka*, in *Poetry and Tales*, 1356.

86   Charles May argued, "Reasoning backward from the fact that the basic desire for Supernal Beauty could only be partially fulfilled by the unity of poetry, Poe argued that the only One capable of achieving absolute unity was God; it therefore followed that the universe itself was a great poem, that is, a fully developed plan or plot (these are controvertible terms for Poe) of God." See May, *Poe: A Study of the Short Fiction*, 15.

87   Elvira Osipova has observed of the change in tone from the scientific section to the conclusion, "In a scientific discourse (he called *Eureka* a 'Discourse'), the clarity of style was deemed by him to be a necessary condition of Truth." See Osipova, "*Eureka* in Russia," 17.

88   Poe, *Eureka*, in *Poetry and Tales*, 1357.

89   Poe, *Eureka*, in *Poetry and Tales*, 1357.

90   Poe, *Eureka*, in *Poetry and Tales*, 1358.

91   Allen Tate called this conclusion Poe's "own descent into the maelstrom" and ended his essay on "The Angelic Imagination" with a stern moral admonition not to become exhausted in our own liberty or we will end our days in the dark like Poe. See Tate, "The Angelic Imagination," in *Recognition* (see n. 2), 254. Tate is wrong, however, in arguing that Poe had circumvented the natural world, for throughout *Eureka* Poe relies upon scientific observation of the natural world to establish a link between the physical and the spiritual.

92   Marie Bonaparte declared that the conclusion to *Eureka* is "the narcissistic and paranoiac paroxysm of mysticism" that expresses Poe's "megalomania." See Bonaparte, *Life and Works of Edgar Allan Poe*, 616.

93   Poe, *Eureka*, in *Poetry and Tales*, 1357.

94   The longing for renewal of loving relationships after death is an experience common to humanity; therefore, it is nothing peculiar to Poe. Richard Kopley, however, has argued that that the longing for reunion with his brother and mother formed an important part of his writing, particularly in *The Narrative of Arthur Gordon Pym*. See Richard Kopley, "Poe's *Pym*-esque 'A Tale of the Ragged Mountains,'" in *Poe and His Times* (see n. 10), 167.

Chapter Seven

1 Susan Jaffe Tane, *Nevermore: The Edgar Allan Poe Collection of Susan Jaffe Tane* (Ithaca, N.Y.: Cornell University Library, 2006), 56. Susan Tane owns Poe's personal copy of *Eureka* in which he made numerous corrections and notes in pencil. This copy remained in New York when he traveled south, and Rufus Griswold took it from Mrs. Clemm when Poe died, so it does not give us Poe's developing thoughts while in Richmond.

2 John Ward Ostrom, Burton R. Pollin, and Jeffrey A. Savoye, eds., *The Collected Letters of Edgar Allan Poe, Volume II: 1847–1849*, 3rd ed. (Staten Island, N.Y.: Gordian Press, 2008), 2:401.

3 Ostrom et al., *Collected Letters*, 2:401.

4 Ostrom et al., *Collected Letters*, 2:387.

INDEX

217

222